50 Best Routes on Skye and Raasay

Ralph Storer is an experienced and respected hillwalker who has hiked and backpacked extensively around the world. Despite being a Sassenach by birth, he has lived in Scotland since studying psychology at Dundee University and has a great affinity for the Highlands, where he can be seen in all weathers roaming the glens and tramping the tops. As well as disappearing into the hills for a regular fix of nature, he also writes novels and sexological non-fiction, and produces darkwave music on his home computer.

Praise for the first edition:

'What an excellent book. Ralph Storer has put together as thoroughly comprehensive a guide to walking and scrambling on Skye as you could wish for.' – *High*

'Informative, evocative and entertaining, this book will inspire you to experience for yourself the adventures awaiting you in the Misty Isle.' – *The Great Outdoors*

'It is a great pleasure to sit back and enjoy the fruits of Ralph Storer's painstaking research.' – *Outdoor Action*

D1152012

By the same author:

100 Best Routes on Scottish Mountains (Little Brown Books)
50 Classic Routes on Scottish Mountains (Luath Press)
Exploring Scottish Hill Tracks (Little Brown Books)
The Joy of Hillwalking (Luath Press)

In *The Ultimate Guide to the Munros* series (Luath Press):

Southern Highlands
Central Highlands South (including Glen Coe)
Central Highlands North (including Ben Nevis)

In the *Baffies' Easy Munros Guide* series (Luath Press):

Southern Highlands
Central Highlands

50 BEST ROUTES

ON

SKYE AND RAASAY

Ralph Storer

Whenever the days are sunny
And the wind's a pleasant breeze,
My heart is turning Skyewards
To the bare rock and the screes.
And oh, for lone Glen Brittle
And a view of the splinter'd ridge,
And a climb on the rough hard gabbro,
And a plunge from the lochan's edge;
Then to stand by the crooning breakers
And watch the setting sun,
And see the shadows turning blue
On Canna, Eigg and Rum.

From *Hill Thirst* (Anon)

BIRLINN

First published in 1996 by David and Charles
This second edition published in 2012 by
Birlinn Limited
West Newington House
10 Newington Road
Edinburgh
EH9 1QS

www.birlinn.co.uk

ISBN-13: 978 1 78027 042 5

British Library Cataloguing-in-Publication Data
A catalogue record for this book is available from the British Library

For Mairet and Dundee University Rucksack Club

DISCLAIMER

Hillwalking, scrambling, coast walking and mountaineering are not
risk-free activities and may prove injurious to users of this book.
While every care and effort has been taken in its preparation, readers
should note that information contained within may not be accurate
and can change following publication. Neither the publisher nor
the author accept any liability for injury or damage of any kind
arising directly or indirectly from the book's contents.

Set in Adobe Garamond Pro at Birlinn

Printed and bound in Great Britain by
Clays Ltd, St Ives plc

CONTENTS

Preface   vii

Introduction   1
     General Description   1
     Geology   3
     History   5
     Natural History   8
     Weather   10
     Visitor Information   12
     Notes on Use of Guide   14

THE CUILLIN

Cuillin Introduction   18

1	Sgurr nan Gillean	25
2	Sgurr Beag and Sgurr na h-Uamha	28
3	Am Basteir	30
4	Bruach na Frithe	32
5	Sgurr a' Bhairnich and An Caisteal	34
6	Sgurr an Fheadain	36
7	The Coire a' Ghreadaidh Skyline	38
8	Sgurr na Banachdich	42
9	Sgurr Dearg	45
10	Sgurr Alasdair	47
11	Sgurr Dubh Mor	50
12	The South Cuillin Ridge	54
13	Bla Bheinn via Coire Uaigneich	56
14	Bla Bheinn via South Ridge	58
15	Sgurr na Stri	60
16	Coruisk via Glen Sligachan	62
17	Coruisk from Elgol	64
18	Coruisk Route Miscellany (1)	67
19	Coruisk Route Miscellany (2)	70

HILL WALKS

20	Glamaig and the Beinn Deargs	72
21	Marsco	74
22	Belig and Garbh-bheinn	76
23	Beinn na Caillich	78

24	The Kylerhea Group	80
25	MacLeod's Tables	82
26	Beinn Tianavaig	84
27	The Storr	86
28	The Fox and the Red Bank	88
29	The Quiraing	90
30	Fingal's Pinnacles	92
31	The Trotternish High-level Route	94

COAST WALKS

Coast Walks Introduction — 96

32	Suisnish and Boreraig	97
33	Limestone Caves of Strath	100
34	Rubh' an Dunain	102
35	Brittle to Eynort	104
36	Eynort to Talisker	106
37	Talisker to Fiskavaig	109
38	MacLeod's Maidens	111
39	The South Duirinish Coast Walk	114
40	Moonen Bay Heights	117
41	Sky Cliff	119
42	The Waternish Peninsula	121

SHORT WALKS

43	Short Walks: South Skye	124
44	Short Walks: Loch Bracadale	132
45	Short Walks: North-east Skye	137
46	Short Walks: Trotternish East	143
47	Short Walks: Trotternish West	150

ISLE OF RAASAY

Raasay Introduction — 154

48	Dun Caan	156
49	Raasay East Coast	158
50	Raasay North End	160

Glossary/Index — 162

Grading System — 168

PREFACE TO THE SECOND EDITION

This guidebook is the result of an enduring love affair with the Isle of Skye, nurtured by the many unforgettable days I have spent on the island in all weathers and all seasons. I first went to Skye to climb the Cuillin, but soon discovered that the entire island was an adventure playground. Most of the secret places I discovered during many years of exploration did not appear in guidebooks and are still unknown to the vast majority of coach-borne and car-bound visitors. The aim of this guidebook is to share the fruits of that exploration with fellow adventurers prepared to leave the roadside.

Ironically, before road transport replaced sea transport as the main mode of travel around Skye, many of the routes pioneered in the first edition were well known. The longest sea cave on Skye, for example, was visited by Boswell and Johnson in 1773, but no longer appears in guidebooks or even on the map.

In the two decades since the first edition much has changed on the island. Population decline has been reversed, helped by the opening of the Skye Bridge in 1995. Visitor facilities might be expected to have changed, but one might have expected less change to the *50 Best Routes* themselves. In some cases routes have had to be re-aligned as a result of changes in land use or the closure or construction of paths. In other places much work has been done in renovating eroded (i.e. boggy and rutted) old paths. Much work still needs to be done.

One might perhaps have expected even less change to the actual scenery, but a landscape as dramatic as Skye's will always be a geomorphological work in progress. Recent years have seen important changes, for example, on the Cuillin Main Ridge and The Storr. To cater for all these changes and include even more exciting places to explore, the second edition has been significantly updated, revised and expanded.

What remains the same and will always remain the same is the island's mysterious allure, encapsulated in the phrase *The Magic of Skye*. May you be as seduced by it as the author continues to be.

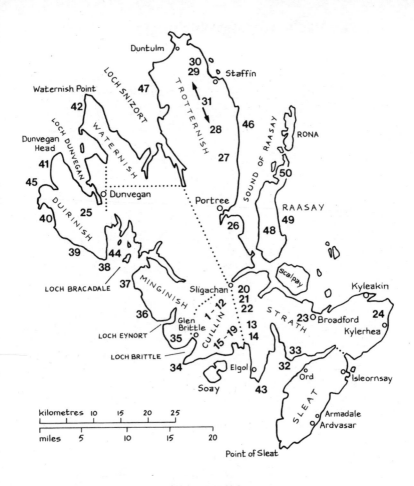

Duntulm

30
29 Staffin

Waternish Point

42 47 31

LOCH SNIZORT

28

TROTTERNISH

WATERNISH

46

SOUND OF RAASAY

RONA

Dunvegan
Head

LOCH DUNVEGAN

27

41

50

45

Dunvegan

Portree

RAASAY

25

26

48

49

DUIRINISH

40

39 44

38

37 MINGINISH

Sligachan

20
21
22

Scalpay

Kyleakin

LOCH BRACADALE

36

1 - 12

CUILLIN

13
14

23 Broadford

STRATH

24

Glen
Brittle

15 - 19

Kylerhea

LOCH EYNORT

35

33

LOCH BRITTLE

34

Elgol

32

Ord

Isleornsay

Soay

43

SLEAT

Armadale
Ardvasar

Point of Sleat

kilometres 10   15   20   25

miles   5   10   15   20

MAP SYMBOLS

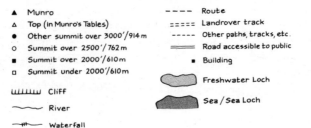

▲ Munro
△ Top (in Munro's Tables)
● Other summit over 3000'/914 m
○ Summit over 2500'/762 m
■ Summit over 2000'/610 m
□ Summit under 2000'/610 m

┴┴┴┴┴┴ Cliff
‾‾‾‾‾ River
‾┼┼‾ Waterfall

- - - - Route
===== Landrover track
- - - - - Other paths, tracks, etc.
═════ Road accessible to public
■ Building

Freshwater Loch

Sea / Sea Loch

viii

INTRODUCTION

General Description

With an area of 640 sq miles (1650 sq km), Skye is the second largest of the Hebridean islands lying off the west coast of Scotland. As the eagle flies it is approximately 50ml/80km long by 7ml/12km to 25ml/40km wide, yet such are the contortions of its shape that the coastline is 400ml/640km long and road distances are always greater than expected.

So indented is the coastline that on the map the island looks like a group of peninsulas joined together in the middle. No place is more than 5ml/8km from the sea, and the nearness of the sea makes walking on Skye a quite different experience from walking in the mainland Highlands. Some say that Skye derives its name from its shape, the name being a modern version of the Celtic *skeitos* or Gaelic *sgiath* (meaning wing). Others derive the name from the Celtic *sci* (cut or indented), the old Gaelic *sgith* (Scots), the Celtic *skia* and *neach* (sword people), the Norse *skith* (a tablet or log used during the Norse occupation) and the Norse *sky* and *ey* (cloud island). Take your choice.

In broad geographical terms there are five peninsulas radiating from the central part of Skye: Duirinish, Waternish and Trotternish to the north, stocky Minginish to the west and the fish-tail of Sleat to the south. The first four of these names are Norse district names, whereas Sleat is a parish name. The bleak moors that form the centre of the island and from which the peninsulas project are of less scenic interest, apart from the old parish of Strath that separates Minginish and Sleat. Part of the island's allure lies in the fact that each of these areas has a character all of its own which is enhanced by the contrasting character of its neighbours.

Most walkers and climbers are attracted to Skye by the Minginish peninsula, for it is here that the Cuillin are to be found. This supreme mountain range contains no fewer than twelve Munros and dominates the island from all angles. The rough gabbro rock of which the mountains are composed is like something out of a climber's dream, and the sharp summit arêtes and fantastic rock shapes it has formed make walking and scrambling in the Cuillin more exciting, challenging and rewarding than anywhere else in the British Isles. For further description see p.18.

Less well-known than the Cuillin but equally spectacular in its own way is the Minginish coastline, where mile upon mile of vertiginous cliff top provides magnificent walks of testing length and remoteness.

After Minginish the second most popular walking area is Trotternish, the most northerly of Skye's peninsulas, where a high mountain backbone running the length of the peninsula erupts on its eastern side into a succession of weird pinnacles and basins. The highest and most popular hill is The Storr (719m/2,358ft) and the most famous pinnacles are those of The Storr and the Quiraing, but off the beaten track other equally fascinating hills and rock basins await the explorer. In addition, an extremely varied coastline on each side of the mountains provides innumerable short but exciting excursions to rocky headlands, sea stacks, caves, natural arches, waterfalls and abandoned castles.

The prize for the most dramatic coastal scenery goes to the Duirinish peninsula in the north-west. Here is to be found the highest sea cliff on Skye (Biod an Athair, 313m/1,028ft), the tallest sea stack (the Mother stack at MacLeod's Maidens, 63m/207ft) and the most beautiful and intricate series of coastal formations to be found anywhere in the British Isles. Inland the remarkable flat hill tops of MacLeod's Tables dominate the landscape from all angles.

Between Trotternish and Duirinish is the least accessible and least frequented of all Skye peninsulas: Waternish. This is a land of empty moors and remote shorelines that appears uninteresting on the map yet on closer investigation reveals many hidden gems, including some fine sea cliffs, stacks and duns.

In the south of Skye the Sleat peninsula makes a dramatic contrast to its northern neighbours. This is 'the garden of Skye', a landscape without mountains where gentle wave-lapped shores are backed by green fields and woods. As with Waternish a glance at the map of Sleat reveals little of interest to the walker, but those who explore on foot will here discover some of the most beautiful coastal scenery on Skye, including the untracked shores of the rocky west coast and some remarkable old castles.

Between Minginish and Sleat the old parish of Strath sprawls across southern Skye with a tremendous variety of scenery, as though trying to incorporate something of all the other areas. After the Cuillin this is the second most mountainous area on Skye, where Cuillin outliers such as Bla Bheinn, which many consider to be the most beautiful mountain on Skye, contrast with the crumbling Red Hills, which provide fine high-level walking of a more relaxed nature than on the Cuillin. Here also there is limestone country to explore and a coastline that includes some notable caves (including the wondrous Spar Cave) and some alarmingly weathered sandstone sea cliffs.

In all, the walker on Skye is spoiled for choice. Its many and varied districts provide a wealth of interesting and exciting walking experiences that are without equal in the British Isles. Add to this the island setting, the magnificent seascapes and the quality of Skye light and there is something here for everyone, enough for anyone. Prepare to be mesmerised by the Magic of Skye.

To bring some order to the complexity of the island landscape, this guidebook organises the walks and scrambles into 50 best routes. It showcases nineteen on the Cuillin (Routes 1-19), eleven on other hills around the island (Routes 20-31) and twelve on coast walks (Routes 32-42). In addition five routes are reserved for a compendium of shorter walks to interesting places (Routes 43-47) and three routes are described on the fascinating neighbouring island of Raasay (Routes 48-50).

Geology

The tremendously varied scenery of Skye reflects a complex geology that has made the island a classic centre for geological study. What follows is a brief walker's guide to this geology, avoiding specialist terms where possible.

The oldest rocks on Skye are found in Sleat, whose surface geology produces low-lying moorland that is more characteristic of the Northern Highlands than the rest of the island. The oldest rock is Lewissian gneiss, a coarse-grained grey rock easily recognised by its gnarled and banded appearance. It was formed up to 3,000 million years ago and today reaches the surface along the east coast of Sleat from Isleornsay to Aird of Sleat.

Over the course of time the gneiss landscape was eroded by rivers whose alluvial deposits formed the Torridonian sandstones and whose deltaic deposits formed the Moine schists of some 800 to 1,000 million years ago. Schist is recognisable by its thin bands of flaky material, treacherous for climbing but attractive when reflecting the light; it occurs mainly in the south-west of Sleat. The sandstone has a much rougher feel and forms the backbone of the Sleat peninsula.

Between 450 and 600 million years ago the sea-level rose, the land that is now Skye was under water and sedimentary rocks were formed on the sea bed: quartzites, shales, grits and limestones. Today these rocks reach the surface in the Ord district of Sleat and on the east side of Strath Suardal south of Broadford, where porous limestone provides dry terrain, lush green grass and caves (Route 33). The limestone contains the earliest fossils found on Skye. Some of the limestone was later metamorphosed into marble, which is still quarried near Torrin.

There is then a gap in the geological history of Skye until the sandstones and conglomerates of 225 million years ago formed on river flood plains, and the limestones, sandstones and shales of 135 to 195 million years ago formed when Skye was again under water. Today these rocks occur around Broadford, in the Strathaird district and around the coast of Trotternish. The younger rocks are abundant in fossils and form the best soils on Skye. In Trotternish they have also yielded dinosaur remains, replicas of which can be seen in the museum at Ellishadder.

The greatest geological upheaval was still to come, for 60 million years ago the land was covered by vast outpourings of lava from fissures in the earth's surface. In the north of Skye wave upon wave of lava flowed to the surface, cooling quickly to form great sheets of fine-grained basalt that today cover over half the island.

The horizontal nature of the lava flows gave rise to the flat-topped summits of MacLeod's Tables and the characteristically rolling countryside of Trotternish. Often the hills and cliffs have a terraced appearance due to weathering between the flows, and this enables individual flows to be traced with ease. The basalt reaches its highest point at The Storr (719m/2,358ft) and also forms the great sea cliffs of the west coast. Cooling fractures often give the cliffs a columnar appearance, as seen most spectacularly at Kilt Rock north of The Storr. Also on this eastern side of the Trotternish mountains underlying rocks have been unable to support the weight of the basalt and some of the largest landslips in Britain have occurred (and still occur), producing chaotic jumbles of pinnacles such as those at The Storr (Route 27) and the Quiraing (Route 29).

The Cuillin were formed from the lava reservoir (magma chamber), which cooled very slowly, producing the extremely hard coarse-grained gabbro that has weathered into the fantastic shapes we know today (see p.18 for further description). The granite Red Hills were formed soon afterwards. Their more rounded shape is the result of the cooling and erosion of a finer-grained type of magma than that which formed the Cuillin.

Since that cataclysmic era the Skye landscape has continued to be changed by weathering and glacial erosion. From two million years ago until c.10,000 years ago ice covered most of Britain, scouring the landscape as it moved slowly westwards. On the Cuillin, glaciers flowed down the mountain sides to form bowl-shaped corries of bare rock. Glens such as Glen Sligachan were chiselled into U-shaped valleys as the ice ground along their bottoms.

After the ice melted, the sea-level changed several times, forming 'raised beaches' around Skye at about 7m/25ft, 15m/50ft and 30m/100ft. Long sea inlets such as Loch Harport are drowned glens. Even today weathering continues to wear down the landscape. In 1987 the famous gendarme on the west ridge of Sgurr nan Gillean disintegrated. In 2004 there was a 4,000 tonne rockfall behind the Old Man of Storr. The Old Man too will one day topple. In 2007 the highest point of the Inaccessible Pinnacle was altered by a lightning strike. Around the coast, weathering of sea cliffs has produced the amazing variety of caves, natural arches and stacks that are such a constant source of wonder to the coast walker.

Such is the geological history of Skye, a continuing process but hopefully one that will not change drastically during your island wanderings.

History

History does not determine the form of a landscape to the same extent as geology, yet it leaves its imprint everywhere, and even a superficial historical knowledge can add much to the pleasures of walking. What follows is a brief sketch of the history of Skye that will place into context any detailed historical references in the main text.

The island was first inhabited by Mesolithic (Middle Stone Age) hunter-gatherers who reached the western isles c.7000–6000BC. The earliest evidence of human presence on Skye is a shell midden (i.e. a heap of discarded shellfish shells) discovered near Staffin in 1988 and dated to 6500BC. Neolithic (New Stone Age) farmers followed c.4000BC. The chambered cairns of Skye (drystone wall burial chambers roofed by a cairn), such as that at Rubh' an Dunain (Route 34), date from this period. The next settlers, c.2000 BC, were the Beaker people, a race of semi-nomadic herdsmen named for their ornate pottery.

During the Iron Age of the late first millennium BC, the Celts of central Europe reached Skye and fortified the island with more than fifty duns (forts), whose ruins remain conspicuous in the modern landscape. Many of these duns were in the form of a circular drystone tower, known as a broch, which had thick double walls up to 15m/50ft high. Between inner and outer walls were small rooms or galleries, sometimes five or six stories high. All Skye brochs are now in a ruinous state, as their stones have been re-used over the centuries for later buildings, but some of the best-preserved are well worth visiting for an insight into prehistoric life (e.g. Dun Beag near Struan in Route 44b).

Another Iron Age structure was the souterrain, a tunnel-like underground passage, used either as a refuge or as a storage space. Good examples, requiring a torch for viewing, can be seen at Kilvaxter (seventeen metres long; NG 389696) and Claigan (ten metres long; NG 238539). Watch your head on the low roofs. Also dating from this period are a number of Druidical sites (the Druids were the Celtic priesthood), such as that at Boreraig (Route 32).

Over the course of time the Celts became polarised into different groups including the Picts of the Highlands and Islands and the Scots of Ireland (Scotti was the Roman word for raiders), each group speaking a different language. The Picts have left their mark on the Skye landscape in the form of incised symbol stones (e.g. Clach Ard near Tote, NG 421491).

Roman Britain repulsed an invasion of combined Picts and Scots in 367, and there was much fighting between various groups all over the Highlands and Islands throughout the fourth and fifth centuries. In the sixth century the Gaelic-speaking Scots invaded and settled in the Islands, gradually turning

Pictland into Scotland. In their wake came St Columba and a number of other (sometimes rival) saints, who converted the locals to Christianity.

From the eighth century onwards Vikings began to settle on the west coast of Scotland, and Skye found itself under Norse occupation as Scandinavian and Scottish kings fought to gain the upper hand. Norwegian supremacy was ended once and for all when the 120-strong fleet of King Haco was defeated at the Battle of Largs by the Scottish King Alexander III in 1263, and the Western Isles were seceded to Scotland by the Treaty of Perth in 1266.

Even then peace was not to be found. The Isles saw themselves as a separate kingdom from Scotland, and under the leadership of the Lord of the Isles there were many rebellions against the Scottish crown in the fourteenth and fifteenth centuries. Constant inter-clan feuds were also a feature of this period. The clan consisted of the children or followers of a chief, who placed themselves under his protection in return for serving him. The two major Skye clans were the MacLeods and the MacDonalds (mac = son), who fought innumerable ferocious battles all over the island.

James IV, the last Gaelic-speaking King of Scotland, abolished the Lordship of the Isles in 1493, but failed to quell the rebelliousness of the chiefs. In 1540 James V decided to demonstrate his power by taking a great fleet to the Isles. He visited both Duntulm Castle (the MacDonald stronghold) and Dunvegan Castle (the MacLeod stronghold), took hostages and anchored in Portree Bay, where the chiefs came to pay their respects. The ensuing peace lasted no longer than James himself, however, who died two years later, and clan fights and rebellions continued apace into the seventeenth century. The last clan battle fought on Skye soil took place in Coire na Creiche in the Cuillin in 1601.

Following the 1688 overthrow by William and Mary of the Stuart King James VII of Scotland (who had also become James II of England when Elizabeth I died), and the Act of Union between England and Scotland in 1707, Skye was much affected by Jacobite attempts to restore the House of Stuart to the throne. The Jacobites were named for Jacobus, the Latin for James. The struggle culminated in the 1745 rebellion led by Prince Charles Edward Stuart ('Bonnie Prince Charlie'). After the disastrous defeat at Culloden in 1746, Prince Charlie's wanderings in the Highlands and Islands, in flight from the English redcoats, became the stuff of legend, fêted in story and song. The few days he spent on Skye have left an indelible mark on the island's folklore, as commemorated in ballads such as the famous Skye Boat Song.

He arrived in Skye from South Uist on 28 June 1746, accompanied by Flora MacDonald and dressed as her maid. They landed in north-west Trotternish at the headland now named Prince Charles's Point and made their way on foot to Portree. From Portree Charlie went to Raasay before returning and heading southwards to the Strathaird coast. To avoid the redcoats he and his guide probably kept well west of Sligachan, forded the River Sligachan below Nead na h-Iolaire, crossed the Mam a' Phobuill beside Marsco, circled round Glas Bheinn Mhor into Srath Mor and followed the shore of Loch Slapin.

Anyone who has undertaken this route will be in no doubt as to Charlie's fitness and hillcraft, especially as he crossed the mountains at night, exclaiming at one point, 'I'm sure the Devil would not find me now!' He was conducted to the cave south of Elgol now named Prince Charles's Cave (Route 46b), from where he was rowed over to the mainland, eventually to escape to safety in France. His route on Skye would make an interesting and unusual backpacking trail.

Following the '45, parliament attempted to eradicate the culture that had spawned rebellion by outlawing weapons, Gaelic and even the kilt. The result was peace in the Isles but the tragic cost was the destruction of a culture that has never really recovered. Some, including Flora MacDonald, emigrated to North America. With peace at last, however, the population of Skye grew steadily in the latter half of the eighteenth century, reaching a peak of 23,000 in 1841. In the Napoleonic Wars the island sent over 10,000 men to Europe, equal to the entire population of Skye today.

Social and economic disaster struck in the mid-nineteenth century, when the kelp industry collapsed and the potato harvest failed. The people became destitute, the landlords bankrupt. Amid scenes of appalling tragedy and hardship, people all over the Highlands and Islands were 'cleared' from their homes, often forcibly, in order to combine small crofts into more profitable larger holdings and make room for sheep, which thrived on the land. One estimate puts the number of people evicted on Skye alone, between 1840 and 1883, at 6,940 families. Thousands emigrated to the colonies, many to perish during the voyage.

The tragedy of the Clearances continues to arouse emotion even to this day. Some blame greedy landlords, others farmers who did not pay rent to bankrupt landlords, others overpopulation, others the fungus that blighted the potato crop. Whatever the causes and the rights and wrongs, anyone who walks the Highlands and Islands today and revels in their solitude cannot help but feel ambivalent about the suffering that has made the land as it is. Wherever you go in Skye you will come across forlorn ruins from the days of the Clearances, notably at the abandoned villages of Suisnish and Boreraig (Route 32).

In the late nineteenth century the people began to fight back against eviction. In 1882 there was a running battle between crofters and police at the Braes south of Portree. Agitation eventually led to the Napier Commission of 1883 and the first Crofters' Act of 1886, whereby crofters were given security of tenure and fair rents. Successive Crofters' Acts in the twentieth century further eased the farmer's lot. Today agriculture remains the main industry on the island, followed by tourism, fishing and forestry. The total population is less than half its 1841 peak of 23,000. As elsewhere in the Islands, young people quit Skye to pursue mainland careers, although the land bridge from Kyle of Lochalsh, opened in 1995, has made the island less isolated and the population has begun to rise again.

The major hope for the future welfare of the island appears to be tourism, although this brings its own set of problems to an island culture. It is now estimated, for instance, that 40% of the population is English by birth. Rural properties bought as retirement homes may eventually lie empty. Other properties have been converted into self-catering establishments for summer visitors, a development that elsewhere in the Highlands and Islands has seen villages become winter ghost-towns. It is to be hoped that the island can survive such an invasion of modern tourism, as the livelihood of many of the inhabitants depends on it.

Tourism has been on the increase ever since the visits of Thomas Pennant in 1772, Dr Samuel Johnson and James Boswell in 1773 and Isobel Murray in 1802, all of whom wrote books about their travels. In 1814 Sir Walter Scott visited Coruisk, and his vivid description of it in *The Lord of the Isles* firmly placed the Cuillin on the tourist map. 'Unclimbable' Sgurr nan Gillean was climbed in 1836 and this paved the way for other first ascents and increasingly difficult rock climbs, a process that continues to this day (see p.22 for a history of Cuillin exploration).

The walker on Skye today is following in the footsteps of some of the greatest climbers, writers and artists of their generations, on ground that has more tales to tell than most. While wandering around the island you may well find yourself as affected as Dr Johnson was when he wrote: 'Far from me be such frigid philosophy as may conduct us indifferent and unmoved over any ground which has been dignified by wisdom, bravery or virtue.'

Natural History

Skye has an immense variety of flora and fauna which reflects its varied topography and diverse habitats. There are, for instance, some 300 common flowering plants and over 300 species of butterfly and moth. To do full justice to such a natural history would require several volumes. This guidebook restricts itself to a brief outline, together with a few more specific details on species likely to be of interest to the non-specialist visitor.

The flora of Skye varies from the flowers of the shoreline to the Alpine and Arctic plants that are found on the mountains, especially in the mineral-rich crevices of the Trotternish hills. Strath limestone provides a rich habitat for lime-loving plants, while the moors of Minginish and northern Skye host a variety of moorland plants such as heather and bog cotton (which at one time was collected as filling for pillows). Trees are not abundant except in coastal Sleat, where birch, oak, hazel and ash are common.

The distribution of birds and animals also varies according to habitat. On the flat coasts herons and orange-beaked oystercatchers never fail to catch the eye, while the sea cliffs play host to a number of large seabirds such as shags and cormorants. Ravens are not uncommon and you may see several types of raptor, including golden eagles, sea eagles and buzzards, which are often indistinguishable from each other to the untrained eye.

The golden eagle is larger than the buzzard (about 80-90cm long compared to the buzzard's 50-60cm), has a 2m wingspan (compared to the buzzard's 1.2m), is less stocky and is more elegant in flight. The white-tailed sea eagle is larger still. With a wingspan of almost 2.5m it is Europe's largest eagle. The species became extinct in Britain when the last one was shot on Skye in 1916 (they were blamed for taking lambs), but in 1975 they were re-introduced on nearby Rum and are becoming an increasingly common sight again on Skye.

Most of the common small animals occur on Skye: mice, voles, shrews etc. Rabbits are abundant on the moors and edges of sea cliffs. There are also foxes, unlike on any other Scottish island. The pine marten arrived from the mainland along with the bridge in 1995, and there have also been possible sightings of the long-extinct wildcat.

Roe deer may be seen in the woods of Strath and Sleat, and red deer can be seen both here and on the Minginish moors, though not in such great numbers as in the sixteenth century, when it was recorded that one thousand were killed in one hunt alone.

On the coast the doglike head of the common seal can often be seen bobbing in the water just offshore; the bulkier grey seal is rarer. Otters are fairly common but not often seen. In the sea itself will be found porpoises, whales, sharks and dolphins.

Reptiles resident on Skye are the common lizard, the slow-worm and the adder. You are unlikely to see an adder, Britain's only venomous snake, but in the author's experience they are more common than they used to be. If you're interested, there's a reptile centre in Broadford (www.skyeserpentarium.org.uk). If you encounter an adder in the wild it will try to stay out of your way and you should try to stay out of its. Eight to ten people are bitten in Scotland every year. If bitten, do not attempt first aid. Apply a dry dressing, immobilise the limb and seek help.

Insects are abundant, notably the cleg and the midge, which ravage visitors from mid-June to late summer. The cleg is a large, persistent horse-fly with a nasty bite, but it can often be spotted before it strikes and certainly immediately afterwards.

Midges are something else. No matter how many are swatted they are never short of kamikaze reinforcements. They prefer boggy ground and damp warm weather, and just love Sligachan and Glen Brittle campsites. As testament to the persistence of the midge, the nineteenth century geologist John MacCulloch once recorded that despite being anchored in the Sound of Soay 1ml/2km from shore, the 'light militia of the lower sky' still managed to nose him out.

Midges hate wind, cold, heat and heavy rain, and (some people claim) certain insect repellents. However, in infestations so bad that the wee beasties batter against a tent like heavy rain (as on a long Sligachan night the author would not wish to repeat), protection will be provided only by a mesh head net and possibly full body armour.

Weather

Skye has a reputation for bad weather that is only in part borne out by the facts. Rainfall is high, averaging 120+cm (50+in) per annum on the coast and 300+cm (125+in) on the mountains, compared to 95cm (40in) in Glasgow and c.60cm (25in) in London and Edinburgh. Average maximum summer temperatures are c.16ºC (60ºF) during the hottest months of July and August. Average annual sunshine is around 1200 hours, considerably lower than in the south and east of Britain but only slightly lower than in the west. Strong winds and gales are common, Skye being directly in the path of the prevailing southerly and westerly winds that blow off the Atlantic.

These figures support the notion of a more inclement climate than on the mainland, but they are not of an order of magnitude that alone will account for Skye's bad weather reputation. It is clear that other factors are at work, one of which is the tendency for visitors to holiday in the late summer, which is nowhere near the driest, brightest and calmest time of the year (see table following).

Another factor is the variability of the weather. Broadford, in the lee of the Cuillin, has around twice as much rainfall as Staffin. Snow is as likely in May as in October. April has been known to be completely dry one year and abnormally wet the next. There may be as much sun in the summer of one year as in the whole of the next.

Such variability makes weather prediction difficult, especially as different localities may experience widely differing weather simultaneously. The mountains of Trotternish may be clear when the mountains of Minginish are enveloped in cloud, the Braes bathed in sunlight beside a storm-ridden Glamaig, the high tops of the Cuillin in sunshine above sea-level cloud in Glen Brittle.

If you go to Skye for a week to climb the Cuillin, you may never see them at all and only surmise their existence from the map, or you may be so seduced by their sun-kissed summits that you yearn for a day of rain simply to recuperate from climbing them. Go expecting a week of squalls, a week of unbroken sunshine and all points in between and you won't be disappointed.

It is this very variability and unpredictability that gives Skye a unique atmospheric quality that is a constant source of surprise and delight. On a hot day in the Cuillin, mist can form in seconds, billowing up from 'nowhere' to engulf a peak. Anvil-shaped clouds can form before your eyes and hang threateningly overhead. Double rainbows are not uncommon. Sunsets can match them for colour. Even a dreich drizzly day can have a delicate translucent quality, and after rain the light has a soft brilliance like nowhere else.

The 'misty isle' myth derives from the incidence of hill cloud, but hills attract cloud everywhere, not just in Skye. Sea-level Skye is notable not for its mist but for the pollution-free clarity of its light. On a clear day on the Cuillin it is even possible to see the remote island of St Kilda, 100ml/160km away beyond the Outer Hebrides.

The unique quality and delicacy of the weather patterns of Skye contribute much to the magic of the island, and many of us who fall under the spell of Skye are quite content to leave things as they are. Or, to put it in the words of an old Skye wish:

> *Geamhradh reodhagach, Earrach ceothagach,*
> *Samhradh breac riabhach, 's Foghar glan grianach.*
>
> *(A frosty winter, a misty spring,*
> *a light and shade summer, and a clear sunny autumn).*

As a rough weather guide the following table shows a monthly comparison of temperature, rainfall, sunshine and wind. The figures are a ranking from 1 to 12. Figures for temperature (1 = hottest, 12 = coldest) and wind (1 = calmest, 12 = windiest) are relatively constant throughout the island. Figures for sunshine (1 = brightest, 12 = dullest) and rainfall (1 = driest, 12 = wettest) vary considerably depending on locality. Where months are shown as being of equal rank, this indicates an averaging that reflects the local variation; thus April is normally drier than June in Staffin but the reverse is true in Broadford.

	Temperature	Rainfall	Sunshine	Wind
JAN	12	8=	11	12
FEB	11	4=	8=	2
MAR	9	4=	6	10
APR	7	2=	3	8
MAY	5	1	1=	1
JUN	3	2=	1=	3
JUL	2	4=	5	6
AUG	1	7	4	4
SEP	4	8=	7	7
OCT	6	8=	8=	9
NOV	8	8=	10	5
DEC	10	8=	12	11

Mountain weather forecasts:

www.mwis.org.uk
www.metoffice.gov.uk/loutdoor/mountainsafety (tel: 09068-500442)
www.metcheck.com/V40/UK/HOBBIES/mountain.asp
www.sais.gov.uk (avalanche conditions)

Webcams:

Kyle of Lochalsh webcam: www.lochalsh.com/webcam.html
A87 road cams at the Skye bridge and at Ard Dorch 6ml/10km north of
Broadford: trafficscotland.org/lev

Visitor Information

Information given here is necessarily subject to change, and if vital should be
verified before travelling to Skye.

Travel information: Private Transport

For many of the best walks on Skye public transport is non-existent or
inconvenient. Most walkers therefore travel to the island by car, especially since
the opening of the road bridge from Kyle of Lochalsh in 1995 and the abolition
of tolls in 2004. To vary a vacation itinerary, there are two car ferries.

The modern ferry from Mallaig to Armadale on Sleat (crossing time 30mins)
provides the shortest route to Skye when coming from the south, but it is also
the most expensive. It carries up to 40 cars on several sailings daily from April
to September, fewer during the winter months. Further information from

Caledonian MacBrayne: www.calmac.co.uk (tel: 0800-066-5000). Head office: Caledonian MacBrayne, Ferry Terminal, Gourock PA19 1QP (tel: 01475-650100).

The Isle of Skye Ferry Community operates 'the world's last sea-going, hand-operated, turntable ferry' from Glenelg to Kylerhea on Sleat (crossing time 5mins). It carries up to six cars and runs every 20mins between10am and 6pm (7pm high season), Easter to mid-October. Further information: www.skyeferry.co.uk (tel: 0800-066-5000).

Should you wish to venture further afield than Skye, CalMac ferries sail from Uig to North Uist and Harris and from Sconser to Raasay (see p.154).

Travel Information: Public Transport

By road Citylink coaches run from Glasgow and Inverness to Uig, with connections from other parts of the mainland. Further information: www.citylink.co.uk (tel: 0871-2663333).

On Skye itself Stagecoach buses connect all major centres (but not Glen Brittle) and operate on a 'hail and ride' basis. A leaflet *Getting Around Skye* is available from tourist information offices. Further information: www.stagecoachbus.com (tel: 01478-612622).

Until 2007 there was a 'postbus' service to more isolated villages, but the postal service on Skye no longer takes passengers.

By rail two of the most scenic railway lines in Britain lead to the doorstep of Skye to connect with ferries or buses. The Highland Railway runs from Inverness to Kyle and the West Highland Railway runs from Glasgow via Fort William to Mallaig. Though neither line is renowned for its speed, both travel through beautiful countryside. For details contact Scotrail: www.scotrail.co.uk (tel: 0845-6015929). There is no railway on Skye itself.

Cars, minibuses, bicycles and taxis can be hired locally. Enquire at tourist information offices.

There is an airstrip at Broadford but there have been no scheduled flights since 1988.

Two websites are useful for journey planning: www.travelinescotland.com/journeyplanner/enterJourneyPlan.do?hss=05yry27510084 (the Traveline Scotland journey planner) and www.highland.gov.uk/yourenvironment/roadsandtransport/publictransport (click on the public transport map link).

Other Information

For travel guides, brochures and other information enquire at Tourist Information Offices: Portree (all year round, tel: 01478-612137); Broadford (May to September only, tel: 01471-822361); Dunvegan (limited winter opening, tel:

01470-521581), and Uig (May to September only, tel: 01470-542404).

Online information on accommodation, restaurants, visitor attractions etc. can be obtained at the following websites among others: www.skye.co.uk, www. holidayskye.com, www.skye-online.co.uk, isleofskyeaccommodation.com.

SHYA Youth Hostels: Broadford, Glen Brittle and Uig. Further information: www.syha.org.uk.

Independent hostels are scattered around the island. Further information: www.hostel-scotland.co.uk.

Caravan and camping sites are also scattered around the island. For up-to-date information consult the above accommodation websites and dedicated camping websites such as www.ukcampsite.co.uk and www.ukcampsitesearch. co.uk/scotland/isle-of-skye.

Two campsites serve the Cuillin: Sligachan (N 485301) and Glen Brittle (NG 414205). For details see p.21.

There are two Mountaineering Club Huts: one in Glen Brittle (owned by the British Mountaineering Council: www.gbmh.co.uk) and one at Loch Coruisk (owned by the Junior Mountaineering Club of Scotland: www.glasgowjmcs. org/coruisk.php).

Small petrol stations will be found in some villages, but without prior knowledge it would be prudent not to rely on finding one off the beaten track, especially on Sundays, out of hours or out of season. The only 24hr petrol station is in Broadford. Portree petrol station is open on Sundays throughout out the year. For up-to-date information enquire at Tourist Information Offices.

Banks: Portree and Broadford.

Shops: Portree is the capital and main shopping centre. There are supermarkets there and in Broadford (and Kyle of Lochalsh). Food may also be obtained at local stores around the island, including Glenbrittle campsite in season.

Notes on the Use of This Guide

General Advice to Walkers

This guidebook is not an instruction manual in hillwalking skills and safety. It assumes that parties will be suitably equipped (good footwear, waterproofs, map, compass etc.) and competent to undertake their chosen itinerary. In case of accident, phone 999. The Skye Mountain Rescue Team is based at Portree Police Station (tel: 01478-612888).

The Mountaineering Club of Scotland website has useful information on safety and the skills required on Scottish mountains: www.mcofs.org.uk (click on the hill walking link).

Many accidents in the Scottish hills are caused by walkers attempting routes outside their capabilities. To enable a more realistic route appraisal, each route in this book has been assigned an at-a-glance difficulty grid. For ease of reference this is explained at the back of this book on p.168. All gradings, assessments and descriptions given in the text are for good summer conditions only. In adverse weather difficulties are compounded and many routes are best avoided, especially if they cross rough and boggy ground. On routes that involve scrambling it is imperative not to attempt anything outwith your capabilities or any move that cannot be reversed if necessary. Particular care is required on the crumbling peaks of Trotternish, and Cuillin routes and difficult coast walks are subject to special considerations (see pp.20 and 96).

Under snow the mountains of Skye should be avoided by those unused to Scottish winter conditions. Snowfall varies greatly from year to year, but in a normal season the hills get their first dusting of snow in October and winter conditions can prevail until after Easter, with pockets of snow lasting even later in sheltered mountain spaces.

Access

Land access in Scotland was revolutionised by *The Land Reform (Scotland) Act* (2003) and the accompanying *Scottish Outdoor Access Code* (2005), which created a statutory right of responsible access for outdoor recreation. Anyone walking in the Scottish countryside should be familiar with the *Code*, which explains rights and responsibilities in detail. Further information from Outdoor Access Scotland: www.outdooraccess-scotland.com.

In connection with the Act, note the following points:

- Respect private property and the privacy of occupants.
- It is illegal to remove or damage flora without the landowner's permission.
- It is illegal to disturb bird nests. Depending on species, these may be occupied from February to August.

The Act extends access rights to wild camping, provided this is done responsibly. Wild camping is characterised by lightweight gear, small numbers and only a few nights spent in one place.

In Scotland the red stag stalking season runs from 1 July to 20 October and the grouse shooting season from 12 August to 10 December, although actual dates vary from locality to locality. There is no stalking on Sundays. On Skye these activities are limited, usually take place in areas not used by walkers and are unlikely to affect any of the routes in this book. Nevertheless, take note of any roadside notices restricting access when activity is taking place. Further information from the Mountaineering Club of Scotland website (see below).

Of more concern to landowners is disturbance to fields, sheep and farm animals by dogs. These are becoming an increasing nuisance on the island and notices to keep them under control proliferate. If you must take a dog with you, keep it on a short lead. Landowners are legally empowered to shoot a dog that is causing disturbance. An owner's advice leaflet is available from Outdoor Access Scotland: http://www.snh.gov.uk/docs/C233791.pdf.

In short, the aim is minimal impact. Please leave the land as you would wish to find it. Further information on all of these topics from the Mountaineering Club of Scotland (McofS): www.mcofs.org.uk (click on the access and conservation link).

Maps

Apart from the Cuillin, OS 1:50,000 Landranger maps are adequate for most Skye walks. Two maps cover the whole island except for the extreme eastern tip: number 23 North Skye and number 32 South Skye. Number 33 Loch Alsh and Glen Shiel covers the eastern tip and number 24 covers Raasay. OS 1:25,000 Explorer maps and Harvey's 1:25,000 map of The Storr enable a more detailed appreciation of the landscape and aid in finding features such as duns and other historical and geographical features. For the complex topography of the Cuillin an even larger scale map is preferable. Harvey's 1:12,500 waterproof map is recommended. Grid references given in the text (all beginning NG) are based on OS maps. Landranger and Explorer maps are indicated for all routes in the form, for example, L32/E411.

Sketch maps are used to show each route's major features but are not intended for use on the hill.

The map symbols used are listed on p.viii.

The classification of mountains as Munros or Tops is based on the 1997 edition of *Munro's Tables*.

Note that river directions, left bank and right bank, in accordance with common usage, refer to the direction when facing downstream.

Measurements

Distances in the text are specified in both miles (to the nearest half-mile) and kilometres (to the nearest kilometre); shorter distances are specified in metres (an approximate imperial measurement is yards).

Heights are specified in both metres and feet. Total amount of ascent for a route is specified to the nearest 10m/50ft but should be regarded as an approximation only.

Route times are notoriously difficult for a guidebook to estimate, owing to differences in fitness levels between individuals, especially on terrain as rugged as the Cuillin's. Those specified in the text (to the nearest half-hour) are based on the time it should take a 'person of reasonable fitness' to complete the route in good summer conditions. They take into account length of route, amount of ascent, technical difficulty, type of terrain and short stoppages, but do not make allowances for long stoppages or adverse weather. They are roughly standard between routes for comparison purposes and can be adjusted where necessary by a factor appropriate to the individual. In winter routes will normally take much longer.

Names

Most Skye names are of Gaelic or Norse origin and many are mispronounced by native English speakers, yet an ability to pronounce them correctly and understand their meaning can add much to the pleasure of walking on Skye. To this end a glossary of pronunciations and meanings has been provided along with the index.

OS spellings have been retained for purposes of standardisation, although they are sometimes incorrect. In this respect, note that names sometimes differ between Landranger and Explorer maps. In addition, some names have become anglicised to such an extent that it would be pedantic to enforce a purist pronunciation on a non-Gaelic speaker. For example, the correct pronunciation of Ben is something akin to *Pyne*, with a soft *n* as in the first syllable of *onion*. Bealach, meaning Pass, is pronounced *byalach*, but many find it hard not to call it a *beelach*. Similarly many find it hard not to pronounce *loch* as *lock*.

Despite these problems the rough phonetic guide given in this book should enable a good attempt at a pronunciation that would be intelligible to a Gaelic speaker. In connection with the guide the following points should be noted: Y before a vowel is pronounced as in *you*, OW is pronounced as in *town* and CH is pronounced as in Scottish *loch* or German *noch*.

Toponymy (the study of place name meanings) is complicated by OS misspellings, changes in spelling and word usage over the centuries, words with more than one meaning and unknown origin of names (Gaelic, Norse, Irish etc). For example, consider the possible meanings of the names Skye (see p.1) and Cuillin (see p.19). Meanings given in the text are the most commonly accepted, even if disputed; some names are too obscure to be given any meaning.

CUILLIN INTRODUCTION

General Description

The Cuillin are unquestionably the finest peaks in the British Isles. They are the perfect miniature mountain range. The geology chapter in the main introduction describes the volcanic formation of the range 60 million years ago, and the slow cooling of the lava to form the coarse-grained gabbro of which the mountains are largely composed. Gabbro is universally acknowledged to be the best climbing rock in the world, and nowhere else does it occur in such quantity or form. It is an extraordinarily rough rock, merciless on skin and clothes but supremely adhesive to feet and other useful parts of the anatomy.

Some of the rock, known as peridotite, is finger-shreddingly sharp. The geologist John MacCulloch vividly described its 'nutmeg-grater-like surface in contact with which the human body may almost defy the laws of gravity'. You are most likely to come across peridotite in upper Coir' a' Ghrunnda (Route 12).

At the other end of the scale the gabbro has been intruded in places by finer-grained basalt dykes. These have eroded more quickly than the rougher gabbro to form conspicuous chimneys, gullies and ladder-like features, such as Waterpipe Gully on Sgurr an Fheadain (Route 6).

The Cuillin landscape is savage and elemental. There are no hillsides of grass or heather here. No plateau summits. The rock forms vertical faces and narrow ridges, some so sharp that the best means of progress is to sit (carefully) astride them (*à cheval*). Many summits can only be gained by rock climbing. Few can be climbed without putting hand to rock.

In form the range consists of a horseshoe-shaped main ridge some 8ml/13km long, with satellite ridges radiating out around deep-cut corries. Along this ridge are strung eleven Munros (separate mountains over 914m/3000ft, as defined in *Munro's Tables* and marked as ▲ in the text), nine further Tops (lesser peaks over 914m/3,000ft, marked as Δ in the text) and numerous other lower tops, which give the Cuillin skyline a jagged and dramatic appearance when viewed from afar. An outlying Munro and Top (Bla Bheinn) bring the total number of Munros and Tops on Skye to twelve and ten respectively. Munro baggers should note that in the latest edition of *Munro's Tables* (1997) Sgurr Dearg lost its long-standing Top status while Knight's Peak (a pinnacle on Sgurr nan Gillean) was controversially elevated to Top status.

Mountaineering in the Cuillin is like nowhere else. To walk and scramble along the narrow ridge from peak to peak, through an otherworldly landscape of remarkable rock formations, with island upon island crowding the western horizon and the whole scene bathed in breathtakingly pure light, is a supreme experience.

The Cuillin corries were gouged out by glaciers during the Ice Age and they typically consist of a flat-bottomed hollow surrounded by steep walls of rock. Sometimes their floors have been scraped smooth by glacial action to form great slabs known as boiler-plate slabs. Boulders removed during this process were sometimes gently deposited elsewhere when the ice melted to form precariously balanced 'erratics'. On a hot day the irresistibly beautiful lochans and streamways that characterise the corries, pure and clear beyond imagining, have put paid to many a well-laid plan.

The faces of the peaks are mainly the preserve of rock climbers. The normal route to the skyline for non-climbers is either via a steeply rising satellite ridge between two corries or via the corrie floor and a stony gully at the back. Descents are by similar routes or perhaps by a scree slope, enabling the walker to linger high late into the evening as the sun sets over the Outer Hebrides.

Around the base of the Cuillin is a sponge-like moor whose water-retaining properties are almost unnatural. This is a prime candidate for The Plain of Ill Luck that, according to legend, barred the way of Cuchullin on his way to Dunscaith Castle (Route 43g). Cuchullin was able to progress only with the aid of a wheel that when rolled before him generated a heat so fierce that the bog dried in its path. Such wheels are unfortunately currently unobtainable on Skye. Paths have improved enormously in the twenty years since the first edition of this guidebook, but a certain degree of humour remains a useful asset during the approach to the peaks.

It has long been held by certain tourist guidebooks that it is from Cuchullin that the Cuillin derive their name, but this is unlikely. More likely meanings of the name include High Rocks (from Norse *Kjölen*), Holly (from Gaelic *Cuilion*, referring to the serrated skyline) and Worthless (from the Celtic, referring to the Cuillin's agricultural potential).

The topographical complexity of the range is such that the descriptions of peaks and walks in the routes that follow will require prolonged study in consultation with a large-scale map. Owing to the complex terrain a large-scale map such as Harvey's 1:12,500 waterproof map is recommended (www.harveymaps.co.uk).

This guidebook describes nineteen routes in the Cuillin. Routes 1–15 cover the entire range from north to south in the form of manageable day trips. Fitter individuals can combine these routes into longer rounds. Routes 16–19 provide a compendium of mix-and-match routes to the supreme mountain sanctuary of Coruisk at the heart of the Cuillin horseshoe. For a detailed description see Route 16.

If you complete all of the routes described here you will have come to know the Cuillin more intimately than most… and still be itching to return.

Advice to Cuillin Walkers and Scramblers

General hillwalking advice is given in the main Introduction on p.14. This section covers considerations specific to walking and scrambling in the Cuillin.

The Cuillin are no place for novice hillwalkers. There are few peaks that can be climbed without putting hand to rock and there are few easy escape routes. In this three-dimensional labyrinth of rock, route-finding is often a problem, to such an extent that in mist the route onwards may be impossible to locate. Even retracing steps to retreat may prove difficult. The problem is compounded by the magnetic nature of the rock, which makes compass readings dangerously unreliable. Mobile phones may not work.

Other problems include loose rock and rubble-strewn ledges, which necessitate constant vigilance. Gabbro blocks are often unstable and rockfall is common. As noted in the Geology section on p.4, important changes have even occurred recently on the main ridge itself, with the loss of the gendarme on Sgurr nan Gillean's west ridge in 1987 and a lightning strike on the Inaccessible Pinnacle in 2007. A rock climber was killed by a displaced rock on the face of Sron na Ciche in 2011.

Atmospheric changes can be sudden. Cloud can appear from nowhere, literally in seconds. In wet weather the roughness of the gabbro helps it retain friction, but this can lead to a false sense of security. Especial care is required where basalt dykes have intruded into the gabbro, as the smoother basalt quickly becomes greasy and slippery.

As noted in the main Introduction, assessments of scrambling difficulty in the routes that follow are necessarily subjective and apply to good summer conditions only. Although great pains have been taken to ensure that gradings are standard across routes, an easy scramble may seem hard to one person and a hard scramble easy to another, depending on individual factors such as physical build, reach and response to exposure.

In short, the Cuillin demand great respect and a high level of mountain craft, and they are best tackled in fine weather only. The first-timer should not only be an experienced hillwalker on Scottish mountains but would do well to seek out the company of someone with Cuillin experience for his or her initial forays onto the peaks. A number of guides are available, with the Inaccessible Pinnacle (Route 9) being the most popular objective requested. For up-to-date details, enquire at Tourist Information Offices or do a web search on 'Cuillin Guide'.

In winter the Cuillin have an Alpine attraction but become serious mountaineering propositions that should be left well alone by walkers. Paths are obliterated by snow, hillsides become treacherous, ridges become corniced, stone shoots become snow gullies, walking becomes more difficult and tiring, terrain becomes featureless in adverse weather, white-outs and spindrift reduce visibility to zero.

Again as noted in the main Introduction, snowfall varies greatly from year to year, but in a normal season the hills get their first dusting of snow in October and winter conditions prevail until after Easter, with pockets of snow lasting even later in sheltered spaces. No-one should venture onto the Cuillin in winter without adequate clothing, an ice-axe, crampons and experience (or the company of an experienced person).

In the following routes almost all ascents should be regarded as Grade 5, because even if scrambling is not involved the terrain is everywhere difficult. If unsure of your abilities or concerned about the terrain, you are recommended to try one of the easier routes first: Bruach na Frithe via Fionn Choire (Route 4) or Sgurr na Banachdich via Coir' an Eich (Route 8). The ascent of Sgurr Dearg via the Bealach Coire na Banachdich also barely requires any scrambling . . . as long as you find the easiest line (Route 9). Outlying Bla Bheinn is also easy to climb from the east (Route 13).

In case of accident phone 999, and remember that mobile phones may not work in the mountains. There are public telephones at Sligachan (NG 485299) and Glenbrittle House (NG 412214), or alert someone local. The Skye Mountain Rescue Team is based at Portree Police Station (tel: 01478-612888).

Valley Bases and Paths

The two main valley bases are Sligachan at the north end of the range (NG 485299) and Glen Brittle at the south end (NG 411206). Sligachan lies on the A87 and can be reached by public transport. Glen Brittle lies 14m/23km away, reached by a single-track road that ends on the coast at Loch Brittle, and requires private transport to reach.

Both bases have seasonal campsites. Sligachan campsite, opposite Sligachan Hotel, is open from the beginning of May to the end of September. Glen Brittle campsite is open from the beginning of April to the end of September and has a campsite shop. Note that Glen Brittle campsite toilets are security-coded all year to prevent use by wild campers and non-campers.

While Sligachan has a hotel (www.sligachan.co.uk), Glen Brittle has a youth hostel (NG 409225), a British Mountaineering Council (BMC) Hut (NG 411216) and other private accommodation (for further details see Visitor Information in main Introduction).

Loch Coruisk is a third possible base at the heart of the Cuillin horseshoe, but there is no road access to it and easy routes from it to the skyline are longer and less numerous. Accommodation is at the Junior Mountaineering Club of Scotland (JMCS) Hut (NG 487196) or by camping wild. All provisions must be carried in.

Freshwater Loch Coruisk lies only a short distance from the sea at Loch Scavaig, across which Bella Jane Boat Trips and Misty Isle Boat Trips ferry passengers from Elgol to facilitate access, either one-way or return. This makes day trips or overnight stays more feasible. Further details: www.beallajane.co.uk (tel: 0800-7313089 or 01471-866244) and www.mistyisleboattrips.co.uk (tel: 01471-866288).

Coruisk is a magnificent spot that demands at least a day-trip visit, but all the standard ascent routes to the peaks begin at Sligachan or in Glen Brittle.

An important path around the foot of the Cuillin links Sligachan and Glen Brittle via the pass known as the Bealach a' Mhaim (NG 447269). At the Sligachan end this path begins at the car park on the A863 Dunvegan road beside the access road to Alltdearg House (NG 480297, signposted 'Glenbrittle'). From here walk along the access road and follow the fence right around the house to reach the banks of the Allt Dearg Mor. An alternative start begins just down the road, 60m west of the Mountain Rescue Base near Sligachan Hotel.

The path holds to the left bank (right-hand side) of the Allt Dearg Mor all the way to the bealach, then it descends beside the Allt a' Mhaim and alongside a forestry plantation into Glen Brittle, reaching the roadside at the Fairy Pools car park (NG 424258) 4ml/6km from the campsite. Campsite to campsite: 8ml/13km, 360m/1200ft, 4hrs.

There is also a useful short-cut in Glen Brittle between Glen Brittle Hut or youth hostel and the campsite. When the road turns sharp right beyond Glenbrittle House, keep straight on along the access road to Cuillin Cottage. Just before the cottage a gate in the fence on the right gives access to a path that skirts the fields to the campsite shop.

History of Exploration

The peaks of the Cuillin are the only mountains in Scotland that have been named for the men who first climbed them, and so the history of their exploration is of more than usual interest. Few walkers of today will ever know the excitement of climbing an unnamed and untrodden peak, yet little more than a century ago the Cuillin were virtually a virgin mountain range. The earliest recorded attempts to climb them were made by the geologist John MacCulloch in the 1810s, but as his favourite mode of ascent was on horseback it is no surprise to learn that he failed seven times in five successive years (blaming the weather, as many still do).

The Cuillin remained unclimbed until the physicist and geologist Professor James Forbes persuaded Duncan MacIntyre, a local forester, to guide him up Sgurr nan Gillean on 7 July, 1836. Forbes returned to Skye again in 1845 and (again with MacIntyre) made the first ascent of Bruach na Frithe. These ascents remained isolated events. Other travellers to Skye contented themselves with a boat trip to Loch Coruisk, firmly placed on the tourist map since the visit of Sir Walter Scott in 1814.

The 1850s saw the first guideless ascent of Sgurr nan Gillean by Inglis and party (1857), the first ascent of Bla Bheinn (from Loch Slapin) by Professor John Nicol and the poet Algernon Swinburne (1857) and the first ascent of Sgurr na Stri by Alpine Club member C. R. Weld (1859). But it was, fittingly, a Skye man, Alexander Nicolson, who took upon himself the fuller exploration of the Cuillin.

Nicolson's first ascent was in 1865, when he was guided up the Sgurr nan Gillean Tourist Route by Duncan MacIntyre's son, then gamekeeper at Sligachan. The many years of adventure that followed culminated in the momentous year of 1873, when Nicolson climbed Sgurr na Banachdich, Sgurr Dearg and Sgurr Alasdair (by the Great Stone Shoot). Before 1873, Sgurr Thearlaich, Sgurr Alasdair and Sgurr Sgumain were all lumped together under the name Sgurr Sgumain, but after Nicolson's feat the highest of the three peaks was named after him.

Nicolson fell in love with the Cuillin and praised them in prose, poem and song. From the late 1860s onwards tourists began to arrive in numbers, with Sligachan Inn as their base and the Sgurr nan Gillean Tourist Route the main attraction. In 1880 brothers Charles and Lawrence Pilkington, two of the greatest mountaineers of their day, climbed the Inaccessible Pinnacle by its east ridge. In 1886 the west ridge fell to Stocker and Parker. In 1887 Charles Pilkington's party climbed the north peak of Sgurr Alasdair, which was named Sgurr Thearlaich after him. In the same year the same party completed the first round of the Coire Lagan skyline, naming the peak south of Sgurr Dearg Pic MacKenzie after one of their number, John Mackenzie. The name survives as Sgurr Mhic Choinnich.

John MacKenzie was the first Cuillin rock-climbing guide. He climbed Sgurr nan Gillean in 1866 at the age of ten, accompanied Tribe on the first ascent of Sgurr a' Ghreadaidh in 1870 and was with Nicolson during that memorable year of 1873. During a climbing career spanning more than fifty years he came to know the Cuillin intimately, and was much sought after for his guiding prowess and congenial company.

His great companion was Professor Norman Collie, who was converted to mountaineering while at Sligachan for the fishing in 1886. Collie became famous for his mountaineering expeditions all over the world, but the Cuillin remained his first love. With MacKenzie he opened up many new rock faces in the Cuillin. They discovered Collie's Ledge on Sgurr Mhic Choinnich in 1888, thereby easing the traverse of that knife-edge summit. They made the first crossing of the Thearlaich-Dubh gap (with King) in 1891, climbed Sgurr Coir' an Lochain (the last unclimbed peak in the Cuillin, with Howell and Naismith) in 1896 and discovered the astonishing rock protuberance known as the Cioch on Sron na Ciche, climbing it in 1906 (MacKenzie named it, Cioch meaning the Breast).

When Collie retired he spent an increasing amount of time at Sligachan, often fishing with his inseparable companion MacKenzie. MacKenzie died in 1934 aged 78. Collie stayed at Sligachan from 1939 onwards, a rather sad figure haunted by Cuillin memories. He died in 1942 aged 83, and at his own request was buried close beside MacKenzie in old Struan cemetery, where their graves can still be visited if you wish to pay your respects. Sgurr Thormaid was named for Collie.

Collie and MacKenzie were part of a new breed of rock climbers who began to appear towards the end of the nineteenth century. In 1889 Swan made the first recorded Cuillin winter ascent (of Bruach na Frithe). In 1895 Kelsall and Hallitt made the first ascent of Waterpipe Gully of Sgurr an Fheadain. In 1898 the last remaining problems on the main ridge were overcome: King's Chimney on Sgurr Mhic Choinnich and the direct ascent of the Basteir Tooth.

The subsequent history of rock climbing in the Cuillin is outwith the remit of this book, but walking history continued to be made. In 1911 Shadbolt and MacLaren made the first traverse of the main ridge (the Great Traverse), from Glen Brittle to Sligachan, in 16¾hrs. Their fitness can be judged by their ascent time of 2½hrs from Glen Brittle to Gars-bheinn. Fell runners of today complete the traverse from Gars-bheinn to Sgurr nan Gillean in under 4hrs (the record, set by Es Tresidder in 2007, stands at a breathtaking 3hrs 17mins). In 1939 the Greater Traverse (including Clach Glas and Bla Bheinn) was accomplished by Charleson and Forde. The first winter Great Traverse took place in 1965.

There are no virgin peaks left in the Cuillin for explorers of today, but to follow in the footsteps of the pioneers will be adventure enough for most. For a vivid account of the history of Cuillin exploration seek out a copy of Ben Humble's classic *The Cuillin of Skye*.

ROUTE 1: SGURR NAN GILLEAN

ROUTE START: Sligachan (NG 483297, L32/E411 or Harvey's Cuillin)

ROUTE LOG: 7½ml/12 km, 1010m/3300ft, 6½ hours

ROUTE OVERVIEW: return mountain scramble (or circular mountain scramble in combination with Route 2). A straightforward

	1	2	3	4	5
Grade	▓	▓	▓	▓	
Terrain	▓	▓	▓	▓	
Navigation	▓	▓	▓		
Seriousness	▓	▓	▓	▓	

approach leads to a hard and exposed final scramble up the south-east ridge of the quintessential Cuillin peak on the misleadingly named Tourist Route.

Sgurr nan Gillean at the north end of the Cuillin is one of the most distinctive and difficult mountains in the range. For the non-climber there is only one way up – the so-called Tourist Route – but do not be misled by the name into thinking this is a mere stroll, for in its latter stages it is a hard exposed scramble that requires care and nerve.

Should you decide in your wisdom to leave the last few metres for another day the ascent is still worthwhile for the typically fine Cuillin scenery and views. And even if you do not reach the top the day need not be summitless, for behind Sgurr nan Gillean at the tail-end of the Cuillin horseshoe are the two smaller peaks of Sgurr Beag and Sgurr na h-Uamha, the former of which is easily reached.

Sgurr nan Gillean's west ridge is not as difficult as Pinnacle Ridge but should be avoided by non-climbers, as even the easiest route up or down it involves exposed rock climbing towards its foot. Until very recently a gendarme astride the ridge here required a heart-stopping traverse above the abyss, but in the winter of 1986-7, to the dismay of all Cuillin lovers and previous guidebook writers, the gendarme disappeared. The scrambly upper section of the ridge can lure the unwary down it, but no-one without rock climbing experience should venture here.

In the famous view of the northern Cuillin from Sligachan, Sgurr nan Gillean is the steep tapering cone on the left, a perfect pyramid of rock. The west ridge (the right-hand skyline) and the north ridge (facing, also known as Pinnacle Ridge) involve rock climbing. The Tourist Route goes across the left-hand skyline to climb the hidden south-east ridge, part of the Cuillin Main Ridge. It is cairned and has a path for much of the way, but it is still difficult to follow in mist.

The route begins just up the A863 Dunvegan road from

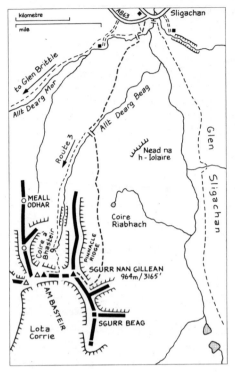

Sligachan Hotel, *c*.60m beyond the Mountain Rescue Base. The initial section of the formerly boggy approach path has been renovated since the first edition of this guidebook and now saves much frustration. After a few hundred metres it reaches a bridge on the Allt Dearg Mor (Big Red Stream) and forks. If masochists wish to know what the path was like prior to renovation, they can reach this point by the old riverbank path that starts opposite the hotel.

Ignore the right branch at the bridge, which continues up beside the stream and crosses the Bealach a' Mhaim to Glen Brittle, and follow the left branch over the bridge. The path crosses the almost flat moor to the Allt Dearg Beag (Little Red Stream), then follows its near bank past beautiful pools and cascades up to a second bridge where it divides again. Again ignore the right branch, which goes to Coire a' Bhasteir (Route 3), and cross the bridge.

The path now crosses the broad flat ridge above the craggy hillock of Nead na h-Iolaire (Eagle's Nest) to reach Coire Riabhach (Brindled Corrie), an untypical shallow heathery Cuillin corrie. Keeping well above the lochan in the bowl of the corrie, it continues up steep stony slopes around Sgurr nan Gillean's east face, bears right beneath the towering pinnacles of Pinnacle Ridge and reaches a higher, smaller corrie whose floor and sides

> *The Cuillin remained unclimbed until the physicist and geologist Professor James Forbes persuaded Duncan MacIntyre, a local forester, to guide him up Sgurr nan Gillean on 7 July, 1836. The route they pioneered has since ironically been dubbed the Tourist Route, more on account of its popularity than the ease of its ascent. The peak was previously considered to be the highest Cuillin and to be unclimbable.*

are a chaotic jumble of crags and boulders.

The path becomes indistinct in places but is well-cairned. It climbs the gully at the back of the corrie onto the boulderfield below the south-east ridge, and reaches the skyline half-way between Sgurr Beag and Sgurr nan Gillean. Here the excitement begins as you turn right to follow the airy crest of the ridge up to the summit platform.

There are many route options at first, but as the steepening summit cone gets nearer the scrambling

From Sligachan the four pinnacles of Pinnacle Ridge cannot be distinguished unless cloud swirls between them and silhouettes them, but from the summit of Sgurr nan Gillean the ridge is seen in all its splendour – a Difficult rock climb with a real mountaineering flavour, requiring the ability to climb down as well as up during its traverse. The fourth pinnacle, known as ▲Knight's Peak, was controversially made a Top in the 1997 revision of Munro's Tables *and is inaccessible to hillwalkers.*

becomes harder and more exposed. On the last 30m/100ft there are only two possible routes: the extremely narrow crest of the ridge or sloping rocks to the left, both of about equal standard. It is at this point that those of a nervous disposition may not wish to proceed, and remember that it will be necessary to descend the same way.

A must-see for all Cuillin lovers is the small climbing museum in Sligachan Hotel. It contains memorabilia, displays, photographs and explanatory panels from the Victorian heyday of Cuillin exploration, together with visitors' books that record visits by the pioneers and others.

The final few metres along the narrow summit ridge are very exposed, especially at a short hiatus where parts of the anatomy other than hands and feet are likely to be put to good use. The ▲ summit itself is an eerie platform from which none of the supporting ridges can be seen, as if it were suspended in the sky. Beyond this eyrie the Cuillin Main Ridge arcs away southwards, peak upon peak. By scrambling just beyond the summit, views of the west ridge and magnificent Pinnacle Ridge can be obtained.

Unless you go rock climbing or decide to take up permanent residence at the summit you must descend via the south-east ridge again. Most summiteers are content to retrace the route of ascent all the way to Sligachan but, as noted above, the two smaller peaks of Sgurr Beag and Sgurr na h-Uamha south of Sgurr nan Gillean at the end of the Main Ridge are worth a closer look (see Route 2).

ROUTE START: Sligachan (NG 483297, L32/E411 or Harvey's Cuillin)

ROUTE LOG: 11ml/18km, 1160m/3800ft, 9hrs (including ascent of Sgurr nan Gillean)

ROUTE OVERVIEW: add-on mountain scramble to Route 1. An (optional) entertaining scramble on the

	1	2	3	4	5
Grade					
Terrain					
Navigation					
Seriousness					

'last nail' in the Cuillin horseshoe is followed by a rough descent amid imposing rock scenery on the wild east side of the range.

The minor peaks of Sgurr Beag and Sgurr na h-Uamha, hidden from view behind Sgurr nan Gillean in the view from Sligachan, complete the north end of the Cuillin horseshoe. Sgurr na h-Uamha in particular is a fine little mountain whose exciting ascent involves a few moves that are even harder than the final section of the Sgurr nan Gillean Tourist Route. If you had qualms about that, be content with a wander out to Sgurr Beag, then go down the way you came up.

The peaks lie only a short distance away from Gillean but, as they fail to reach Munro height, they are unjustly ignored by 'Tourist Routers' and are equally unlikely to be climbed for their own sake from Sligachan. Following an ascent of Gillean, however, they offer more sport, dramatic views of the higher peak and the option of a different return route to Sligachan.

The stony summit of Sgurr Beag is only a short walk away from the foot of Gillean's south-east ridge and on its far side easy slopes of grass and stones descend to the Bealach a' Ghlas-choire. Across the bealach the beautiful conical peak of Sgurr na h-Uamha forms a fitting 'last nail' in the Cuillin horseshoe. The two-tiered north ridge that rises from the bealach is sharp enough to quicken the pulse of the most experienced scrambler. On closer view the first tier provides easy scrambling on satisfying gabbro blocks, with little exposure. The second tier is hard. Handholds are excellent but there's a brief section that involves a few moves of Moderate rock climbing standard. The route goes initially left,

> The Bloody Stone is a curious, huge, isolated boulder, some 10m/30ft high. Its name derives from a traditional tale of yet another bloody battle between the feuding MacDonalds and MacLeods on yet another godforsaken patch of remote moorland. Depending on which account you read, the victorious MacDonalds either piled up MacLeod bodies around the stone or divided the spoils of battle here. In this wild and lonely spot, the story certainly has resonance.

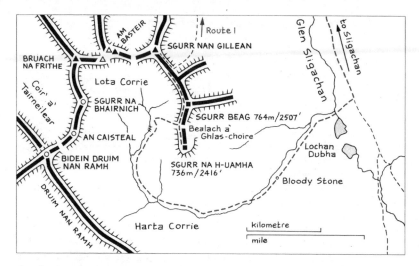

then back right and straight up the centre of the face towering overhead.

WARNING. As on the final section of Gillean's south-east ridge, this second tier should be attempted by expert scramblers only. Do not go further than your abilities allow and do not attempt anything you won't be able to reverse.

Once back on the Bealach a' Ghlas-choire, a descent westwards into the remote mountain fastness of Harta Corrie provides a way back to Sligachan through some of the wildest and least trodden parts of the Cuillin. Note, however, that the terrain is rocky, steep and awkward and the route requires sure-footedness and good routefinding ability.

Steep broken slopes, requiring care, lead down into Lota Corrie, a small green oasis hemmed in by the peaks of the northern Cuillin and from which a tremendous water chute, the longest in the Cuillin, falls into upper Harta Corrie. The descent into Harta Corrie continues to require care. Numerous small crags have to be outwitted but the line of least resistance is without technical difficulty. The best route down keeps to the left of the water chute and is cairned, but you may find the cairns difficult to locate.

Upper Harta Corrie is another impressive spot beneath the eastern buttresses of An Caisteal, whose huge walls of rock, over 300m/1000ft high, hang overhead like curtains. On easing ground at last, a further short descent leads to the lower corrie, a deep U-shaped trench that curves around the rocky flanks of Sgurr na h-Uamha to meet Glen Sligachan. A path is picked up on the right bank of the river and this leads past the Bloody Stone at the corrie mouth. The path eventually joins the excellent Glen Sligachan path (Route 16), which leads back 3½ml/6km to Sligachan.

ROUTE 3: AM BASTEIR

ROUTE START: Sligachan (NG 483297, L32/E411 or Harvey's Cuillin)

ROUTE LOG: 7ml/11km, 930m/3050ft, 6hrs

ROUTE OVERVIEW: return mountain scramble. A complex approach to a secluded corrie is followed by an exposed scramble to

	1	2	3	4	5
Grade	■	■	■	■	■
Terrain	■	■	■	■	
Navigation	■	■	■	■	■
Seriousness	■	■	■	■	■

the summit of one of the Cuillin's most imposing peaks. The scrambling is mostly straightforward but, following recent rockfall, there is a harder section that may put the summit itself just out of reach.

West of Sgurr nan Gillean the Cuillin Main Ridge and two side ridges enclose secluded Coire a' Bhasteir to form one of the most majestic skylines on Skye. At the back of the corrie the Main Ridge rises steeply from the Bealach a' Bhasteir to form the east ridge of Am Basteir, then falls away vertically to the dramatic Basteir Tooth. The east ridge is a hard scramble that has become even harder in recent years owing to rockfall, but it remains the easiest way to the summit (or near-summit) of this most impressive rock peak.

From Sligachan follow the Sgurr nan Gillean Tourist Route (Route 1) as far as the fork at the bridge over the Allt Dearg Beag. Instead of going left over the bridge, continue on the path up the right-hand side of the stream towards Coire a' Bhasteir. Approaching the corrie the stream flows through the Basteir Gorge, whose high rock walls merge on the right into slabs at the foot of the north-east ridge of Sgurr a' Bhasteir.

A cairned route across the slabs climbs through the gorge, cutting across the shoulder of the ridge. There are one or two places where easy, slightly exposed scrambling is required, and it is important not to lose the line of cairns, especially in mist. On exit from the gorge, more cairns lead into the bowl of the corrie, where a secret lochan is surrounded by towering peaks. Shaded from the sun for most of the year, this is a dramatic spot that merits a trip in its own right, even if you forego an attempt on Am Basteir.

> The △Basteir Tooth is a fantastic rock tower on the main Cuillin ridge, well seen from Sligachan. Along with Knight's Peak of Sgurr nan Gillean it is one of a pair of Tops (as defined in Munro's Tables) that are inaccessible to walkers. It resembles the blade of an axe and it is this that gives Am Basteir, the peak that hangs over it, its evocative Gaelic name meaning The Executioner.

A path crosses the stream at the lochan's outflow, outflanks the band of crags at the back of the corrie on the left and reaches the foot of the summit cliffs of Am Basteir, which soar menacingly overhead. Climb the boulder ruckle to their left to reach the Bealach a' Bhasteir, where you will want to pause to survey the east ridge that rears dauntingly skywards in front of you.

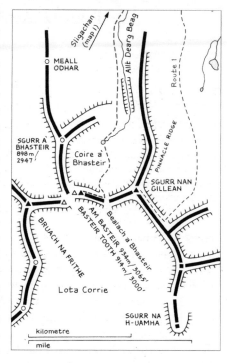

Surprisingly the ascent initially involves mostly walking and easy scrambling, albeit along a narrow exposed crest, with any hard sections easily bypassed on ledges on the Lota Coire side (beware loose rubble on ledges). If only it continued in a similar vein, but around two-thirds of the way up you are faced with a 'Bad Step' – a 3m/10ft vertical rib directly on the crest that must be descended by facing inwards. It used to be a nerve-racking scramble anyway, but recent rockfall, perhaps induced by scrambler erosion, has turned it into a tricky little rock climb. You will perhaps need no advice to turn back at this point.

> *Beyond Am Basteir's summit it is possible to continue a short distance to the top of the western cliffs, to view the top of the Basteir Tooth. This involves a hard scramble down a wall and across a slab, easier on the way back.*

N.B. An alternative route to the notch beyond the Bad Step is developing. When the ridge begins to steepen on ascent, go left below the crest on an indistinct path and across slabs. **WARNING.** This is an exposed and hard scramble that requires good routefinding ability on rock. It should be attempted only by confident, expert scramblers, who should remain aware that the route must be reversed on descent.

If you do make it to the far side of the Bad Step, Am Basteir's small ▲ summit platform is soon reached without further ado.

ROUTE 4: BRUACH NA FRITHE

ROUTE START: head of Glen Brittle (NG 424258, L32/E411 or Harvey's Cuillin) or Sligachan (NG 447269)

ROUTE LOG: 6½ml/11km, 890m/2900ft, 6hrs

ROUTE OVERVIEW: circular mountain scramble. An easy scramble up a shattered ridge puts you atop one

	1	2	3	4	5
Grade					
Terrain					
Navigation					
Seriousness					

of the best viewpoints on the Cuillin Main Ridge, with a number of descent options that pass through stunning rock scenery.

When climbed via Fionn Coire, Bruach na Frithe is one of the most easily reached summits in the Cuillin, yet it is of no less character for that and is a great viewpoint. Leaving the Fionn Coire route for descent, scramblers will find that the narrow, shattered north-west ridge offers a more exhilarating ascent, devoid of any unavoidable hard moves, although the rock is basalt and should be avoided when wet. In its lower reaches the ridge divides into two spurs, and the shallow basin between them contains the most featureless terrain in the Cuillin.

The path between Sligachan and Glen Brittle crosses the Bealach a' Mhaim at the foot of the ridge and gives easy access from either starting point. The Glen Brittle approach from the Fairy Pools car park at the head of the glen is the shorter. From the lochan on the bealach, climb the more westerly of the two spurs. Grassy slopes lead up over a couple of levellings, then stonier slopes climb more steeply to the point where the two spurs join.

Above here the ridge quickly narrows and soon becomes rocky. The scrambling is in the easy-to-moderate category, and with judicious routefinding most of it could even be avoided. The crest of the ridge has some hard moves but

The ascent of Bruach na Frithe via Fionn Choire, described here on descent, vies with the ascent of Sgurr na Banachdich (Route 8) as the easiest ascent route to the summit of a Cuillin Munro. The route is nevertheless rough and crosses featureless terrain, so it is still necessary for Cuillin tenderfoots to take care and keep an eye on the weather.

there is always an easier line to the right. The hardest section is where the ridge rears up steeply about half-way along, and there is some exposure here. Bypass paths on the right (the south-west face) can be used to avoid this steepening, but take care not to wander out along rubble-strewn ledges to dead-ends. The view from the ▲ summit is one

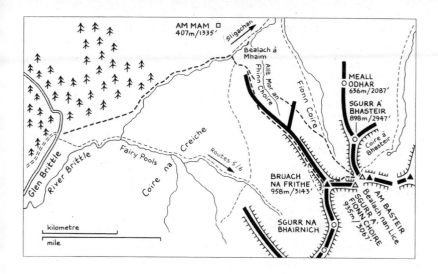

of the finest in the range, with the savage rock peaks around Coire a' Bhasteir cleaving the sky in Dolomitic splendour.

To descend, first go down the east ridge to the gap between Bruach na Frithe and Sgurr a' Fionn Choire. This is no more than a stony walk, although there's a spot of easy scrambling on the crest to begin with should you wish. Beyond the gap the rock bastion of ΔSgurr a' Fionn Choire blocks the way onward but an easy traverse path contours around it to the Bealach nan Lice beneath the Basteir Tooth. From here it is worth wandering out along the narrow south ridge of Sgurr a' Bhasteir immediately beyond to study the Tooth and also Pinnacle Ridge of Sgurr nan Gillean.

There's more than one way down from the Bealach nan Lice. If you're still seeking excitement (and heading for Sligachan), follow a path beneath the Basteir Tooth and descend scree slopes beyond into Coire a' Bhasteir, then reverse the first section of Route 3 through the Basteir Gorge to Sligachan.

For an easier way down, take the stony path that descends slopes of boulders and scree into Fionn Coire, an untypically grassy but charming Cuillin corrie with an attractive shelf of small lochans. Once into the bowl of the corrie, if heading down to Glen Brittle, cross into the basin between the two spurs of the north-west ridge and regain the Bealach a' Mhaim. If heading for Sligachan, continue down the path to rejoin the Bealach a' Mhaim path north of the bealach.

Note also that expert scramblers can find an exciting way down by descending Bruach na Frithe's south ridge (see Route 5).

ROUTE 5: SGURR NA BHAIRNICH AND AN CAISTEAL

ROUTE START: head of Glen Brittle via Bruach na Frithe (NG 424258, L32/ E411 or Harvey's Cuillin)

ROUTE LOG: 6½ml/11km, 980m/3200ft, 7hrs (including ascent of Bruach na Frithe)

ROUTE OVERVIEW: add-on mountain scramble to Route 4. A

	1	2	3	4	5
Grade					
Terrain					
Navigation					
Seriousness					

sensational scramble, with a few moves of rock climbing standard, traverses one of the sharpest summits in the Cuillin.

South of Bruach na Frithe the Cuillin Main Ridge crosses the two minor peaks of Sgurr na Bhairnich and An Caisteal, and their traverse makes a thrilling (and harder) add-on to the ascent of Bruach na Frithe (Route 4). Once across, a descent can be made down Coir' a' Tairneilear back to the Fairy Pools car park at the head of Glen Brittle.

Leaving the summit of Bruach na Frithe, the south ridge becomes quite narrow, but remains easier than the north-west ridge used by Route 4, requiring only one or two short scrambles that can be awkward when wet. Sgurr na Bhairnich, the next top along, is also easily reached by a short ascent, with any moderate moves on the ridge crest avoidable on the right.

A steep descent on rubble-strewn ledges then leads down to the deep cleft between Sgurr na Bhairnich and An Caisteal. A short distance down, a 5m/16ft vertical descent to the head of a gully can be bypassed on the left, after which it is best to keep left and hold to the steeply descending crest. Ledges on the right look more tempting initially but become awkward lower down.

An Caisteal (well deserving its Gaelic name The Castle) rears above the cleft in such an improbable fashion that most scramblers will rightly think twice before tackling it. The ascent begins with a polished vertical wall whose holds, though good, force you off-balance.

> At the first bend in the river as you turn into Coire na Creiche (Corrie of the Spoils) are a number of grassy mounds formerly topped by cairns that commemorate those who fell in the Battle of Coire na Creiche in 1601. This spot was once known as Tom nan Tighearnan (Knoll of the Lords). The battle has a place in history as the last battle ever fought on Skye soil between the MacLeods and the MacDonalds, and the corrie is named after the division of the spoils following the defeat of the MacLeods.

WARNING. For a few moves the grade approaches Moderate rock climbing, so only those who are sure of their ability should attempt it. Above the wall there are no comparable difficulties but, if you don't wish to tackle it, a stony gully on the right provides an escape route down to Coir' a' Tairneilear.

Once past the wall the route veers left until beneath An Caisteal's imposing summit buttress, then it regains the crest of the ridge by a gully on the right. The final section to the summit, which looks impossibly sharp and exposed from Sgurr a' Bhairnich, turns out to be a short 'stroll' along a sensational path.

The descent of the far side of An Caisteal to the Bealach Harta (called Bealach Coir' a'

Tairneilear in older guidebooks) is mostly no more than a moderate scramble, but it too has its moments. First, a couple of notches must be negotiated. The first can be turned on rubble-strewn ledges to the left, the second by a step across the void a few metres down on the right. Then the ridge continues narrow but easy until a vertical knob of rock called An Turaid (The Turret) blocks the way to the bealach. This can be bypassed by an exposed but easy traverse along a ledge on the left or by descending to easier slopes on the right.

Continued progress south of the Bealach Harta is blocked by the attractive triple-topped summit of Bidein Druim nan Ramh, whose traverse involves intricate route-finding and rock-climbing, so leave the ridge at the bealach to descend scree slopes into Coir' a' Tairneilear. Cairns indicate the best line if you can find them. Once into the corrie, a path follows the right bank of the stream all the way down to Coire na Creiche and the Fairy Pools car park (see also Route 6).

ROUTE 6: SGURR AN FHEADAIN

ROUTE START: head of Glen Brittle via Bruach na Frithe (NG 424258, L32/ E411 or Harvey's Cuillin)

ROUTE LOG: 5½ml/9km, 640m/2100ft, 5½hrs

ROUTE OVERVIEW: circular mountain scramble. A unique and exciting scramble climbs beside the

	1	2	3	4	5
Grade					
Terrain					
Navigation					
Seriousness					

vertiginous Waterpipe on a basalt peak that thrusts out from the main Cuillin ridge.

South of Bruach na Frithe the wide open spaces of Coire na Creiche are backed by the peaks of Sgurr na Bhairnich, An Caisteal and Bidein Druim nan Ramh on the main Cuillin ridge. From Bidein a short spur juts out to the imposing pyramid-shaped peak of Sgurr an Fheadain to divide the upper corrie into two: Coir' a' Tairneilear to the north and Coir' a' Mhadaidh to the south. Sgurr an Fheadain soars above the flat floor of Coire na Creiche, its face split by the deep Waterpipe Gully that gives the peak its name (Peak of the Waterpipe). On sunny days the true stature of the peak is masked by the higher peaks that rise behind it on the main ridge, but on stormy days the summit often stands proud against a backdrop of swirling cloud.

An ascent via the exciting north-west spur left of Waterpipe Gully has a real mountaineering feel to it. Although the scrambling is no more than moderate if the crest is adhered to, the route rises through some spectacular rock scenery and gives a fine sense of achievement. It should be undertaken by experienced scramblers only, as the rock is often loose and the exposure above Waterpipe Gully is considerable. Note also that the rock is mainly basalt and should be left well alone when wet. Beyond the summit a continuing scramble along the south-east ridge enables a fine circuit to be made.

The foot of the peak is reached by a path from the Fairy Pools car park at the head of Glen Brittle. The path, signposted Glen Brittle, forks almost immediately. Branch right on a renovated section of path that descends to the River Brittle and continues up the bank of the river, now called the Allt Coir' a' Mhadaidh, into Coire na Creiche. After half an hour or so it passes the Fairy Pools, a series of waterfalls and rock pools that form perhaps the finest stretch of streamway in the Cuillin.

Further up (NG 450252), the path is crossed by a less distinct path that traverses from the Bealach a' Mhaim across the flanks of Bruach na Frithe's north-west ridge and makes a useful access route from Sligachan to Coire na

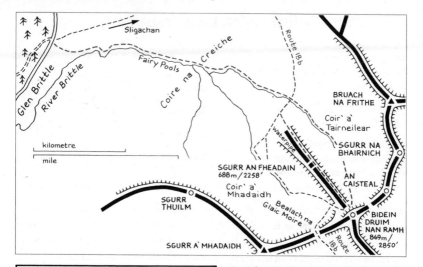

Creiche. To the right it climbs to the Bealach na Glaic Moire, the lowest pass to Coruisk on the Cuillin Main Ridge (see Route 18b).

At the foot of Sgurr an Fheadain, just beyond the path junction, to the left of the lowest point, a broad grassy rake pushes up into the cliffs. The scrambling begins on slabs to the left of this. Once above the slabs, aim right to gain the north-west spur and then climb skywards. There are numerous choices of route and the excitement increases as height is gained.

Over the summit the route continues along the south-east ridge. A rock buttress is outflanked by an easy scramble on the right to reach a small bealach, then another easy scramble climbs to the shattered ridge itself, which provides a pleasant walk down to the saddle below Bidein Druim nan Ramh. From here you can descend either side, left (north) into Coir' a' Tairneilear or right (south) into Coir' a' Mhadaidh.

The slopes of scree and rubble falling into Coir' a' Tairneilear provide much the easier way down and, once down, you'll soon regain the outward approach path beside the stream. Coir' a' Mhadaidh is a more attractive corrie if you can find the route down into it, with a fine waterfall and pool and huge walls of rock all around. The key to the descent is an awkward stone shoot (cairned at the top) at the near end of a grassy terrace that descends diagonally from the Bealach na Glaic Moire. For details see Route 18b.

ROUTE 7: THE COIRE A' GHREADAIDH SKYLINE

STARTING POINT: Glen Brittle
Youth Hostel (NG 409225, L32/E411
or Harvey's Cuillin)

ROUTE LOG: 6ml/10km,
1340m/4400ft, 8½hrs

ROUTE OVERVIEW: circular
mountain scramble. A long, hard and
sustained scramble over three Cuillin
Munros, with some stimulating situations.

	1	2	3	4	5
Grade					
Terrain					
Navigation					
Seriousness					

South of Coire na Creiche (Route 6) the next great corrie gouged out of the Cuillin is beautiful Coire a' Ghreadaidh, whose pools and waterslides can be irresistibly inviting on a hot day, when the rocks are baked by sunlight reflected from the surrounding corrie walls. Ghreadaidh means either Clear Water or Mighty Winds, and either can be appropriate. The corrie headwall, forming part of the Cuillin Main Ridge, crosses the three massive Munros of Sgurr a' Mhadaidh, Sgurr a' Ghreadaidh and Sgurr na Banachdich. Between Sgurr a' Ghreadaidh and Sgurr na Banachdich is the smaller peak of Sgurr Thormaid.

The traverse of the corrie headwall, over the three Munros, is one of the most continuously exciting in the Cuillin. When combined with the long side ridges that run out to Sgurr Thuilm and Sgurr nan Gobhar to form the north and south bounding arms of the corrie respectively, the round of the corrie skyline is aesthetically as well as technically pleasing, with some fine situations and a real mountaineering flavour. **WARNING**. The route requires competence on exposed hard scrambles, good route-finding ability, stamina and a more than usual degree of commitment, even for the Cuillin.

From Sgurr a' Ghreadaidh in the centre of the corrie headwall a short spur juts out to the minor peak of Sgurr Eadar Da Choire (Peak Between Two Corries) to divide upper Coire a' Ghreadaidh into two. The summit of this lower peak is rarely trodden, as reaching it from Sgurr a' Ghreadaidh involves rock climbing, while a rubble-strewn ascent from the corrie hardly appeals.

Another prominent skyline feature is the notch of An Dorus between Sgurr a' Mhadaidh and Sgurr a' Ghreadaidh. The gully leading up to the notch provides the only easy access to the Main Ridge in the whole of the corrie, although progress from it along the ridge in either direction then involves immediate scrambling.

The route into the corrie begins at Glen Brittle Youth Hostel, from where a path follows the left bank (right-hand side) of the tumbling burn (Allt a' Choire

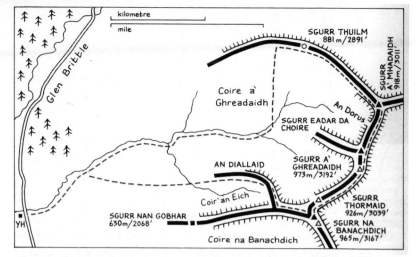

Ghreadaidh). The initial section, up which tourists go waterfall-watching, has been much improved since the first edition of this guidebook. It climbs into the flat bowl of the corrie to the picturesque waterslides at its back.

Your first objective, high on the corrie's northern arm to the left, is the outlying summit of Sgurr Thuilm. It's a shapely enough top whose separation from the main Cuillin ridge gives it good views of the main peaks, but it bears few features of interest, and reaching the summit is somewhat tedious. The west shoulder can be reached from the mouth of Coir' a' Ghreadaidh or more directly by a moorland crossing from Glen Brittle, but this would mean missing the path up to the waterslides. Less arduously (although it may not seem so at the time), a route can be made from the waterslides directly up steep slopes of grass and scree to the saddle seen above on the summit ridge.

From the summit, descend the narrow but gentle south-east ridge to another saddle where it abuts sharply against the steep north-west ridge of Sgurr a' Mhadaidh. Now the fun starts in earnest. Sgurr a' Mhadaidh has four tops, the highest of which fortunately lies at the top of the north-west ridge. The three

> *The prominent notch at the low point on the skyline of Coire a' Ghreadaidh is known as An Dorus (The Door). It is reputed to be an historically important pass used in the days of clan warfare, but this is difficult to believe. It can be reached on the Coire a' Ghreadaidh side by a gully of scree and rubble, but chockstones in the gully on the Coruisk side force you out onto a loose and exposed rock wall. Despite its siting on current maps, the actual location of the pass is open to debate, and some old maps and guidebooks located it elsewhere.*

lower tops lie to the east, outwith Coire a' Ghreadaidh, so the exposed rock climbing required to traverse them can remain of academic interest to non-climbers.

The climb up the north-west ridge attacks the leftmost of two rock ribs and is a hard and exposed scramble. An initial very steep section is bypassed on the right, then there is an adrenaline-pumping section on the crest before an easier line can again be taken on the right. The best line is difficult to find (even on repeated visits!). Higher up, summit crags bar a direct ascent to the summit and it is necessary to take a more roundabout route. A cairn marks the start of a path that traverses right and runs all the way across to a point on the south ridge just below the summit, from where an easy scramble soon puts you atop the narrow ▲ summit crest. You'll want to pause here, if only to take in the stunning view of Loch Coruisk.

N.B. If you deem the ascent of Sgurr a' Mhadaidh from the saddle below Sgurr Thuilm to be a tad *too* exciting, and if you can handle route-finding on steep, rough ground, it is possible to traverse scree slopes beneath the cliffs of Sgurr a' Mhadaidh to reach the gully below An Dorus. A cairn on the saddle marks the start of the traverse. The scramble from An Dorus, up Mhadaidh's south ridge to the summit, is much less taxing than the scramble up the north-west ridge (see below).

Note also that you can omit Sgurr Thuilm as well as Sgurr a' Mhadaidh's north-west ridge by climbing directly from Coire a' Ghreadaidh to An Dorus. From the waterslides continue up beside the stream, with traces of path on each bank, into the upper corrie at the foot of An Dorus. The left bank (right-hand side) path takes a short cut across the flanks of Sgurr Eadar Da Choire into the stony gully below An Dorus. Cairns mark the best line if you can find them. When the gully forks half way up, scramble up the scree and rocks of the left branch to reach the notch. The right branch leads to the Eag Dubh (see below).

Heading southwards from the summit of Sgurr a' Mhadaidh around the Coire a' Ghreadaidh skyline, bouldery slopes lead down to a moderate scramble on solid clean rock into An Dorus. On the far side of the notch another moderate scramble, less daunting than it looks, begins the ascent to the extremely narrow summit ridge of Sgurr a' Ghreadaidh. Once out of An Dorus the ascent is mainly a walk as far as another deep cleft known as the Eag Dubh (Black Cleft), which is easily passed. A hard slabby scramble then leads up to the Wart, a large rock bastion that is bypassed by an unexpectedly easy walk on the Coire a' Ghreadaidh side to reach the ▲ summit of Sgurr a' Ghreadaidh immediately beyond.

The ridge now narrows in sensational fashion over Ghreadaidh's △ South Top (a Top in *Munro's Tables*) to provide a long, knife-edge scramble that is hard,

The classic Cuillin view: Sgurr nan Gillean (Route 1), Am Basteir (Route 3) and Sgurr a' Bhasteir (Route4) from Sligachan

Sunlight highlights Sgurr na h-Uamha (Route 2), with Sgurr nan Gillean behind right, viewed from Captain Maryon's Cairn (Route 15)

Traversing beneath Sgurr a' Fionn Choire, with Bruach na Frithe behind right, at Easter (Route 4)

The twin summits of Sgurr a' Ghreadaidh from Sgurr na Banachdich (Route 7)

Sensational scrambling on the Centre Top of Sgurr na Banachdich (Route 8), with Sgurr Dearg (Route 9) behind right

The Coire Lagan skyline from Glen Brittle. From left to right: Sgurr Dearg (Route 9), Sgurr Mhic Choinnich, Sgurr Alasdair (Route 10), Sgurr Sgumain and the Sron na Ciche face.

The Great Stone Shoot drops from the bealach between Sgurr Thearlaich and Sgurr Alasdair, with Sgurr Mhic Choinnich further left and Sgurr Sgumain further right (Route 10)

Looking across Coir' a' Ghrunnda from Sgurr nan Eag (Routes 11 and 12). The highest peak is Sgurr Alasdair, the peak on the right is Sgurr Dubh na Da Bheinn

Gars-bheinn from Sgurr a' Choire Bhig (Route 12)

Bla Bheinn from Torrin (Route 13)

Loch Scavaig, Loch Coruisk and the Cuillin from Sgurr na Stri (Routes 15-19)

Glamaig and Beinn Dearg Mhor from Sligachan (Route 20)

Belig and Garbh-bheinn from Beinn Dearg Mheadhonach, with Bla Bheinn behind (Route 22)

Macleod's Tables: Healabhal Bheag from Beinn na h-Uamha (Route 25)

Ben Tianavaig (foreground), with The Storr behind; telephoto from Glamaig (Route 26)

Sunset above the clouds from the Cuillin Main Ridge

dramatic and totally absorbing. The view of Coruisk beneath your feet will be forever ingrained in your memory. The sustained scrambling requires constant care and attention and much physical and mental effort. It needs to be taken slowly and savoured. Beyond the South Top the ridge descends more steeply to the bealach below Sgurr Thormaid, but all major difficulties are avoidable on the Coire a' Ghreadaidh side.

Across the bealach the minor peak of △Sgurr Thormaid (another Top in Munro's Tables) looks impressively steep but yields easily to a frontal assault. *En route* you pass three rock 'teeth', the last of which overhangs. A path on the Coire a' Ghreadaidh side bypasses them all. The easiest line over Sgurr Thormaid's summit keeps to the left on the way up and to the right on the descent of the far side. The scrambling is reasonably exposed but much easier than anything encountered so far on Sgurr a' Mhadaidh and Sgurr a' Ghreadaidh.

Once over Sgurr Thormaid you arrive at the Bealach Thormaid below ▲Sgurr na Banachdich, the third and final Munro of the day. Despite its sharp summit crest, Banachdich ranks alongside Bruach na Frithe as one of the easiest of all Cuillin peaks to reach, as its rough western slopes, described below, are reasonably gentle by Cuillin standards. From the Bealach Thormaid the ascent via the north ridge is easy provided you keep to broken slopes of loose scree and rocks on the Coire a' Ghreadaidh side of the crest. (For a more exciting route up via the south ridge see Route 8.)

From the summit numerous cairned lines leave the Cuillin Main Ridge to descend the mountain's stony western slopes and complete the round of the Coire a' Ghreadaidh skyline. Around 150m/500ft down they reach a small plateau where two ridges diverge: west to Sgurr na Gobhar and north-west to An Diallaid, giving a choice of routes down. The many cairns confuse rather than help, especially in mist, when the small plateau can be a confusing place. A descent over An Diollaid is straightforward, while the west ridge involves more scrambling and is described in Route 8.

The quickest and easiest route down, and the one by which the ascent of Sgurr na Banachdich is barely more than a walk, goes via the small bowl of Coir' an Eich (Horse Corrie) between the two ridges. A well-worn route descends stony slopes into the corrie, crosses to the left bank of the Allt Coir' an Eich and descends to meet the Allt Coire a' Ghreadaidh path to complete another memorable Cuillin round.

Sgurr na Banachdaich occupies a prominent position at the centre of the Cuillin Main Ridge. It is both one of the best viewpoints and, ascended by Coir' an Eich, one of the easiest to reach. Peaks crowd the skyline, but it is the aerial view over Loch Coruisk that will linger longest in the memory.

ROUTE 8: SGURR NA BANACHDICH

ROUTE START: Glen Brittle Hut (NG 411216, L32/E411 or Harvey's Cuillin)

ROUTE LOG: 6mkl/10km, 1010m/3300ft, 6hrs

ROUTE OVERVIEW: circular mountain scramble. An enterprising approach leads to a sensational

	1	2	3	4	5
Grade					
Terrain					
Navigation					
Seriousness					

scramble over a rock tower on one of the Cuillin's most underrated peaks.

From Sgurr na Banachdich southwards to Sgurr Dearg the Cuillin Main Ridge encloses Coire na Banachdich, a large open corrie with a fine shape but whose bounding side ridges (the west ridge of Sgurr na Banachdich to the north and the west ridge of Sgurr Dearg to the south) surround the corrie with mainly featureless slopes of broken crag and scree. On the plus side Coire na Banachdich boasts the longest waterfall in the Cuillin and, at the low point on the corrie headwall between the two Munros, a bealach (Bealach Coire na Banachdich) that provides both an easy route to Coruisk (Route 19a) and a relatively easy approach to Sgurr Dearg.

The route described here takes the most spectacular route up Sgurr na Banachdich by climbing its multi-topped south ridge above the Bealach Coire na Banachdich and descending its long west ridge to the subsidiary peak and eyrie of Sgurr nan Gobhar.

The main path into the corrie begins c.50m south of Glen Brittle Hut beside sheep pens. From parking spaces opposite the Hut another path takes a short cut to it. The path climbs diagonally right to the Allt Coire na Banachdich, which has been bridged since the first edition of this guidebook, and continues up the stream's left bank (right-hand side).

The ascent route passes the longest waterfall in the Cuillin, the Eas Mor (Big Waterfall), which plunges 24m/80ft into an enormous open gorge at the foot of Coire na Banachdich and is a marvellous sight when in spate. It must have looked spectacular on a certain day in 1855, when a waterspout broke at the head of the corrie and flooded Glenbrittle House to a depth of over 3m/10ft.

N.B. If you're starting from Glen Brittle campsite, upper Coire na Banachdich can be reached more directly by an indistinct path that begins a few metres up the Coire Lagan path (see Route 9). When the Coire Lagan path bears right over a

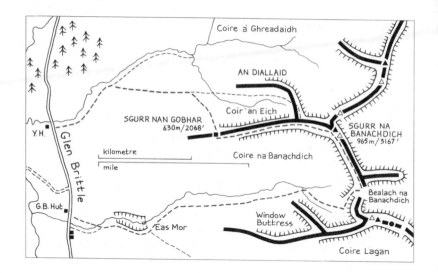

stream, the indistinct path forks left to make a rising traverse across the moor to the Allt a' Mhuilinn. It follows the right bank of this stream, crosses the path from Glen Brittle Hut to Coire Lagan and climbs to a conspicuous cairn-shaped boulder at the foot of the south-west ridge of Sgurr Dearg. From here cut left into Coire na Banachdich to join the main path.

Continuing up the left bank of the Allt Coire na Banachdich above the bridge, the path soon reaches the waterfall and gorge of the Eas Mor, where you'll want to pause for views. At the head of the gorge the path forks. Ignore the right branch, which crosses the moor to Coire Lagan (see Route 9) and stay with the left branch, which hugs the riverbank a while longer before taking to the moor well away from the river.

The path eventually rounds the foot of Window Buttress (the spur on the right) to reach the foot of a fine deep-cut gorge on the right. Ahead rears Coire na Banachdich's craggy headwall, split by the chasm of Banachdich Gully, and this forms a formidable barrier. The route to the Bealach Coire na Banachdich outflanks the crags by veering right towards Sgurr Dearg and following the main stream through the deep-cut gorge. A cairned line climbs the slabs on the right bank (left-hand side) of the stream. The going is rocky but easy, with no scree to hinder the ascent. Looking back, note the hole on the crest of Window Buttress that gives the buttress its name.

One line of cairns continues straight up a scree gully onto the stony summit dome of Sgurr Dearg, but the main route cuts back left above the crags at the back of the corrie, traversing to the bealach across a broad bouldery shelf. It is important to pay attention to route-finding and follow the cairns. Should you need to descend this way, the shelf will be found by descending the boulder ruckle below the bealach until the crags on the left give way to bouldery slopes. At this point traverse left across the shelf to pick up the line of cairns down into the corrie.

From the bealach it is possible to descend to Coruisk (Route 19a) or climb rough but easy slopes to the stony dome of Sgurr Dearg (see Route 9). For Sgurr na Banachdich the route goes left up the peak's south ridge. If taken direct the crest of the ridge develops into a hard and thrilling scramble. Traversing below the crest on the Coire na Banachdich side can avoid the hardest sections, but the line is not always obvious and it is easy to get into difficulties on rubble-strewn ledges.

The route begins as an easy walk along a narrow shattered ridge over a subsidiary top. The rock then improves over the narrow South Top to reach the tower-like △Centre Top and the most sensational scrambling. From the gap between the two tops you can traverse ledges on the left (Coire na Banachdich side) and omit the Centre Top altogether but, as noted above, care is required not to be led out onto even more difficult ground.

The ascent of the Centre Top involves the negotiation of a difficult section near the start (easily bypassed on the left) and, higher up, a narrow rib of large blocks that require dramatic step-ups. On the descent of the far side the only hard section is a short wall near the foot, which is steep but has good holds. From the gap beyond the Centre Top the final section of ridge to the ▲summit of Sgurr na Banachdich becomes a shattered crest once more and involves mostly easy scrambling, with any awkward bits easily avoidable on the Coire na Banachdich side.

To descend from Sgurr na Banachdich, follow cairns down the mountain's stony western slopes to a small plateau at the junction of the west ridge leading out to Sgurr nan Gobhar and the north-west ridge leading to An Diallaid. As described in Route 7, the easiest route down from here descends Coir' an Eich between the two ridges. The narrow ridge to Sgurr nan Gobhar, described here, makes a more satisfying end to the round, with an enjoyable mixture of walking and easy scrambling. The summit of Sgurr nan Gobhar itself is a fine eyrie at the end of the ridge which makes a wonderful evening viewpoint within easy reach of Glen Brittle.

The easiest line down to the glen descends the south-west shoulder, keeping to slopes of scree and rubble on the south side of crags and a large gully. The going isn't great but is certainly easier on descent than ascent, and from its foot a short tramp across the moor soon rejoins the outward path beside the Allt Coire na Banachdich.

ROUTE 9: SGURR DEARG

ROUTE START: Glen Brittle
campsite (NG 414205, L32/E411 or
Harvey's Cuillin)

ROUTE LOG: 5ml/8km,
990m/3250ft, 6hrs

ROUTE OVERVIEW: circular
mountain scramble. An essentially
straightforward scramble is rendered

	I	2	3	4	5
Grade					
Terrain					
Navigation					
Seriousness					

exciting by tremendous exposure and perhaps the most dramatic surroundings in
the whole Cuillin.

South of Coire na Banachdich (Route 8) lies the rock playground of Coire
Lagan, whose skyline round is a classic climber's test piece with situations
worthy of an Alpine route. The ascent of Sgurr Dearg at the start of the round,
however, involves no hard scrambling and provides a route through perhaps the
most spectacular situations in a mountain range full of spectacular situations.
The route can be started either at Glen Brittle Hut or campsite, but the latter
has the better approach paths. Note also that you can reach the summit more
easily via the Bealach Coire na Banachdich, as described in Route 8.

From the campsite go through the gate beside the toilet block and take the
renovated Coire Lagan path up the hillside and across the moor to just past Loch
an Fhir-bhallaich (this point can also be reached by a path from Glen Brittle
Hut – see Route 8). Leave the path when you think fit to pick a route up Sgurr
Dearg's steep south-west shoulder on scree, rubble, more scree, scree + boulders
etc. The ascent requires determination until it eases off over a minor top (Sgurr
Dearg Beag) to reach a narrow section of ridge just below the summit, which
requires slightly exposed but no more than moderate scrambling.

The Δsummit is a short sharp arête that is one of the most awesome spots on
the Cuillin Main Ridge, for looming even higher is the preposterous blade of
rock known as the ▲ Inaccessible Pinnacle ('In Pin' to its friends). This mighty
monolith teeters some 24m/80ft above the south-east slopes of Sgurr Dearg,
overtopping the summit by about 8m/26ft to form the most difficult Munro in
Scotland. Its sensational situation above abysmal drops on each side has been
known to cause more than one normally rock-steady ridge wanderer to hug the
ground for confirmation of its solidity.

Climbers undertaking the round of the Coire Lagan skyline will ascend the
facing (west) ridge of the In Pin (graded Difficult) and descend its far (east) ridge
(graded Moderate) but, fortunately for others, it can be bypassed on a broad

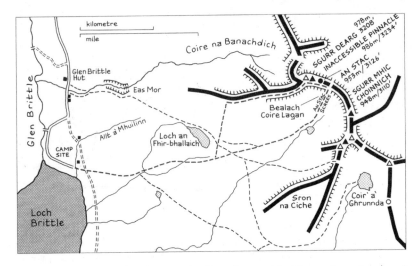

ramp that runs around its base on the Coire Lagan side. Descend rough ground to the neck of rock between Sgurr Dearg and the 'In Pin', with vertiginous drops left to Coruisk, and follow the ramp round to the foot of the pinnacle's east ridge. The going hardly constitutes a scramble, yet the situation and the occasional rubble on the ledge will cause most walkers to negotiate this section in a less than upright posture. Take care to continue left around a corner (cairn), rather than right down some tempting scree that leads to crags, and regain the crest of the ridge at the Bealach Coire Lagan.

The next peak along is ▲Sgurr Mhic Choinnich. Munro-baggers will be tempted to make the return trip to its summit, which requires no more than moderate scrambling, but the ridge crest is perhaps the sharpest in the Cuillin and incredibly exposed. From the Bealach Coire Lagan, descend scree slopes (An Stac Screes) to the heart of Coire Lagan, a beautifully glaciated corrie, wonderfully wild and rocky, in whose upper bowl a lovely lochan nestles among enormous boiler-plate slabs. The path down to Glen Brittle descends from the right-hand corner of the lochan. It is a pleasant descent across the moor, with the climber's playground of Sron na Ciche cliffs to your left (Route 10) and in front of you the endless sea.

> *Munro baggers unable to climb the In Pin may choose to question its status, because in the original 1891 edition of Munro's Tables it was listed as a Top of Sgurr Dearg. It was not elevated to Munro status until 1921 and was never climbed by Sir Hugh himself. Poor Sgurr Dearg was demoted to Top status in 1921 and deleted from the Tables altogether in 1997.*

ROUTE 10: SGURR ALASDAIR

ROUTE START: Glen Brittle campsite (NG 414205, L32/E411 or Harvey's Cuillin)

ROUTE LOG: 5ml/8km, 970m/3200ft, 6½hrs

ROUTE OVERVIEW: circular mountain scramble. An absorbing scramble visits the highest peak in the

	1	2	3	4	5
Grade					
Terrain					
Navigation					
Seriousness					

Cuillin, the Great Stone Shoot and the finest rock face in the British Isles.

Coire Lagan is bounded on its south by a side ridge that runs from Sgurr Thearlaich over Sgurr Alasdair, Sgurr Sgumain and Sron na Ciche. Sgurr Alasdair is a beautiful pointed peak that makes a fitting highest Cuillin, even though its summit is composed of basalt rather than gabbro. For non-climbers there are only two routes to the top: via the south-west ridge from Sgurr Sgumain and via the Great Stone Shoot.

The Great Stone Shoot is the normal route of *descent* for climbers completing the round of Coire Lagan. At one time its 400m/1300ft of scree provided the fastest descent in the Cuillin, but its upper section is now very steep and bare and requires care. The most stable ground lies close by the rock walls on either side. As an ascent route it is not to be recommended to friends, but it does

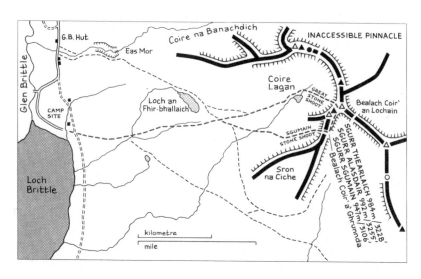

provide the only way to the highest summit in the Cuillin which involves no more than easy scrambling.

The scree begins at the back of the corrie beyond the lochan and ascends to the gap between Sgurr Thearlaich and Sgurr Alasdair. The ascent should be avoided in mist, when it is possible to lose one's bearings on the featureless terrain of the lower scree slopes and veer too far right towards Sgurr Sgumain. From the top of the stone shoot a short, easy but somewhat exposed scramble leads to the airy summit.

The ascent of Sgurr Alasdair's south-west ridge from Sgurr Sgumain is a far more interesting and pleasant route, provided you are good at route-finding on rock and can handle hard scrambling. The route described here climbs Sgurr Alasdair by this ridge and descends by the Great Stone Shoot.

There are two ways up Sgurr Sgumain: one via the cliff top of Sron na Ciche and one via the cliff foot. The cliff-top route takes the Coir' a' Ghrunnda path (Route 11) as far as the foot of the south-west slopes of Sron na Ciche, then climbs up uniform slopes of grass and outcrops to reach the flat stony summit plateau and the Bealach Coir' a' Ghrunnda beyond (between Sron na Ciche and Sgurr Sgumain). The view from the plateau, both over the cliff edge and out to sea, is stunning, but the cliff-foot approach (described next) is even more spectacular, giving a glimpse of a world of rock rarely seen by the walker.

From Glen Brittle campsite, as for Route 9, go through the gate beside the toilet block and take the renovated Coire Lagan path up the hillside and across the moor. Beyond Loch an Fhir-bhallaich a rougher path from Glen Brittle Hut crosses from left to right. Branch right along it to reach the foot of the Sgumain Stone Shoot beneath the Sron na Ciche cliffs and climb it to the Bealach Coir' a' Ghrunnda on the skyline. The going, on scree and rubble, isn't the greatest, but the surroundings are immense. As you climb, crane your neck skywards to view the remarkable wall of clean contorted gabbro that towers 300m/1000ft overhead. There is nothing like it anywhere else in Britain. Note the markings on the rock that indicate the start of classic climbs.

Hidden above the huge boulders in the Sgumain Stone Shoot is the most extraordinary piece of rock in the Cuillin – The Cioch (The Breast), a wodge of rock that seems to have been affixed to the cliff face as an afterthought.

The Cioch and the great slab to which it clings can be viewed by a short moderate scramble that goes diagonally right up a shelf from the foot of the boulders. It is possible to reach the foot of the Cioch by continuing along the shelf across a gully, although this involves an awkward exposed move around a rib of rock. You may be able to obtain a view of it more easily by scrambling up the rubbly slopes on the other side of the stone shoot.

Around two-thirds of the way up the stone shoot, in the vicinity of the Cioch, are some enormous boulders that have fallen from the cliff face above, some of them alarmingly recently. Scrambling up and around them gives a welcome respite from the loose terrain.

At the Bealach Coir' a' Ghrunnda you get your first view of Coir' a' Ghrunnda and its sandy-shored loch only 140m/460ft below. The route down to the corrie is easy and can be linked with either of the Coire Lagan approaches to the bealach to make a scenic round (see Route 11).

> *Munro Top baggers should note that the Munro of Sgurr Alasdair has two subsidiary Tops: Sgurr Sgumain, crossed on the ascent route described, and Sgurr Thearlaich, which lies on the opposite side of the Great Stone Shoot to the parent peak. Reaching the summit involves very hard scrambling on rock that has seen recent rockfall. After taking a look you may well decide to leave the ascent for another day.*

The ascent of ∆Sgurr Sgumain from the bealach follows an easy path up the bouldery summit dome. The route onwards up Sgurr Alasdair's towering southwest ridge is less easy. It involves hard scrambling and route-finding on loose rock and should be attempted by experienced scramblers only.

Even reaching the Bealach Sgumain, between Sgumain and Alasdair, can be a problem if the correct line is not found. An immediate short sharp scramble up an exposed rib of rock leads to a narrow ridge that ends in a steep drop to the bealach. This drop can be turned by an easy scramble on either side. The right (Coir' a' Ghrunnda) side looks more obvious but lower down there is a move across a slab that can be awkward when greasy. All difficulties between Sgurr Sgumain and the Bealach Sgumain can be avoided if necessary by quitting the crest of the ridge at the foot of the rib and descending ledges on the Coire Lagan side to reach a path that traverses to the bealach.

A gendarme on the Bealach Sgumain is easily passed on the right by a path that leads away from the crest of the ridge to a chimney at the foot of Sgurr Alasdair's summit cliffs. On the crest itself the scrambling becomes increasingly difficult and soon reaches a Bad Step – a 4m/12ft wall, graded a Severe rock climb.

The only way onwards for scramblers is via the well-worn chimney further right. It's a hard scramble but the holds are good. The angle eases above the chimney but remains steep, and care is required to find the best line up shattered slopes, trending back left onto the crest to reach the ▲ summit.

After suitable R&R continue over the summit for a short, exposed but easier scramble down to the head of the Great Stone Shoot and descend into Coire Lagan to pick up the route back down to Glen Brittle.

ROUTE 11: SGURR DUBH MOR

ROUTE START: Glen Brittle campsite (NG 414205, L32/E411 or Harvey's Cuillin)

ROUTE LOG: 6ml/10km, 970m/3200ft, 7hrs for return route 1 (add 1½hrs for 2a and 2b, and 3 hours for 2c)

	1	2	3	4	5
Grade					
Terrain					
Navigation					
Seriousness					

ROUTE OVERVIEW: circular mountain scramble. A beautiful secret corrie and a sharp peak hidden beyond its headwall combine to produce one of the most scenic of all Cuillin scrambles.

The next corrie south of Coire Lagan is Coir' a' Ghrunnda, which is at the same time the wildest and most beautiful of all Cuillin corries. Its large sandy-shored lochan, at 697m/2287ft the highest in the range, is hemmed in by high peaks and hidden behind a barrier of vast boiler-plate slabs that guard its entrance. The rocks at the back of the corrie are incredibly rough but easy to clamber up, giving easy access to the one Munro on the Cuillin horseshoe that lies off the main ridge to the east, overlooking Loch Coruisk: Sgurr Dubh Mor. The main problem in climbing it is not reaching the summit from the corrie but, thanks to those boiler-plate slabs, reaching the corrie in the first place.

The route into the corrie begins at Glen Brittle campsite on the Coire Lagan path (see Route 10). Follow the path for c.800m, to some rock pavement beside the gorge of a small stream, then branch right across the stream. On the far side, two paths continue: a high path and a low path. The less distinct high path branches left to contour beneath the south-west shoulder of Sron na Ciche, but don't worry if you miss it. The more distinct low path stays low down on the moor, making a gentle rise to an obvious fork. Ignoring the right branch here, which continues towards Coruisk (Route 18a), branch left to climb more steeply up the hillside. Both approach paths meet to cut steeply around a corner, where a clamber up an earthy gully beside a rock wall exits into the confines of the lower corrie.

Once into the corrie the rock scenery is outstanding. The lower part consists of a rising trough floored by wave upon wave of boiler-plate slabs, which seem to flow down the corrie in the manner of the glacier that formed them. Walls of clean rock rear skywards all around. The skyline ahead is merely the lower lip of the upper corrie, behind which hides the lochan. As you gain height a wonderful view opens up back through the jaws of the corrie across Soay to Eigg and Rum.

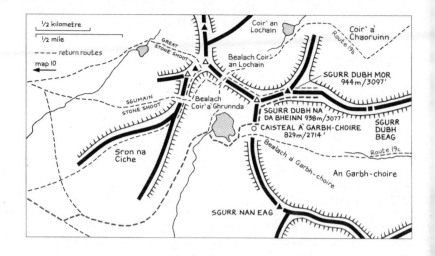

The path keeps high on the left at the foot of the walls of gabbro that form the south-east face of Sron na Ciche. You may wish to leave the path to explore the central boiler plates, in order better to appreciate their immensity, but avoid trying to scramble up the centre of the corrie, as tempting lines may lead to difficulties.

The path aims for the foot of the waterfall, seen above on the skyline, which tumbles out of the lochan. It becomes rougher as it gains height, especially when it has to negotiate a huge boulderfield immediately before the waterfall. Either follow it up, around and down the boulderfield, or pick your own way across. The normal route from the foot of the waterfall climbs a steep groove on the left beside awkward slabs, but many walkers are deterred here by a few moves on rock that is often wet and greasy. Once up, cairns indicate the best continuing line to the lochan.

On the right of the waterfall a small path points the way to an easier ascent that climbs straight up for a few metres before rising left around a corner and trending back right, following the line of least resistance. There are other obstacles above here but none that can't be outflanked without too much difficulty.

Above the waterfall you emerge into the secret bowl of the upper corrie, cupped high beneath the Cuillin ridge. The craggy slopes of the surrounding peaks make a savage setting for the highest and largest of all Cuillin lochans, whose clear waters and shores of clean rock and sand make it irresistible on a hot day.

Owing to the height of the corrie and the broken terrain there are several easy routes up to the skyline. Such is the complexity of the terrain that you may wish to study a map in conjunction with the following descriptions.

The left-hand rim of the corrie is formed by the ridge that runs over Sron na

Ciche, Sgurr Sgumain and Sgurr Alasdair to Sgurr Thearlaich. The Bealach Coir' a' Ghrunnda, at the top of the rubbly slope on the left between Sron na Ciche and Sgurr Sgumain, is only 140m/460ft above the lochan and can be linked with a descent of the Sgumain Stone Shoot to make a fine round (see Route 10).

At the back of the corrie the Cuillin Main Ridge runs from Sgurr Thearlaich across Sgurr Dubh na Da Bheinn and Caisteal a' Garbh-choire (the rock bastion that towers over the lochan) to Sgurr nan Eag. The south-west shoulder of Sgurr nan Eag forms the right-hand rim of the corrie.

Between Sgurr Thearlaich and Sgurr Dubh na Da Bheinn a slope of boulders and scree climbs to the Bealach Coir' an Lochain, giving an easy route to Coruisk (Route 19b). Note also that, on return to Glen Brittle via this bealach, either from Coruisk, Sgurr Dubh Mor or Sgurr nan Eag (Route 12), it is possible to traverse beneath the Alasdair-Thearlaich crags to the Bealach Coir' a' Ghrunnda or the Bealach Sgumain (see Route 10) without much loss of height.

The most interesting route up to the main ridge, and to still hidden Sgurr Dubh Mor, climbs to the next gap to the right, between Sgurr Dubh na Da Bheinn and Caisteal a' Garbh-choire. This involves some delightful easy scrambling on large boulders that are the roughest in the Cuillin. The rock is peridotite, described by an early guidebook writer as 'absurdly and painfully adhesive'. Watch out for your fingers and clothes. The exit onto the skyline goes through a window formed by a leaning slab.

Further right, a cairn at the far right-hand corner of the lochan marks the start of a route up to the Bealach a' Garbh-choire between Caisteal a' Garbh-choire and Sgurr nan Eag's north ridge. There are traces of path and the scrambling required is minimal; this makes it the most popular way to the skyline for access to the South Cuillin Ridge (Route 12).

The bealach is linked to the gap

> The Cuillin Main Ridge north of Bealach Coir' an Lochain, rising to Sgurr Thearlaich, is a no-go area for walkers as it contains the famous Thearlaich-Dubh Gap – a great cleft in the ridge that is a polished Very Difficult rock climb on each side. It is possible to reach the south side of the gap from the bealach by an increasingly hard scramble along the ridge. The crux is a couple of spectacular steps up a steep and exposed nose that most scramblers will not relish the thought of reversing.
>
> An early climbers' guidebook recommended that not all members of a climbing party descend into the gap at once in case they should remain there forever. It is, however, possible to scramble into the gap by the gully that falls from it to the Coir' a' Ghrunnda screes, although why anyone but guidebook writers who know no better would want to do so is perhaps best not discussed in polite company.

on the Sgurr Dubh na Da Bheinn side of Caisteal a' Garbh-choire by a path that traverses the base of Caisteal a' Garbh-choire on the far (An Garbh-choire) side, and from either end there is an easy descent to Coruisk via An Garbh-choire (Route 19c).

Further right still, it is possible to make a relatively easy and more direct route up onto the north ridge of Sgurr nan Eag.

For Sgurr Dubh Mor it is first

POSSIBLE RETURN ROUTES from Coir' a Ghrunnda skyline: (1) Reverse the outward route by descending Coir' a' Ghrunnda. (2) Traverse beneath the Alasdair-Thearlaich cliffs to the Bealach Coir' a' Ghrunnda and (a) descend the Sgumain Stone Shoot (Route 10), (b) descend along the cliff top of Sron na Ciche and down its south-west shoulder or (c) climb Sgurr Alasdair and descend the Great Stone Shoot (Route 10).

necessary to climb its subsidiary Top Sgurr Dubh na Da Bheinn. The broken but shapely summit is easily reached from either left or right: either from the Bealach Coir' an Lochain to the left (north) or the gap between it and Caisteal a' Garbh-choire to the right (south). A frontal assault from the corrie should be avoided owing to craggy ground. From the Bealach Coir' an Lochain the ascent is no more than a rough walk on peridotite blocks, with any difficulties easily avoided on the Coir' a' Ghrunnda side. From the gap between Sgurr Dubh na Da Bheinn and Caisteal a' Garbh-choire the ascent is of a similar nature. The actual crest gives harder scrambling but any difficulties are again easily bypassed on the Coir' a' Ghrunnda side.

From the △summit of Sgurr Dubh na Da Bheinn the traverse eastwards along the connecting ridge to Sgurr Dubh Mor makes an exciting scramble. A short easy descent leads to the saddle between the two peaks, then it is necessary to keep right (An Garbh-choire side) to find a practicable line. On the final section follow scratch marks and cairns. The scrambling is mostly moderate with one or two moves that some may find hard.

The ▲ summit of Sgurr Dubh Mor is a narrow crest with a cairn at one end and a mossy tuft of grass perched precariously at the other, beyond which the ridge continues level for some distance before descending towards Sgurr Dubh Beag. The ascent of the ridge from Coruisk ('doing the Dubhs') is a classic rock climb graded only Moderate but with some tremendous situations. For a taster, wander out along the level section of ridge on beautiful clean slabs of gabbro. They give exhilarating scrambling that is never more than moderate. You can reach the end of the level section, from where the ridge drops away steeply to Sgurr Dubh Beag, before returning to the summit of Sgurr Dubh Mor.

Now . . . do you have the time and energy to undertake the easy South Cuillin Ridge (Route 12) as well? Then . . . which way down? See sidebar for options.

ROUTE 12: THE SOUTH CUILLIN RIDGE

ROUTE START: Glen Brittle campsite (NG 414205, L32/E411 or Harvey's Cuillin)

ROUTE LOG: 9ml/14km, 1270m/4150ft, 9hrs return by outward route or 4½hrs add-on to Route 11

ROUTE OVERVIEW: return mountain scramble (or add-on to

	1	2	3	4	5
Grade					
Terrain					
Navigation					
Seriousness					

Route 11). A magnificent skyline stravaig traverses the easiest section of the Cuillin Main Ridge, with the best views in the range.

The southern end of the Cuillin Main Ridge, south of Sgurr Dubh na Da Bheinn, is the easiest lengthy section of ridge in the whole range and provides a wonderfully airy walk and easy scramble. The approach is as for Sgurr Dubh Mor in Route 11, gaining the Main Ridge north (left) or south (right) of Caisteal a' Garbh-choire from Coir' a' Ghrunnda. In fact the route could be combined with the ascent of Sgurr Dubh Mor.

From the Bealach a' Garbh-choire south of the Caisteal, the route first climbs Sgurr nan Eag's north ridge. If you keep to the crest the ascent is more than a scramble on occasion, but all difficulties are avoidable on the right to give exhilarating scrambling of all grades on firm blocks of gabbro. A path further right makes the ascent barely more than a walk. The ▲summit of this most southerly of the eleven Munros on the Main Ridge is the third of three tors and lies at the far end of a 400m long level summit ridge.

The route onwards to Sgurr a' Choire Bhig and Gars-bheinn, the two peaks at the extreme south end of the Main Ridge, also involves barely any scrambling at all, but even the most committed scrambler must agree that it is a delightful high-level walk, with wonderful views over Loch Coruisk on one side and Soay Sound on the other. The walk begins with a 150m/500ft descent of Sgurr nan Eag's south-east shoulder. If you wish, by keeping to the cliff top overlooking An Garbh-choire, scrambling of all grades can be

From Coruisk, Gars-bheinn's east ridge gives a straightforward and scenic ascent. Reaching the foot of the ridge can be problematical owing to rocky ground above the shore, but this can be circumvented if necessary by an approach via An Garbh-choire (see Route 19c). Higher up, the ridge narrows pleasantly, and towards the summit passes some fine crags overlooking Coire a' Chruidh. Boat trips put this route within day-walk distance of Elgol.

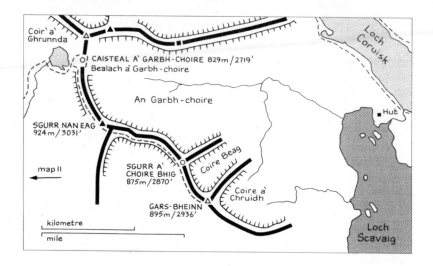

sought (more enjoyable on the return journey than in this direction). One deep chimney on the crest (for which the mountain is named Notched Peak) can be crossed by a dramatic rock bridge.

The 100m/330ft rise to Sgurr a' Choire Bhig begins gently, then narrows towards the summit. The crest of the ridge is barely more than an exposed walk but a path below the crest on the right takes an even easier line. A short descent of 35m/120ft follows, where it is necessary to put hand to rock at times, and then the main ridge ends with a very pleasant stroll out to Gars-bheinn. Beyond the summit there are no more Cuillin, only the boundless sea.

For the return route to Coir' a' Ghrunnda, see Route 11 sidebar on p.53.

Additional South Cuillin notes

Between Sgurr nan Eag and Gars-bheinn the main ridge rims the shallow hollow of Coire nan Laogh, whose lack of features makes it perhaps the dullest of all Cuillin corries to both climbers and walkers, despite harbouring a few off-the-beaten-path climbs and scrambles. A way up the featureless southern flank of Gars-bheinn can be made from Glen Brittle campsite by following the Coruisk coast path (Route 18a) as far as the corrie's stream (Allt Coire nan Laogh), then striking uphill on some of the most tedious scree in the Cuillin.

This route can be used to vary the approach to Gars-bheinn, but it is terminally frustrating and involves a long walk across the moor. It is used mainly by climbers intent on spending the night on Gars-bheinn prior to attempting the traverse of the Cuillin Main Ridge the following day. At the summit you can see the stone walls they have constructed to shelter their bivouac spots.

ROUTE 13: BLA BHEINN VIA COIRE UAIGNEICH

ROUTE START: head of Loch Slapin (NG 561217, L32/E411 or Harvey's Cuillin)

ROUTE LOG: 6ml/10km, 960m/3150ft, 6hrs

ROUTE OVERVIEW: circular mountain walk. A straightforward ascent through rocky surroundings

	1	2	3	4	5
Grade					
Terrain					
Navigation					
Seriousness					

leads to the summit of a Cuillin outlier that many consider to be more attractive than any on the Main Ridge.

When viewed across Loch Slapin from near Torrin the bold gabbro peak of Bla Bheinn presents one of the most compelling mountain sights in Britain. That great pioneer of Cuillin exploration, Alexander Nicolson, considered it to be the shapeliest mountain on Skye. Several poets have been moved by it to put pen to paper. 'Queen of mountains fair though stern' wrote William Ross in the eighteenth century, while Alexander Smith began his lengthy Victorian eulogy with the line, 'O wonderful mountain of Blaavin'. Such praise is worth keeping in mind as you toil up the stony summit slopes.

Bla Bheinn has a dramatic appearance from all angles, with the fearsome north face of the east ridge and the soaring rock tower of Clach Glas providing some classic rock routes. For ordinary mortals there are two easy routes to the summit in fine weather: via the south ridge and via Coire Uaigneich from the east. The south ridge route (Route 14) is the more scenic of the two, while the Coire Uaigneich approach described here is shorter and affords close-up views of the rock scenery.

The unappealing gully on the south side of the dip between North and South Tops, known as Great Gully, provides a rough route to or from Coire Uaigneich but is not recommended. It was perhaps by this gully that, unusually, Bla Bheinn was first ascended in 1873 by the poet Algernon Swinburne and Professor of English John Nichol, who otherwise seem to have been more interested in alcoholic adventures.

Neither route need involve more than elementary handwork, although both give ample scope for scrambling of all grades. The only potentially awkward section is between Bla Bheinn's two tops, so sensitive hillwalkers may prefer the Coire Uaigneich route, which climbs directly to the summit (North Top) and avoids the trickier South Top.

The route begins at the bridge over the Allt na Dunaiche on the

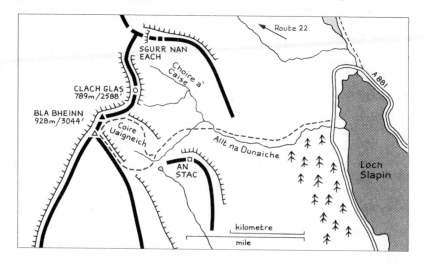

B8083 Broadford-Elgol road. There's a car park just around the corner to the south, from where a path leads to the bridge. Take the path on the left bank (right-hand side) of the river up into Choire a' Caise, past some fine pools and waterfalls.

The path bears left across the Allt na Dunaiche and climbs steeply beneath the towering east face of Bla Bheinn into the bowl of Coire Uaigneich, which is unusually rich in Alpine flora owing to a small outcrop of Jurassic limestone. The path curves into the heart of the corrie, then turns sharp right to climb towards the skyline of the east ridge. It is indistinct in places but well cairned.

Once onto the east ridge the path meanders up stony slopes (with optional scrambling) to the ▲ summit, with occasional glimpses of Clach Glas seen across the yawning gullies of the north face. The summit perches at the edge of the cliffs and affords a superb view of the main Cuillin ridge across the deep trench of Srath na Creitheach.

A different descent route, and one that will appeal to Top baggers, can be made by first crossing to the lower △South Top, which lies only 200m away across a shallow dip but whose negotiation requires some handwork. After an easy descent to the dip, the obvious line up the South Top is along a ledge that gives an easy if slightly exposed scramble. An earthy gully a few metres down to the left provides an easier route (see also Route 14).

From the South Top, descend the steep stony south-east slopes of the mountain to a small lochan at their foot. An indistinct path will be found in places. Cairns bear left in front of the lochan to mark a further stony descent into Coire Uaigneich. Alternatively, continue to the dip a short distance beyond the lochan and descend grass slopes. Once into the corrie, rejoin the outward route.

ROUTE 14: BLA BHEINN VIA SOUTH RIDGE

ROUTE START: Kilmarie (NG 545172, L32/E411 or Harvey's Cuillin)

ROUTE LOG: 8ml/13km, 1100m/3600ft, 6½hrs

ROUTE OVERVIEW: circular mountain walk. Although this is not the shortest route to the summit of mighty Bla Bheinn, it is certainly the most pleasant and scenic.

	1	2	3	4	5
Grade					
Terrain					
Navigation					
Seriousness					

The Coire Uaigneich route up Bla Bheinn (Route 13) is the shorter and more popular of the two walkers' routes up the mountain, but the south ridge route described here is the more scenic and aesthetically pleasing. The ridge rises attractively in one clean sweep from the beautiful bay of Camasunary, giving superb views of the main Cuillin ridge across Srath na Creitheach and providing a surprisingly dry ascent

> *Energetic rock climbers can combine the traverse of Bla Bheinn and Clach Glas with the traverse of the Cuillin Main Ridge to form the Greater Cuillin Traverse, a major test of mountaineering skill and stamina that involves nearly 4300m/14,000ft of ascent. It wasn't completed until 1939, by Charleson and Forde, well after the Golden Age of Cuillin exploration in Victorian times.*

even after rain. In many ways it provides a unique Cuillin ascent, much of it on grass, and it was famously described by an early guidebook as 'delightfully easy'. Should you wish, there's also plenty of opportunity for scrambling *en route*.

The route to the foot of the south ridge begins on a Land Rover track, signposted Camasunary, that leaves the A881 Broadford-Elgol road 400m south of Kilmarie. There are parking spaces opposite the start of the track. The track crosses the shallow bealach of Am Mam south of Bla Bheinn to the house at Camasunary on Loch Scavaig. At the large cairn on Am Mam, the sharp crest of the south ridge comes into view for the first time, rising evenly and invitingly from seashore to mountain top. Its sharp crest and purity of line do much to enhance the grandeur of the superb view across Camasunary Bay to the Cuillin.

Twenty metres before the hairpin bend on the descent to Camasunary (cairn), branch right on a path that cuts across the hillside and crosses the Abhainn nan Leac, which has some picturesque waterfalls, to the foot of the south ridge. Leave the path a couple of hundred metres beyond the river, at a large cairn on a boulder, and take the path that climbs the ridge.

The lower part of the ridge consists of steep grass slopes leading to the craggy brow above. The path bypasses the crags on the right to reach the increasingly rocky upper ridge, whose solid gabbro is a pleasure to negotiate. Scrambling of all grades can be sought or avoided almost altogether by keeping to the path, which takes the line of least resistance. The ridge eventually merges with the south-east slopes of the mountain to culminate at the stony dome of the △South Top.

The ▲summit (North Top) lies 200m away across a short dip whose negotiation involves some easy scrambling. The easiest route descends a steep earthy gully to just below the dip. A more direct and interesting route involves an easy if slightly exposed scramble along a ledge on the left near the top of this gully. From the dip the summit, with its unrivalled views of the main Cuillin ridge across Srath na Creitheach, is reached without difficulty (see also Route 13). In adverse weather, return via the route of ascent. If in doubt, the easiest line is unfailingly to the left (east). In fine weather a return via the lochan-studded plateau of Slat Bheinn makes a delightful contrast to the ascent route. From the South Top descend the stony south-east slopes of the mountain that rim Coire Uaigneich, as for Route 13. From the small lochan at the foot of the slopes a pleasant stroll across the flat, grassy plateau, with its many clear moorland lochans, leads back to Am Mam and the Land Rover track back to Kilmarie.

> 'And over all broods the mighty mass of Blaaven, gleaming with rich purple, its clefts white with dazzling snow-wreaths, and wisps of cloud stealing around its secret top. It is a mountain among mountains, a king among them all, whose magic influence fills the heart...'
>
> J. A. MacCulloch (The Misty Isle of Skye, 1905)

ROUTE 15: SGURR NA STRI

ROUTE START: Sligachan (NG 486298, L32/E411 or Harvey's Cuillin)

ROUTE LOG: 15ml/24km, 580m/1900ft, 8hrs

ROUTE OVERVIEW: return hill walk. A long but easy walk leads to a perfectly sited miniature mountain at the heart of the Cuillin.

	1	2	3	4	5
Grade		▓			
Terrain		▓			
Navigation			▓		
Seriousness		▓			

The extremely complex and rocky mountain of Sgurr na Stri, which stands at the mouth of Loch Coruisk, is a minor hill by Cuillin standards but of such rugged grandeur, in such a perfect situation and boasting such stunning views that its ascent is highly recommended. The route to it from Sligachan is itself a magnificent walk along probably the best path in the Cuillin, but its length should not be underestimated. In times past it was possible to hire a pony at Sligachan, but today the journey must be done under your own steam.

Begin at the old bridge at Sligachan and follow the path southwards along Glen Sligachan between the rounded Red Hills and the jagged Black Cuillin. The first feature of interest reached is the Clach na Craoibhe Chaoruinn (Stone of the Rowan Tree), which stands beside the path on the right a short distance beyond the Allt na Measarroch. After 3½ml/6km the path passes the deep trench of Harta Corrie, in whose mouth can be seen the curious Bloody Stone (see Route 2).

After a further ½ml/1km or so the path forks at the foot of Am Fraoch-choire. The left branch goes past Loch an Athain into the jaws of Srath na Creitheach below Bla Bheinn and leads to Camasunary and beyond (see Route 17). The right branch leads to Sgurr na Stri across the broad flats of upper Srath na Creitheach, a remote basin that has an air of spaciousness unequalled in the Cuillin. The conjunction of the flat floor of the strath and the steep western wall of Bla Bheinn behind gives the place the appearance and scale of an Alpine cirque. The path climbs to a large cairn on the low ridge of Druim Hain, from where

From a wild camp at Coruisk, or as part of a day-trip by boat from Elgol, the capable scrambler should be able to find an entertaining route to the summit of Sgurr na Stri directly from the lochside. A steep route involving less route-finding and scrambling can be found by starting along the Sligachan path at the foot of Coire Riabhach, and still easier routes will be found further up the path (including the easy route described from Druim Hain).

the sparkling waters of Loch Coruisk and Loch Scavaig are seen for the first time.

The main path appears to go straight on at the cairn, but this leads only to a viewpoint (worth the short detour). The true path goes left for a short distance to another large cairn, then forks. Keep left for Sgurr na Stri (the right branch descends to Coruisk – see Route 16). The path crosses the hillside below Sgurr Hain and after about 20 minutes passes Captain Maryon's Cairn, which can be seen 100m below on the right. This 2m/7ft stone pyramid was erected in memory of the captain after his body was found here in 1946, two years after his disappearance.

Five minutes further along, a stream drains a shallow grassy depression on the left that offers an easy way up to the complex series of rocky knolls that form the summit of Sgurr na Stri. The two most southerly knolls are the highest – one an eyrie above Camasunary, the other an eyrie above picturesque Loch Coruisk. The views in all directions are perfection.

The easiest and quickest return route is by the outward route, but energetic walkers should not miss the opportunity to descend to Coruisk and explore before returning (see Route 16). Experienced Cuillin walkers may wish to consider the more serious return route to Sligachan over the Bealach na Glaic Moire (Route 18b).

Sgurr na Stri's name (meaning Peak of Strife) is said to derive from an eighteenth-century boundary dispute between the MacLeods and MacKinnons, each of whom laid claim to the land on which the mountain stands. A compromise was agreed, but the dispute was soon forgotten as the land was of no use to either clan. Could there be a more fitting example of the pointlessness of the clan feuding that blighted Skye for centuries?

ROUTE 16: CORUISK VIA GLEN SLIGACHAN

ROUTE START: Sligachan (NG 486298, L32/E411 or Harvey's Cuillin)

ROUTE LOG: 15ml/24km, 380m/1250ft, 8hrs

ROUTE OVERVIEW: return hill walk. A long but easy walk to the most spectacularly sited loch in the British Isles. Simply breathtaking.

	1	2	3	4	5
Grade	■				
Terrain		■			
Navigation	✓				
Seriousness	■		■		

For sketch map see Routes 15 and 21

If the Cuillin of Skye are the crowning glory of British mountains, then Loch Coruisk is the jewel in the crown. Cradled in the long narrow basin of Coir' Uisge (Water Corrie) at the heart of the remote eastern side of the range, it is justly famed for its rugged yet picturesque scenery. The loch itself is studded with islands and fringed with sandy bays. Around its rocky shores tower the vertiginous parapets of the Cuillin, from where streams tumble into wild corries. Beyond the isthmus at the mouth of the loch lap the emerald waters of Loch Scavaig, itself fringed by attractively craggy shores. At Coruisk the forces of nature have run wild.

Coruisk is at its most colourful when slanting sunlight highlights its intricate forms, but it is at its most glorious and dramatic on a stormy day, when the crashing waters of loch and sea and the foaming mountainsides are a truly awesome sight. The difficulty of reaching Coruisk when rivers are in spate, however, should not be underestimated.

'The mountains rose so perpendicularly from the water's edge, that Borrowdale, or even Glencoe, is a jest to them . . . It is as exquisite a savage scene as Loch Katrine is a scene of romantic beauty . . . Though I have never seen many scenes of more extensive desolation, I have never witnessed any in which it pressed more deeply upon the eye and the heart.'

Sir Walter Scott on Loch Coruisk (from his journal, 1814)

The Coruisk River and its tributaries at the head of the loch, the Abhainn Camas Fhionnairigh at Camasunary, the Allt a Chaoich at the foot of An Garbh-choire and the River Scavaig (which is normally crossed on stepping stones) are all impassable in spate. Coir' Uisge did not receive its Gaelic name for nothing. The waters of the loch have been known to rise 2½m/8ft in one day.

Tourists came to Coruisk to stand

and stare long before the Cuillin were climbed. Sir Walter Scott came in 1814 while on a yachting tour of the west coast of Scotland. At his exhortation the painters William Danielson and J. M. W. Turner followed, and their paintings encouraged others. They came by boat across Loch Scavaig, as many still do, but to appreciate Coruisk to the full it must be explored on foot.

The best lochside view is obtained from the south-east shore (the arrival point from Sligachan), from where the prospect up the loch to the splintered Cuillin skyline is exquisite. A short distance further away is the mouth of the loch, where the River Scavaig, only 400m long and renowned as one of the shortest rivers in the world, cascades into the sea at Loch na Cuilce, the inner bay of Loch Scavaig where Elgol boats arrive. The best viewpoint here is the knoll on the small peninsula that juts out into Loch Scavaig. In dry weather the River Scavaig can be crossed dryshod on stepping-stones at the mouth of Loch Coruisk. On the far side, hidden by a crag, is the Junior Mountaineering Club of Scotland's hut, with wild camping possible nearby.

Walkers who have time to spend at Coruisk will find much to do. It is possible to walk all the way around the loch in about two hours, excluding stops to view the islands, explore the sandy bays and gawp at the mountain scenery. There is a boggy path all the way; the south side provides slightly easier going as the north side is narrow and rutted.

At the head of the loch is a rugged amphitheatre of rock whose scale and complexity is such that the peaks on the main ridge above are indistinguishable to the inexperienced eye. The floor of the corrie is a combination of boulders and tussocky heather that makes heavy going, but indistinct paths wend their way through the wilderness, providing access to the skyline (see Routes 18 & 19).

Other places to explore include the Elgol coast path, on which the renowned Bad Step is only a few minutes walk away around Loch Scavaig (Route 17). Ascents unique to Coruisk include Sgurr na Stri (Route 15), Gars-bheinn via its east ridge (see Route 12) and Meall na Cuilce, a scramblers' viewpoint that offers stunning views of the whole area.

Eschewing a boat ride from Elgol, the standard walking routes to Coruisk begin at Elgol (Route 17) and Sligachan (described here). Each has merit. Both are recommended.

The Sligachan route follows the path along Glen Sligachan to the second fork on Druim Hain, as described in Route 15. While the left branch goes straight on to Sgurr na Stri, the right branch curves down through upper Coire Riabhach. Below the lochan in the corrie, several paths continue down to the shores of Loch Coruisk. Stay nearer the stream for a spot of slabby scrambling or stay further away for easier going.

ROUTE 17: CORUISK FROM ELGOL

ROUTE START: Elgol (NG 516135, OS Landranger 32, L32/E411 or Harvey's Cuillin)

ROUTE LOG: 12ml/19km, undulating, 8hrs

ROUTE OVERVIEW: difficult return coast walk. Perhaps the finest coast walk in the British Isles leads to incomparable Coruisk. The route merits its Grade 4 rating for the Bad Step.

	1	2	3	4	5
Grade	█	█	█	█	
Terrain	█	█	█		
Navigation	█	█		█	
Seriousness	█	█	█		

The view of the Cuillin horseshoe from the hilly village of Elgol is one of the most celebrated on Skye. In summer, boats ferry passengers from Elgol jetty across Loch Scavaig to Coruisk, but the grandeur and remoteness of this unique mountain fastness are best appreciated on foot.

In terms of mountain scenery there is no finer coast walk in the British Isles than that around the shores of Loch Scavaig. Paths from Elgol and Kilmarie join at the lonely bay of Camasunary and continue all the way to Coruisk, but the route is not without its adventurous moments. In particular there is at least one major river crossing which may be impracticable after rain, and towards Coruisk the renowned Bad Step provides a sting in the tail that will keep the adrenaline flowing throughout the walk. Despite the low level of the route, the walk there and back can be tiring. The effort required can be reduced by booking a boat passage back. For further details see p.22.

The building of the Kilmarie-Camasunary track by the army in 1968 was part of a scheme to 'improve' access to Coruisk. The proposal became a conservation cause célèbre when it was discovered that the intention was also to build bridges over the Abhainn Camas Fhionnairigh and the River Scavaig and to dynamite the Bad Step. The bridges were built but soon destroyed by the elements. The Bad Step was thankfully left inviolate so that future generations can continue to enjoy the wildness of Coruisk.

There are two car parks in Elgol, but the upper car park has a maximum 4hr stay, so park in the lower car park down by the jetty. The route begins as a short access road to some houses, signposted Camasunary, several hundred metres back up the B8083 at the top of the hill. From the road-end a path continues across the hillside below Bidein an Fhithich, descends to cross a stream, then wends its way across the grassy hillside of Ben Cleat some 60m/200ft above the shore. The walk is delightful, with Soay on one's left, the Cuillin drawing ever closer and the white house at Camasunary ahead acting as a homing beacon.

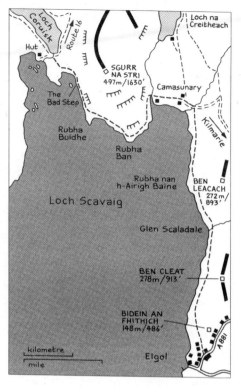

The path next descends to the meadows at the foot of Glen Scaladal before climbing around the slopes of Ben Leacach to 60m/200ft again above vegetated cliffs at the water's edge. There is some exposure, but if you find yourself overlooking a precipice with no obvious way forward you have missed the true path a few metres back. Easier slopes are reached at the headland of Rubha na h-Airighe Baine, and from then on the path keeps low down by the shore to Camasunary (Bay of the Fair Shieling). Camasunary is one of the most beautiful bays on Skye, its wide sandy beach backed by luscious green meadows which are in turn backed by the savage rock faces of Sgurr na Stri and Bla Bheinn. This spot is well worth a visit even should you go no further (3½ml/6km from Elgol).

Beyond Camasunary the route becomes more exciting. At the west end of the bay is a fine bothy, then the first obstacle is encountered almost immediately in the form of the Abhainn Camas Fhionnairigh. At low tide the river can be forded at its confluence with a smaller stream just upriver from the remains of the old bridge. At high tide the river is flooded beyond here at least as far as the island at NG 509191, and a longer detour will be necessary to ford it.

On the far side the path follows the shoreline around the craggy slopes of Sgurr na Stri. There is now gabbro underfoot (as well as plenty of bog). At Rubha Ban (White Headland), Gars-bheinn comes into view across Loch Scavaig and the scenery becomes increasingly wild towards the next point (Rubha Buidhe, Yellow Headland), where the path cuts through a defile right of a rocky knoll, isolated from the main hillside. The top of the knoll provides a spectacular view of Loch na Cuilce, the rocky inner basin of Loch Scavaig where the Elgol boats arrive, with the waters of Loch Coruisk just visible beyond. On a stormy day there can be few wilder prospects than this, with the turbulent waters of Scavaig crashing against the many islets, and the Cuillin wreathed in swirling cloud beyond.

> 'Where a wild stream, with headlong shock
> Came brawling down its bed of rock
> To mingle with the main.'
>
> Sir Walter Scott on the River Scavaig
> (The Lord of the Isles, 1815)

Coruisk looks close at hand now, but chaotic terrain on the western slopes of Sgurr na Stri makes the going slow. At two points boiler-plate slabs curve into the sea. The path rises over the top of the first but can find no way around the second – the infamous Bad Step, the negotiation of which is a moderate scramble with some exposure above deep water.

Follow cairns down to the water's edge and clamber over huge blocks of rock that have fallen from the overhang above. Scramble round a corner and up a sloping crack, using finger holds on the slab above the crack for safety. Half-way up the crack go left along another horizontal fault onto easier ground. The temptation to continue straight on up the crack is what gets people into difficulties. The Bad Step is enjoyable or nerve-racking depending on your point of view. If in doubt leave it for another day and journey to Coruisk by a different route.

Once past the Bad Step it is only a few minutes walk to the shores of Loch Coruisk (2½ml/4km from Camasunary). Note that to reach the JMCS Hut and the west side of Loch Coruisk it is necessary to cross the River Scavaig on stepping stones at the mouth of the loch. For a truly magnificent trip, if transport can be arranged, walk out of Coruisk by a different route, either to Sligachan or Glen Brittle. If returning to Elgol on foot, evening light on Rum (if you're lucky) will ease the journey homeward.

Alternative Route Start (Kilmarie)

Camasunary can be reached more easily from the B8083 Broadford-Elgol road by a Land Rover track that begins 400m south of Kilmarie (NG 545172) and crosses the low bealach of Am Mam, as for Route 14 to Bla Bheinn. The track is easier, drier, faster and around a mile shorter each way than the Elgol path, but it climbs higher, is less appealing to walk on and affords no views westwards until the summit of Am Mam is reached. The Elgol route is more aesthetically pleasing, but because of its comparative ease and shortness the Kilmarie track has now become the more popular approach route to Coruisk.

Following on from Routes 16 & 17, Routes 18 and 19 are a compendium of five further routes linking Coruisk to Glen Brittle and Sligachan, from which to pick and mix. All involve handwork, rough terrain and navigational difficulty and should be considered serious propositions. Note also that in wet weather, when burns are in spate, Coruisk can become a trap from which only dry weather will spring you.

Maps: all routes to Coruisk use L32/ E411 or Harvey's Cuillin.

The grid (right) and maps apply to all five routes. Distance/ascent/time shown applies **one-way only**.

	1	2	3	4	5
Grade					
Terrain					
Navigation					
Seriousness					

ROUTE 18a: To/from Glen Brittle campsite (NG 414205) via **the coast route**.

ROUTE LOG: one-way 7ml/11km, 300+m/1000+ft, 4+hrs

This is the only route from Glen Brittle to Coruisk that does not involve a crossing of the Cuillin, but it should not be taken lightly. It involves difficult route-finding on craggy slopes and one spot of slabby scrambling on the shores of Loch Scavaig that some may find awkward.

The route begins at Glen Brittle campsite and initially follows the Coir' a' Ghrunnda path (Route 11). Avoid all left-branching lines up into Coir' a' Ghrunnda and keep straight on around the foot of the Cuillin to the Allt Coir' a' Ghrunnda. The path continues to the Allt Coire nan Laogh but increasingly deteriorates. Beyond the Allt Coire nan Laogh a frustrating three-dimensional maze of crags drops from Gars-bheinn to the seashore and complicates finding a route around the headland above Ulfhart Point and Rubha a' Gheodha Bhuidhe to Loch Scavaig.

One route rises gently up a grassy terrace onto rocky ground and continues around the 300m contour. Another goes straight on around the 225m contour before rising to that height. If you come across any cairns, it might be judicious to follow them. The point all lines are aiming for is the top of the gorge of the Allt an Fhraoich (named only on E411), where the stream takes a right-angled turn (NG 481178).

Beyond here, avoid the temptation to descend too early. Stay high, climbing down and up if necessary, before taking an obvious diagonal line down towards the shore beyond Eilean Reamhar. If you're lucky, a path reappears and takes an even shallower line down than expected, eventually reaching the shore in the vicinity of the Allt a' Chaoich (the Mad Burn). Beyond the Mad Burn a section of boiler-plate slab by the shoreline involves a short moderate scramble that may be awkward when wet and greasy. Once past here, Coruisk is only a few minutes' walk away.

In the direction Coruisk to Glen Brittle, the correct route is even harder to find.

ROUTE 18b: To/from Sligachan (NG 486298) via **Bealach na Glaic Moire** (NG 453238).

ROUTE LOG: one-way 9½ml/15km, 900m/2950ft, 6½hrs

This 760m/2492ft bealach between Bidein Druim nan Ramh and Sgurr a' Mhadaidh at the head of Coir' a' Mhadaidh is the lowest pass to Coruisk on the main Cuillin ridge. The route over it is marked on E411 and is the shortest way between Sligachan and upper Coir'-uisg. In combination with Glen Sligachan (Route 16) it makes a magnificent round trip from Sligachan, but do not let the dotted line on the Explorer map mislead you into thinking there is a path. The route is steep, stony, awkward and a much harder proposition than the low-level path along the glen.

In the direction Loch Coruisk to Sligachan, take either of the lochside paths to the head of the loch and Coir'-uisg. The south side of the loch gives slightly easier going. The level floor of Coir'-uisg is a combination of boulders and tussocky heather that makes heavy going, but a cairned path will be found on the left bank (right-hand side) of the stream that bears right beneath the crags of Druim nan Ramh into the broad gully of the Glac Mhor (Big Defile). The bealach is at the head of this gully.

The gully rises past crags that guard the high corrie of Coir' an Uaigneis and splits into two branches. The left (south) branch deposits you at the Sgurr a' Mhadaidh end of the bealach and is easier on ascent, with grass and rocks to ease the stony going. The right (north) branch deposits you at the Bidein Druim nan Ramh end of the bealach and its loose stones are perhaps easier on descent. From the bealach it may be tempting to explore along the main ridge, but progress in either direction soon involves rock climbing.

To descend into Coir' a' Mhadaidh, first trend diagonally right from the Sgurr a' Mhadaidh end of the bealach down a broad grassy shelf beneath the crags of Bidein Druim nan Ramh. From the north (Bidein) end of the bealach this shelf can be reached by descending diagonally right until a short stone shoot gives access.

The traverse along the shelf is necessary to bypass the corrie's craggy headwall

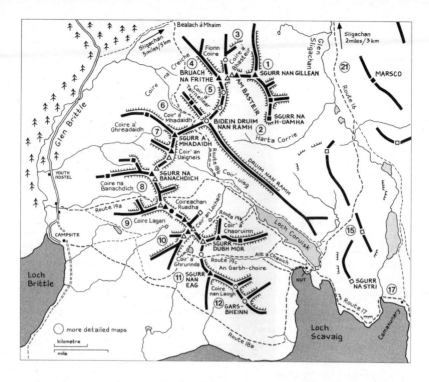

and reach a stone shoot in the far eastern corner of the corrie (the right-hand corner on descent) beneath the south-east ridge of Sgurr an Fheadain. Keep descending diagonally until you reach the head of the stone shoot (cairn; difficult to find in mist), then descend directly into the bowl of the corrie. The descent is stony, expletive-inducing but safe.

Lower down, pick up a path on the right bank of the developing stream and continue down beside a short gorge to reach a grassy area. Bear right here to follow a cairned line away from the stream beneath the cliffs of Sgurr an Fheadain. The route marked on E411 continues down beside the stream but is longer and less straightforward than the right-branching route. At the foot of Sgurr an Fheadain the route joins a path that makes a rising traverse across the flanks of the north-west ridge of Bruach na Frithe to the Bealach a' Mhaim, and then it is downhill all the way beside the tumbling Allt Dearg Mor to Sligachan.

In the reverse direction, from Sligachan to Coruisk, the ascent of the stone shoot in Coir' a' Mhadaidh is purgatorial.

ROUTE 19: CORUISK ROUTE MISCELLANY (2)

Maps: all routes to Coruisk use L32/
E411 or Harvey's Cuillin.

The grid (right) and maps apply to all
routes. Distance/ascent/time shown
applies **one-way only**.

	1	2	3	4	5
Grade					
Terrain					
Navigation					
Seriousness					

ROUTE 19a: To/from Glen Brittle Hut (NG 411216) or campsite (NG 414205) via **Bealach Coire na Banachdich** (NG 443218).

ROUTE LOG: one-way 6ml/10km, 850m/2800ft, 5hrs

This 851m/2791ft bealach between Sgurr na Banachdich and Sgurr Dearg connects Coire na Banachdich on the Glen Brittle side to Coireachan Ruadha on the Coruisk side and provides technically the easiest way to Coruisk from Glen Brittle (Route 18a coast route included). The route is marked on E411, but do not let the dotted line on the map mislead you into thinking there is a path. See Route 8 for a description of the Coire na Banachdich side.

Starting at Coruisk, follow the stream that bears left around the leaning tower of Sgurr Coir' an Lochain into the large hollow of Coireachan Ruadha. This corrie is one of the largest and remotest in the Cuillin, and Sgurr Coir' an Lochain is probably the least ascended peak in the range. Historically it lays claim to being the last peak not only in the Cuillin but also in the whole British Isles to receive a first ascent (in 1896). A cairned path will be found on the right bank (left side) of the stream. Higher up, keep well to the left of the stream to outflank waterfalls, then cut back right into the upper corrie and pick a route up steep slopes of boulders and scree at the back to reach the bealach.

ROUTE 19b: To/from Glen Brittle campsite (NG 414205) via **Bealach Coir' an Lochain** (NG 452205).

ROUTE LOG: one-way 7ml/11km, 850m/2800ft, 5½hrs

This 855m/2806ft bealach between Sgurr Thearlaich and Sgurr Dubh na Da Bheinn connects Coir' a' Ghrunnda on the Glen Brittle side to Coir' an Lochain on the Coruisk side, two of the wildest corries in the Cuillin. The Coir' a' Ghrunnda side of the bealach is a slope of boulders and scree, easily reached from the bowl of the corrie. See Route 11 for a description of the more difficult route from Glen Brittle to Coir' a' Ghrunnda.

Coir' an Lochain is a high (580m/1900ft) and remote corrie, so well guarded by crags that it is best approached from neighbouring Coir' a' Chaoruinn by a hidden terrace. Coir' a' Chaoruinn is a shallower corrie from which several streams descend over slabs to the head of Loch Coruisk. Starting at Coruisk, take the path along the south shore of the loch and climb left into Coir' a' Chaoruinn beside its first (southernmost) stream. The slabs cannot be avoided altogether but the line of least resistance has little difficulty.

At about 400m/1300ft a large leaning slab on the right marks the start of a cairned terrace that makes a curious rising traverse around the slabby north-east slopes of Sgurr Dubh Mor to emerge in Coir' an Lochain a short distance below the lochan. There are no more secret places in the whole Cuillin. The route to the Bealach Coir' an Lochain goes up grass and rocks at the back of the corrie to finish in a stone shoot. In the direction Glen Brittle to Coruisk, to find the terrace below the lochan on descent, follow cairns down to the right (east).

ROUTE 19c: To/from Glen Brittle campsite (NG 414205) via **Bealach a' Gharbh-choire** (NG 454201).

ROUTE LOG: one-way 6ml/10km, 800m/2600ft, 5hrs

This 797m/2614ft bealach between Caisteal a' Garbh-choire and Sgurr nan Eag connects Coir' a' Ghrunnda on the Glen Brittle side to An Garbh-choire on the Coruisk side. See Route 11 for a description of the Coir' a' Ghrunnda side.

Starting at Coruisk, there are a number of routes into An Garbh-choire. One follows the shore of Loch Scavaig as far as the stream beyond the Allt a' Chaoich (short moderate scramble required) then climbs the right-hand side of this stream into the lower corrie. An easier route begins half-way along the south-west side of Loch Coruisk, climbs the shallow corrie of tussocky grass and heather on the south side of the Dubh slabs and crosses the low ridge at its head into lower An Garbh-choire.

More interestingly, from c.700m along the south-west side of the loch, cut back up a shallow depression onto the south-east ridge of Meall na Cuilce for an easy and scenic scramble over the top into the corrie.

Once into the corrie, follow the path up the right-hand side of the stream towards Caisteal a' Garbh-choire, the unmistakable rock fortress seen ahead on the skyline. The path finds an easy route up the craggy steepening that separates the lower from the upper corrie but then becomes lost in a narrow V-shaped defile choked with gargantuan boulders whose negotiation requires nimbleness and humour. This upper section has a savage charm that may not be fully appreciated until you reach the skyline. The corrie is not named The Rough Corrie for nothing. The bealach is the gap on the main ridge left of the Caisteal.

Route 20: Glamaig and the Beinn Deargs

ROUTE START: Sligachan (NG 487299, L32/E411 or Harvey's Cuillin)

ROUTE LOG: 7ml/11km, 1230m/4050ft, 6½hrs

ROUTE OVERVIEW: difficult circular hill walk. A tough ascent is rewarded with glorious views and ridge walking on the Red Hills in the shadow of the Black Cuillin.

	1	2	3	4	5
Grade	▨	▨			
Terrain	▨	▨	▨	▨	
Navigation	▨	▨			
Seriousness	▨	▨			

Across the trench of Glen Sligachan the rounded granite peaks of the Red Hills line up incongruously against the bold gabbro peaks of the Black Cuillin. Ascents are tough – the geologist John MacCulloch named the hills Red after their long fans of granite scree. Once up, however, Red Hillwalking has much to recommend it. There are easy ridges to wander along and the views are superb.

Glamaig, one of only two Corbetts on Skye, is the epitome of Red Hill architecture. From Sligachan it appears as an enormous cone-shaped mountain that dominates the moor, and the view from the summit is exceptional even by Skye standards. A continuation across the ridges of the neighbouring Beinn Deargs gives the best round in the Red Hills.

The very steep, unrelenting, scree-riddled ascent of Glamaig from Sligachan requires more than the usual amount of motivation, but a direttissima line does have a certain purist (some might say masochistic) appeal. There is no best way across the moor to the foot of the mountain, so begin at the lay-by 100m east of Sligachan bridge.

Because of its steepness the ascent demands care. Grass rakes can be used to ease the going lower down, but these too require care, especially when wet, as a slip would propel you glenwards with increasing velocity. Aim right of the broken crags as viewed from Sligachan and do not expect to stay upright all of the way.

> In 1899, Gurkha soldier Havildar Harkabir Thapa reached the summit of Glamaig from the old bridge at Sligachan in 37 minutes, followed by a descent of 18 minutes. In bare feet! The current up-and-down record, set in 1997 by Mark Rigby, stands at 44 minutes 41 seconds.

From the summit, which is called Sgurr Mhairi (Mary's Peak), descend south-east down scree runs to well-named Bealach na Sgairde (Scree Pass). Care is required in mist as the high ground trends east towards crags. The broken slope leading to the bealach is further right and is again very steep. From the bealach the equally steep, stony ascent of over 300m/1000ft to the summit of Beinn Dearg Mhor looks monstrous, but secure good-sized rocks enable you to bound up in true Gurkha style and the north ridge and summit are soon reached.

Beyond the summit the going becomes increasingly pleasant as the stony ridge leads on across the shallower Bealach Mosgaraidh to Beinn Dearg Mheadhonach. The fine, narrow summit ridge here is a few hundred metres long and has a cairn at each end; the far one is the summit.

The descent back to the moor follows a rough path down Mheadhonach's summit boulderfield and along the

level ridge of Druim na Ruaige, where welcome patches of turf appear underfoot to add some spring to the step. From the end of the ridge bear right down steep grass slopes into Coire na Sgairde, where the Allt Daraich is as inviting as any Cuillin burn, and where in summer dragonflies of many colours add to the picturesqueness of the scene.

The view from the summit of Glamaig demands superlatives. Westwards is beautiful Loch Bracadale on the far side of the island, northwards is the coast of Trotternish and the whole of Raasay, eastwards are Scalpay and the islands of the Inner Sound, while southwards lie the inimitable Cuillin, with Bla Bheinn looking especially magnificent.

Lower down, a path follows the left bank of the Allt Daraich beside a wooded gorge that has some fine waterfalls and pools. The path is unmaintained and can become boggy after rain, but when dry it gives a pleasant end-of-day descent to meet the Glen Sligachan path (Route 15) close to Sligachan.

Route 21: Marsco

ROUTE START: Sligachan (NG 487299, L32/E411 or Harvey's Cuillin)

ROUTE LOG: 8½ml/14km, 730m/2400ft, 5½hrs

ROUTE OVERVIEW: circular hill walk. A steep but screeless ascent in the Red Hills leads to the summit of an attractive isolated mountain and prominent viewpoint.

	1	2	3	4	5
Grade	■	■	■		
Terrain	■	■	■		
Navigation	■	■			
Seriousness	■	■			

The solitary sentinel of Marsco is the most isolated and attractive of the Red Hills. Separated from Beinn Dearg Mheadhonach to the north by a 280m/920ft bealach and from Garbh-bheinn to the south by a 320m/1050ft bealach, its conical summit provides a much-photographed backdrop to the view along Glen Sligachan. When bathed in the warm glow of the evening sun, it may even distract attention from the shadowy Black Cuillin across the glen. Although geologically similar to Glamaig and the Beinn Deargs, it is a much sturdier mountain that can be climbed without resort to the scree that bedevils its neighbours.

There are two possible routes to the summit, one beginning at Loch Ainort to the east and one beginning at Sligachan to the north. The Loch Ainort approach is the shorter of the two but is mostly pathless and has no Cuillin views. The more aesthetic and rewarding approach begins at Sligachan, from where the north-west ridge that forms the route of ascent can be seen in its entirety.

From Sligachan, follow the excellent Coruisk path along Glen Sligachan (see Route 15) for c.2ml/3km, to a fork just before the Allt na Measarroch. Leave it here to branch left up a rougher, boggier, less distinct path along the near bank (left-hand side) of this stream. The path continues to Mam a' Phobuill, a pass that leads over to Loch Ainort, where it becomes lost among sheep paths.

The buttress on the west face of Marsco, seen in profile from Sligachan, is known as the Fiaclan Dearg (Red Tooth) and it yields the only sound rock of any quantity in the whole of the crumbling Red Hills. Its other claim to fame is that the first climb here was put up by Noel Odell, who was the last person to see Mallory and Irvine disappear into the cloud on Everest in 1924.

When the path begins to level out onto the pass, leave it to head for the skyline up the steep, grassy hillside on the right. This will take you up the near side of Coire nan Laogh, Marsco's only corrie scooped out of the west side of the hill, directly to the north-west ridge and narrow summit. Higher up, the slope becomes very steep indeed, with some exposure, and you may well want to use hands for balance.

The excellent all-round view from the summit includes the entire horseshoe Cuillin Main Ridge spread before you across the yawning depths of Harta Corrie. Note especially the distinctive colourings of Am Fraoch-choire beneath your feet, where the green grass slopes of Marsco meet the red rocks of Ruadh Stac to the south.

For an alternative return route that provides a more gentle (though still steep) descent, continue over the top of Marsco and down the south-east ridge to a dip before the minor south-east top. Turn left (north) here to follow a line of old fence posts down around the east rim of Coire nan Laogh to Mam a' Phobuill, to regain the path along the Allt na Measarroch.

The ascent to Mam a' Phobuill follows in the footsteps of Bonnie Prince Charlie on his flight across Skye in 1746 following his defeat at the Battle of Culloden. He used this pass to cross the Red Hills, avoiding the English redcoats stationed at Sligachan. Perhaps it was here that he had to be pulled waist-deep out of a bog and exclaimed, 'I'm sure the Devil would not find me now!'

N.B. It is also possible to extend the day by a descent south into Am Fraoch-choire and Glen Sligachan. The extremely rough direct descent into the corrie from the dip before the south-east top is not recommended, but a continuation over the top and down the lower south-east ridge makes an interesting way down, with the waters of Am Fraoch-choire's beautifully clear stream beckoning below.

ROUTE 22: BELIG AND GHARB-BHEINN

ROUTE START: head of Loch Slapin (NG 562224, L32/E411 or Harvey's Cuillin)

ROUTE LOG: 6ml/10km, 1110m/3650ft, 7hrs

ROUTE OVERVIEW: circular mountain scramble. A varied, exploratory horseshoe round combines good scrambling on narrow basalt ridges with some tough scree and close-up views of impressive gabbro rock architecture.

	1	2	3	4	5
Grade	■	■	■	■	
Terrain	■	■	■		
Navigation	■	■	■		
Seriousness	■	■			

The trio of craggy peaks at the head of Loch Slapin (Belig, Garbh-bheinn and Sgurr nan Each) make a rewarding scramble, but note that the summits are basalt, less adhesive than Cuillin gabbro, and best avoided when wet. As with Marsco (Route 21), there are two possible approach routes, one beginning at Loch Ainort to the north and one beginning at Loch Slapin to the east. Both are of approximately equal length but the Loch Slapin approach sports a much greater variety of dramatic and picturesque scenery.

Begin at the head of Loch Slapin, where parking is possible at the roadside or on the east side of a bridge. Cross the grassy flats above the road to reach the Allt Aigeann at the point where (except after heavy rain) it disappears curiously into its stony bed. Sheep paths lead up both banks of the stream to the foot of the south-east ridge of Belig, where the ascent begins on short, sheep-cropped grass.

At c.250m/800ft the ridge steepens appreciably among small crags then becomes rockier and more interesting. A prominent rock tower yields to a direct scramble (easier on the right, harder and more exposed on the left) or can be avoided altogether on the right. Above here the crest of the ridge develops into a delightfully easy scramble, quite narrow and exposed in parts, but with no unavoidable problems. A flat, grassy section is reached before a final rise to the summit.

The route onwards to higher Garbh-bheinn, one of only two Corbetts on Skye, begins with a steep descent of Belig's south-west ridge to the intervening Bealach na Beiste. The upper part of the ridge

> Bealach nam Beiste (Pass of the Beast) is named for the legendary water horse of Loch na Sguabaidh, which was killed here by a MacKinnon. The beast had a penchant for attractive girls and left plain girls alone, such that to be chased by him was good for a girl's self-confidence (as long as he didn't catch her).

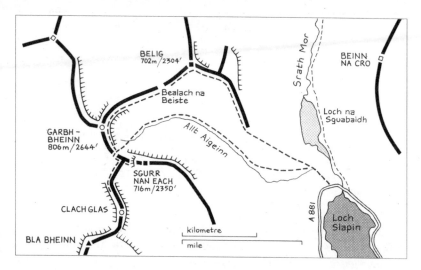

would provide an interesting scramble were it not for a loose drystone wall on the crest that makes it necessary to resort to an indistinct path below on the right (north). Lower down, the ridge broadens onto loose, stony slopes that give rough going. Similar awkward slopes rise from the bealach to Garbh-bheinn, but scrambling opportunities develop again near the summit.

The round continues down Garbh-bheinn's south-east ridge. This requires care at the top, where it is steep, broken and loose. Rockier ground lower down, on approach to the bealach below Sgurr nan Each, gives better footing and enables the descent to develop into another pleasant scramble. The scree slopes that descend left (east) of the bealach are the descent route, but it is first worth exploring further along the skyline towards Sgurr nan Each.

Half-way up Sgurr nan Each's west ridge, a level side ridge branches right towards Clach Glas. Above this junction the ridge to Sgurr nan Each narrows suddenly across gabbro slabs to become a dead-end for walkers at an impassable rock tower. The easier side ridge leads to the improbable rock tower of Clach Glas, known as the Matterhorn of Skye. Wander out along the ridge as far as the bealach at the foot of the tower, which looks spectacular from close up as it soars 162m/532ft overhead, bristling with classic rock climbs.

When you have finished exploring, descend the screes below the Garbh-bheinn-Sgurr nan Each bealach into the glen of the Allt Aigeann, which is one of the most beautiful streamways on Skye. Just before it turns to descend into the lower glen, at a tiered waterfall, there are a series of pools and cascades that are breathtakingly beautiful, and all the way down the glen there are pools and waterfalls that make the descent to your starting point a constant delight.

ROUTE 23: BEINN NAN CAILLICH

ROUTE START: Coire-chat-achan (NG 619227, L32/E411 or E412, or Harvey's Cuillin)

ROUTE LOG: 5ml/8km, 980m/3200ft, 5hrs

ROUTE OVERVIEW: circular hill walk. A steep boulder hop develops into a horseshoe ridge walk with superb and varied views.

	1	2	3	4	5
Grade		■	■		
Terrain			■		■
Navigation	■	■	■		
Seriousness		■	■	■	

Of Skye's two Beinn na Caillichs, that to the immediate west of Broadford is the higher and more imposing, its bald grey dome towering over the moorland, capped by a huge cairn that is visible for miles around. The shortest and time-honoured ascent begins from near the ruins of the old MacKinnon house at Coire-chat-achan, at the end of the minor road that leaves the A87 just north-west of Broadford. Park with consideration at the road-end turning circle.

The foreshortened view from Coire-chat-achan of the steep stony slopes of the Caillich is enough to give anyone, not just Samuel Johnson, pause for thought, and one may well feel the 'lethargy of indolence' that Boswell noted in his journal here. Fortunately, the ascent is nowhere near as steep and formidable as it looks. The rock has weathered into larger blocks than on the Red Hills further west and, once up, a fine horseshoe ridge walk leads onwards around the rim of Coire Gorm to Beinn Dearg Mhor and Beinn Dearg Bheag, giving a trio of summits equal to Loch Slapin's (Route 22).

Just beyond the road-end is a small stream whose banks provide perhaps the best going across the moor to the Caillich's foot. When the stream peters out, aim for the right-hand skyline. Once onto the bouldery hillside, any way up is as good as any other, so choose whichever boulder ruckle appeals and start boulder-hopping.

Coire-chat-achan means Corrie of the Place of Wildcats, this being the last stronghold of wildcats on Skye before their extermination. However, there have been recent sightings of possible wildcats, as opposed to smaller feral tabbies, so they may be back.

Be patient with the convex slope and the unexpectedly grassy summit will be reached without excessive effort. Beneath the huge cairn is said to lie a Norse princess, entombed here at her own wish so that she could forever face the land of her birth. Hence the hill's name, meaning Mountain of the Old Woman.

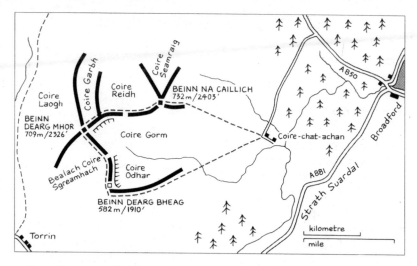

From the west end of the summit plateau a ridge, whose start may be awkward to locate in mist, leads off around the tight horseshoe of Coire Gorm. It descends pleasantly on grass and boulders to a bealach, then narrows attractively above steep corrie headwalls on each side to reach the stony summit of Beinn Dearg Mhor. N.B., this is a different Beinn Dearg Mhor from the one next to Glamaig in Route 20 – keep up!

Continuing the round, steep featureless scree slopes descend to the Bealach Coire Sgreamhach. In mist great care is required if the correct line is to be found. On the far side

It was from Coire-chat-achan that traveller Thomas Pennant climbed Beinn na Caillich in 1772 to make the first recorded ascent of any mountain on Skye. He was less than enamoured to find its sides 'covered with vast loose stones' and the summit view to be 'of desolation itself'. It was from here also that, during his 1773 tour of the island with James Boswell, Samuel Johnson made his famour one and only remark on the mountains of Skye: 'The hill behind the house we did not climb. The weather was rough and the height and steepness discouraged us.'

of the bealach a short rocky re-ascent gains the summit of Beinn Dearg Bheag.

To complete the horseshoe, descend the gentle ridge that curves down from Beinn Dearg Bheag's summit around Coire Odhar, picking up a path among the heather and boulders. Go straight off the end of the ridge down steep heathery slopes, cross the mouth of Coire Gorm and make a beeline back across the moor to your starting point. The going is rough but the sweeping panorama ahead lures you homewards, with the island of Pabay set like a jewel in the sea.

ROUTE 24: THE KYLERHEA GROUP

ROUTE START: Bealach Udal (NG 756206, L32/E412)

ROUTE LOG: 4ml/6km, 760m/2500ft, 4½hrs

ROUTE OVERVIEW: return hill walk. A rough tramp with good coastal views bags the two hills that dominate the eastern tip of Skye.

	1	2	3	4	5
Grade	▓	▓			
Terrain	▓	▓	▓		
Navigation	▓	▓			
Seriousness	▓				

At the eastern tip of Skye, dominating the straits of Kyle Akin and Kyle Rhea, stand the two commanding viewpoints of Sgurr na Coinnich and Beinn na Caillich (N.B., a different Caillich than Broadford's in Route 23). From the Glenelg-Kylerhea ferry their steep slopes give an impression of great height, yet they are easily climbed from the 279m/915ft Bealach Udal at the high point of the twisting road that links Kylerhea to Broadford.

The direct ascent of Sgurr na Coinnich from the Bealach Udal involves very rough going on tussocky grass and heather strewn with boulders. Easier going will be found further east, on the south ridge, so it is better to begin a few hundred metres east of the bealach, at the top of the steep descent to Kylerhea. There are parking spaces 130m down the road from a gated track to a satellite mast.

Begin by climbing diagonally right, staying left of a prominent buttress, to gain the south ridge. From the roadside, faced with some of the roughest terrain on the island, it doesn't look much like a ridge, but the going gets easier as height is gained. Once the ridge is reached, the going becomes very pleasant on short turf. Look for a beautiful lochan hidden in a hollow (NG 760209).

Higher up, another lochan (NG 759220) marks the start of the broad summit ridge, at the far end of which lies Coinnich's highest point. From the summit there are tremendous views all round the compass.

Beinn na Caillich is separated from Sgurr na Coinnich by the deep Bealach nam Mulachag, such that reaching this second summit involves a descent and re-ascent of

> *While bridge-building has destroyed otter habitats in the Kyleakin area, peaceful Kylerhea retains one of Britain's most thriving otter populations. An actively managed Otter Haven has been established by the Forestry Commission, together with a trail to a viewing hide. The signposted track to the car park (NG 786212) leaves the roadside not far above the ferry, and the path from there to the viewing hide is a 2½ml/4km return trip.*

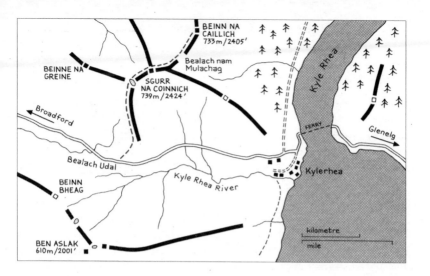

just over 150m/500ft, which must be repeated in reverse on the return journey. From Sgurr na Coinnich, Beinn na Caillich appears as a steep stony dome, but a route to the summit can be picked out on grassy rakes to ease the going. The ascent is worthwhile if only for the unrivalled summit views of the kyles and Loch Alsh.

Like the name of Broadford's Beinn na Caillich (Mountain of the Old Woman), the name of Kylerhea is also said to derive from a summit burial. Legend has it that here is buried Grainnhe, wife of Fionn, chief of the Fiennes, together with a pot of gold and jewels filled to the brim in her honour.

N.B., Ben Aslak (610m/2001ft) on the opposite side of the Bealach Udal is a less imposing hill than its two neighbours, but its attractive and complex summit makes a good objective for a short tramp. Beginning on the track to the satellite mast, climb heathery slopes towards the summit of Beinn Bheag, then cut left across the Kylerhea River onto Aslak's north-west ridge. Short turf and rock ease the ascent to the broad and knobbly summit ridge, which has good views, a top at each end and a fine lochan in the middle (2½ml/4km, 340m/1100ft, 2½hrs).

The straits of Kyle Akin and Kyle Rhea are traditionally named for Acunn and Readh, two brothers of the legendary Fiennes, a race of powerful hunters and fighters. Readh was drowned during an unsuccessful attempt to leap his strait. Both are said to have been buried at Glenelg.

ROUTE 25: MACLEOD'S TABLES

ROUTE START: near Orbost (NG 256445, L23/E407)

ROUTE LOG: 7ml/11km, 750m/2450ft, 5½hrs

ROUTE OVERVIEW: circular hill walk. Steep ascents contrast with peculiar flat summits on the crossing of two of Skye's most recognisable hills.

	1	2	3	4	5
Grade	■	■			
Terrain	■				
Navigation		■	■	■	
Seriousness	■				

Healabhal Mhor and Healabhal Bheag are curious truncated hills that are more familiarly known as MacLeod's Tables. Whatever the legendary derivation of their shape, geologists have a more prosaic explanation – it reflects the horizontal stratification of the basalt lavas of which they are composed.

Of the two, Healabhal Mhor

> *So flat are the summits of Healabhal Mhor and Healabhal Bheag, it is as though their summits have been lopped off by some supernatural force. Legend has it that this is precisely what happened – in order to provide a bed and table for St Columba when he was turned away from the door of a local clan chief.*

(Big) is the more often climbed, being closer to Dunvegan and having the larger summit plateau, but Healabhal Bheag (Little) is the more interesting hill. The best starting point for the round of both hills is on the road that runs south from the B884 to Orbost, at a right-angled bend where the road crosses a small stream. An anti-clockwise trip gets most of the moor work done with at the beginning.

> *Tired of hearing of the splendours of Holyrood Palace during a visit to the King's court in Edinburgh, a MacLeod chief boasted that he had an even more spacious banqueting hall and invited a number of mainland lords to an evening feast . . . on the summit of Healabhal Bheag. With the flat summit as his table, a starry sky as his ceiling and clansmen with flaming torches as his candelabra, one assumes the point was made. Hence MacLeod's Tables.*

On the north side of the stream is a farm track and you can park at its start (without obstructing the gate). Deer fencing provides an immediate initial obstacle. Follow boggy ground up beside its right-hand side then head westwards across the rough moors of Glen Osdale, gain the broad east ridge of Healabhal Mhor and follow it to the summit. The ridge is enlivened by one or two rock bands and has fine views over Loch Dunvegan,

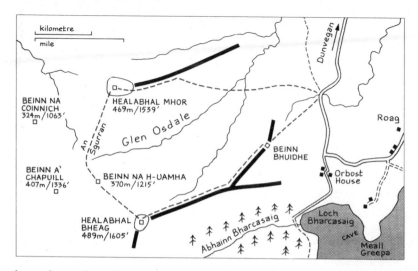

but it has to be said that its most appealing attribute is its brevity.

The uniform steepness of the grassy upper slopes of Healabhal Mhor accentuate the flatness of the mossy summit plateau. The summit cairn, surprisingly large considering the lack of building material, lies at the far right-hand corner. The view is notable for its non-existence, for the edges of the table form a truncated horizon. On a hazy day you could be on a platform in the sky that has no visible earthly support.

> For an easier day out, the two hills can be climbed separately. Healabhal Mhor is best ascended by its north-east ridge from the track to Osdale farm off the B884 (NG 245462). Healabhal Bheag is also best ascended by its north-east ridge, reached by climbing around the edge of a forestry plantation from Loch Bharcasaig south of Orbost House (NG 257431).

To continue the round, descend to a saddle, cross an intermediate minor hill top (named Beinn na h-Uamha on E407) and climb steep grass slopes to the summit of Healabhal Bheag. The summit plateau is not as vast as Healabhal Mhor's but is equally table-like, and the view over Loch Bracadale is stunning.

To complete the round, descend Healabhal Bheag's north-east ridge. This soon narrows onto the top of an impressive buttress, which in the evening casts a perfect pyramidal shadow onto the moor below. Avoid the buttress on steep broken slopes to the left and continue down the ridge past one or two rises. Go over Beinn Bhuidhe or bypass it on the right to reach the deer fence and, keeping it to your left, follow it down to a roadside gate 200m around the bend from your starting point.

ROUTE 26: BEN TIANAVAIG

ROUTE START: Penifiler (NG 489417, L23/E409 or E410)

ROUTE LOG: 4½ml/7km, 440m/1450ft, 4hrs

ROUTE OVERVIEW: circular hill and coast walk. A mixture of rough moor and springy turf characterise a combined hill/coast walk on an isolated hilltop and viewpoint that forms its own peninsula on the Sound of Raasay.

	1	2	3	4	5
Grade	▦	▦			
Terrain	▦	▦			
Navigation	▦				
Seriousness		▦			

Ben Tianavaig is the high point of the peninsula to the immediate south of Portree and is a magnificent viewpoint for Raasay and the east coast of Skye. In appearance it has much in common with the hills of Trotternish to the north, with uniform, mostly unbroken slopes on the west (giving the hill an attractive pyramidal shape) and tiers of cliffs formed by landslips on the east. The upper slopes are composed of porous gravel, with large expanses of short turf that remains remarkably dry even in wet weather. Once above the flanking moor, the pleasant terrain and summit views make the ascent far more rewarding than you would expect from such a lowly hill.

The shortest route to the summit is from Tianavaig Bay to the south, but a more interesting circuit combines an ascent with an exploration of the coastline at the hill's northern foot. The route begins at Penifiler, reached by a minor road that branches off the B883 Braes road. At the road-end (roadside parking just before) ignore the track on the left and head north-east across the moor, following a line of telegraph poles through a shallow moorland gap. The gap is very marshy, so keep to its right-hand side, cross a small stream on the far side and bear slightly right to reach the coast above lonely Camas Ban (White Bay), where easy grass slopes descend to the shoreline.

Despite its Gaelic name, Camas Ban is a broad, cliff-flanked strand of almost black sand. Ruins reflect its former importance as a source of lignite. From the bay a good path runs westwards over small shoreline crags to a larger, stonier bay. At the

Ben Tianavaig's northern sea cliffs are holed at sea-level by large caves such as Tom Cave and the Scarf Caves, but unfortunately there is no shoreline access to them (you can study them through binoculars from across Portree Bay). Beyond the skerries described in the text is a long stony beach, and beyond that a nightmarish sheep path, suitable only for those with cloven feet, continues along a perilous grass shelf to a dead-end.

end of this more crags force you up onto a broad grass shelf some 20m/65ft above the sea, where a good sheep path provides excellent coast walking close to the cliff edge. Soon another bay is reached, enclosed by skerries, where a great variety of sea birds gather to pass the time of day. It is worth descending to the bay to explore the rock pavement at the water's edge, where rock buttresses project seaward like fingers. There are even a few small caves to investigate.

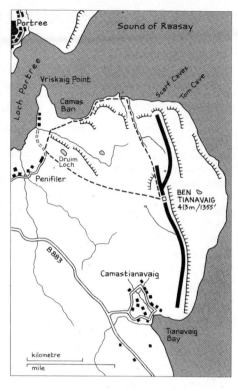

Leave the coast at this point for the ascent of Ben Tianavaig. Two streams come down to the shoreline. Climb the hillside between them, passing some ruined dwellings a short distance up. Continue directly to the summit. The going, as noted above, is excellent.

The summit is perched close to the edge of the broken cliffs of the east face and is one of the best viewpoints on the east coast of Skye, with an incomparable panorama of Raasay. In the basin below are a number of pinnacles similar to those at the Storr and Quiraing. To return to Penifiler, go straight down Ben Tianavaig's steep western slopes, negotiating one or two easy rock bands on the way. Plan your descent route at the summit, aiming left of the line of small cliffs to the left of Loch Meallachain, for once onto the flat moor, navigation is difficult.

> *If transport can be arranged, a one-way crossing of Ben Tianavaig from north to south makes an attractive proposition. From the summit, instead of descending back across the moor to Penifiler, continue southwards along the grassy cliff-top, bearing right lower down to reach parking at Tianavaig Bay just off the B883 (NG 508389).*

ROUTE 27: THE STORR

ROUTE START: Storr Forest (NG 509529, L23/E08 or E409, or Harvey's Storr)

ROUTE LOG: 3½ml/6km, 550m/1800ft, 4+hrs

ROUTE OVERVIEW: return hill walk. A visit to the weird rock pinnacles of the highest mountain in

	1	2	3	4	5
Grade	■	■			
Terrain	■	■			
Navigation	■	■	■		
Seriousness	■	■	■		

north Skye is followed by an ascent to its summit above disintegrating cliffs.

It is at The Storr that the backbone of the Trotternish peninsula begins to erupt into the contorted forms for which it is renowned. The view of The Storr across Loch Fada and Loch Leathan from the coast road north of Portree is one of the most photographed on Skye, with the summit cliffs of the mountain given scale by the Old Man at their foot. The Old Man is only one of a number of extraordinary pinnacles that ring the basin known as the Sanctuary, and the walk up to it, on an excellent re-surfaced path built since the first edition of this guidebook, is one of the most popular excursions on Skye.

The path begins at the car park at the foot of the hill and climbs through the Storr Woodlands to reach open ground beneath the Old Man. An improved path continues up the hillside to a fork. Leaving the right branch for descent, climb left to a second fork where the main path goes right, for a short scrambly climb to the base of the Old Man.

Before visiting the Old Man, take the almost level left branch at the second fork to the south end of the Sanctuary for the best view of the pinnacles, which include not only the Old Man but also the equally improbable Needle – a fragile wedge of rock with two 'eyes' left by fallen blocks. The Old Man stands half-way along the Sanctuary and can be reached from this south end, although recent rock falls mean that you do so at your own risk. Alternatively, return to the second fork and reach the Old Man on the main path. It teeters 50m/165ft above its plinth and is undercut all around. The rock is so flaky that it comes away in your fingers.

Behind the Sanctuary tower the 200m/650ft rotten summit

> *'Here is a scene for dark tragedies; here might lurk the fabulous creatures of the Celtic mythology; here might rise the altars of some horrid and ghastly faith, propitiating the gloomy powers with human sacrifice.'*
>
> J. A. MacCulloch on the Sanctuary
> (*The Misty Isle of Skye, 1905*)

cliffs of The Storr, split into five buttresses by deep dark gullies. The direct route to the summit from the Old Man follows a path behind the Needle and through the northern half of the Sanctuary, but a large rockfall in 2004 has made the area unstable and there are warning notices to this effect. The alternative is to descend the hillside below the Old Man to find paths that traverse to meet the direct path further along.

The path climbs diagonally right around the foot of the cliffs to gain the skyline, then it turns back left (south) along the cliff-top to head for The Storr's summit. Higher up, a grassy gully breaches some small crags, where a spot of

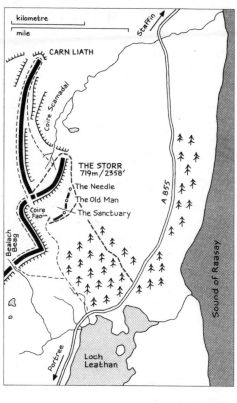

handwork may be required, to deposit you on the summit plateau not far from the trig-point.

> 'The Old Man may be climbable but we didn't make an attempt.' – Victorian climber Harold Raeburn's famous throwaway remark, expressing an understandable reluctance to rope up. Don Whillans made the first ascent in 1955 by the north-west face. Other routes have been added since, but the alarming state of the rock rightly deters most rock climbers.

A detour along the north ridge to the castellated rocky eminence of Carn Liath adds interest to the return trip. The impressive northern cliffs of Carn Liath, hidden on approach, sport the cleanest climbing rock on the Storr, and beneath them is perhaps the most chaotic terrain in all Trotternish. Regain the main path by contouring back across the hillside below the north ridge, above a line of crags in Coire Scamadal.

ROUTE 28: THE FOX AND THE RED BANK

ROUTE START: Loch Cuithir (OS 23, NG 476596, L23/E408 or Harvey's Storr)

ROUTE LOG: 4ml/6km, 520m/1700ft, 3½hrs

ROUTE OVERVIEW: circular hill scramble. A short circuit around a corrie skyline sports enough

	1	2	3	4	5
Grade	▓	▓	▓		
Terrain	▓	▓		▓	
Navigation	▓	▓			
Seriousness			▓	▓	

scrambling and routefinding problems to make it a challenging round with an exploratory air.

North of The Storr the hilly spine of the Trotternish peninsula gives an excellent end-to-end walk characterised by gentle slopes on the west and an almost continuous line of cliffs on the east. The cliffs are incredibly complex owing to landslips, and the scenery created by these geological contortions is of such interest that three distinct areas are recommended for more detailed investigation (Routes 28-30).

Heading northwards, the first points of interest reached are Sgurr a' Mhadaidh Ruaidh (Fox Peak) and Baca Ruadh (Red Bank). These hills are unusual for Trotternish in that they thrust out steep stubs of ridges to the east, enclosing Coir' an t-Seasgaich, and the short round of the corrie skyline makes an interesting and at times challenging route with plenty of opportunity for scrambling.

Access is by an unsurfaced road that runs westwards from the A855 Portree-Staffin road through the village of Lealt to Loch Cuithir at the foot of the massive eastern buttress of Sgurr a' Mhadaidh Ruaidh. The road was originally built to aid mining operations at the loch, but nature has reclaimed the land and the area is now very picturesque. The road is quite rough but can normally be driven

Loch Cuithir is floored with diatomite, a chalky earth with many industrial applications. The diatomite deposit was originally over 13m/40ft thick and over 20 acres in extent, and was mined several times, most recently from the end of the Second World War to the 1960s, when the operation became uneconomic. To permit mining, Loch Cuithir had to be drained, and the group of reedy lochans that remain today are the only remnants of what was once a large loch. The diatomite was transported by rail to Inver Tote for drying (see Route 46d). What remains now lies underwater again, and there is little of the mining operation still to be seen except some old brickwork and the line of the railway.

if you take it steady. You won't want to walk it, as this would add 6ml/10km each way to the trip.

From Loch Cuithir the route to the summit of Sgurr a' Mhadaidh Ruaidh begins by crossing grassy terrain to the foot of the ridge that forms the left-hand skyline. This ridge abuts against rotten cliffs that offer no way up. Further left, however, on the far side of a shallow corrie, is another ridge whose broken slopes provide an easy, if sometimes earthy, scramble to the summit, in situations that are perhaps not for those of a sensitive disposition. The summit itself is perched airily at the cliff edge above Loch Cuithir and offers grand views of the undulating Trotternish ridge and the vast flatlands of eastern Trotternish.

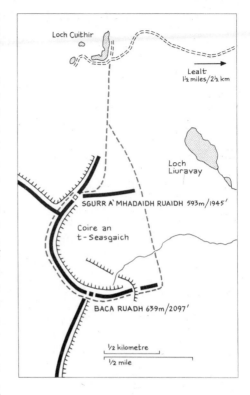

Baca Ruadh is easily reached by a pleasant stroll around the curving plateau rim above Coir' an t-Seasgaich, then things become more exciting again. Descend eastwards, straight over the edge (!) and down steep grass slopes, to reach the top of Baca Ruadh's eastern buttress. Crags bar a direct descent from here, but they are easily negotiated by a gully a short distance along on the right. Lower down, another hidden line of crags bars the way but these again are easily outflanked a short distance along on the right, by a shelf that slants down right to easier ground.

To avoid all problems on descent, keep to the steep grass slopes that descend from the summit to the right of the buttress, although these are best avoided when wet as the grass is very slippery. From their foot, contour round the foot of the buttress, cross rough ground at the mouth of Coir' an t-Seasgaich, contour round the foot of Sgurr a' Mhadaidh Ruaidh and re-cross the moor to Loch Cuithir.

ROUTE 29: THE QUIRAING

ROUTE START: Bealach Ollasgairte (NG 440679, L23/E408 or Harvey's Storr)

ROUTE LOG: 5½ml/9km, 570m/1850ft, 4+hrs

ROUTE OVERVIEW: circular hill walk with optional scrambling. An exploration of the pinnacled recesses

	1	2	3	4	5
Grade	▓		▓		
Terrain	▓				
Navigation		▓			
Seriousness	▓				

of one of the natural wonders of Scotland is followed by a cliff-top walk to view them from above.

In the north of the Trotternish peninsula, beneath the cliffs of Meall na Suiramach, stands a ghostly labyrinth of rock spires known as the Quiraing. Visitors have come here to be thrilled or terrified for a century or more. In the heyday of Victorian tourism, guides led tours through the narrow corridors between the spires. On a driech day, with the wind shrieking around the rocks, it can be an eerie place indeed, but when the sun shines there are few more exciting places to explore.

> *The view from the Table, with pinnacle crowding upon pinnacle, resembles nothing less than a Chinese print. In former times the grassy table-top hosted an annual midsummer shinty match, but today it is the preserve of sheep. Surprisingly for Skye, there is no legend to explain the Quiraing's formation, so you can make up your own.*

The route begins at the car park on the Bealach Ollasgairte, at the high point of the hill road that links Uig on the west coast to Staffin on the east coast. A fine path clings to the hillside beneath the crags of Maoladh Mor and takes an almost level route north-east into the Quiraing. Here the 36m/120ft Needle stands opposite the castellated rocky eminence known as the Prison (whose entertaining summit ridge scramblers may wish to explore). The main path continues past the Needle, but the most fantastic formations lie hidden on the hillside above it.

> *From the cliff-top north of Meall na Suiramach the short return trip further north to the summit and north top of Sron Vourlinn is recommended. The spacious cliff-top walk leads to superb seaward views from the end of the Trotternish Ridge to the isles of Harris and Lewis.*

To scramble deep into the heart of the Quiraing, leave the

main path for a rough side path that climbs steeply left of and behind the Needle, crosses the gully on its right and squeezes between two rock pillars to emerge into a fantastic pinnacled defile. The path meanders up this secret, claustrophobic sanctuary and deposits you on the curious Table, a 36m/120ft by 18m/60ft flat expanse of grass beneath the summit cliffs of Meall na Suiramach. After visiting the Table, retrace your steps to the main path or take a steep, rough shortcut to it down the gully right (north) of the Table (keep right at a fork halfway down).

The path continues northwards along the foot of the main cliff face through complex country. Ignore all right-branching paths, which lead down to Loch Hasco (see Route 30), and cross the neck of land at the foot of the south-west ridge of Leac nan Fionn. The path eventually reaches the plateau north of Meall na Suiramach at a break in the cliffs (NG 449704).

Once onto the plateau, turn south to return to the car park along the plateau rim, where grassy going makes for a fine cliff-top walk with magnificent views over the Quiraing to Staffin Bay and the offshore islands. Away from the cliff edge the plateau is mossy, yielding and best avoided (except for the easily bagged summit of Meall na Suiramach). Beyond Suiramach the cliff edge becomes less well delineated and it is best to keep high, contouring along sheep paths, until a way can be made down the steep grass slopes of Maoladh Mor to the car park.

On the south side of the Bealach Ollasgairte, amid yet more amazing landslip scenery, the lump of Cleat (Cliff) towers over two hidden lochs. View the sights by making the 217m/712ft ascent to the cliff-top summit of Bioda Buidhe above Cleat.

Route 30: Fingal's Pinnacles

ROUTE START: near Flodigarry (NG 464710, L23/E408 or Harvey's Storr)

ROUTE LOG: 3ml/5km, 270m/900ft 3+hrs

ROUTE OVERVIEW: circular hill walk with optional scrambling. An easy walk across pinnacled hillsides optionally includes plenty of enjoyable scrambling opportunities.

	1	2	3	4	5
Grade	▓				
Terrain	▓				
Navigation		▓	▓		
Seriousness	▓				

To the north and east of the Quiraing (Route 29), around the flanks of Leac nan Fionn (Fingal's Tombstone), landslips have created an astonishingly contorted terrain, full of knolls, crags, pinnacles and hidden lochans. To explore the area, begin on a gated cart track that leaves the A855 coast road just south of Flodigarry (signposted to the Quiraing; parking area just beyond).

After barely 100m you'll reach Loch Langaig, which lies in a hollow hidden from the roadside and commands an impressive view of the precipices of Leac nan Fionn's east face. The track circles the loch on the right and continues as a path to Loch Hasco, another fine loch that nestles at the foot of the steep hillside beneath the cliffs. Note the rock tooth that projects from the hillside up on the right.

Left (south) of Loch Hasco a defile climbs to another hidden loch (Loch Fada), but the route to the summit of Leac nan Fionn continues straight on, following a fence below the crags of the south-west ridge to the neck of land where the ridge abuts against the cliffs of Meall na Suiramach. Note the rock needle high up on the crest of the ridge.

Double back to climb the ridge to the summit of Leac nan Fionn. A number of obstacles give enjoyable scrambling if you are so inclined, otherwise simply bypass them on gentle grass slopes to the left. The first obstacle is a rock tower that provides a short sharp scramble to the clump of grass that crowns its summit. Above here grass rakes rise between crags, right of which is the rock needle that was seen from below. The needle gives an easy scramble but good luck to anyone who dares to place more

The landslips explored on this route are among the largest in Britain, extending 1½ml/2km to the coast, where material is constantly being carried away by the sea. They were caused by the collapse of great cliffs on the eastern edge of the lava cap that covered Trotternish 60 million years ago.

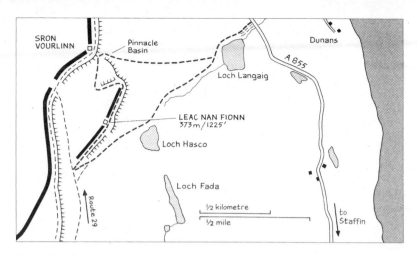

than a hand on its airy top.

Beyond here, at the cliff edge above the east face, lies Leac nan Fionn's level grassy summit. The east-face cliffs are split into four buttresses of approximately equal height. The rightmost (south) buttress is separated from the rest by a shallow notch, but can be reached by a moderate exposed scramble.

A descent northwards enables a circular route to be made via one of

After the Storr the second highest summit in Trotternish is Hartaval (NG 480551, 668m/2192ft) to its immediate north-west. With a rounded summit guarded by miles of boggy moorland, it attracts few visitors. The easiest way to bag it, should you wish to do so, is to reach it from the Storr, despite a steep descent and re-ascent across a low 489m/1605ft bealach.

the unsung wonders of Trotternish – Pinnacle Basin. First make for the saddle that separates Leac nan Fionn from Sron Vourlinn. The direct descent is barred by cliffs but these are easily outflanked on the left (west). Once onto the saddle, aim for a small lochan and a wall just beyond, then descend over the lip of the saddle into the secret hollow of Pinnacle Basin. Here pinnacles rise from the hillside like prehistoric standing stones, each with an individual character that gains from its group setting. The most impressive pinnacle is undercut all around and is reminiscent of the Old Man of Storr. There is plenty of climbing and scrambling to be done hereabouts.

On leaving the basin, aim diagonally right down the steep hillside to rejoin the approach path above Loch Langaig. On the way you should pass the rock tooth seen during the approach walk, and this provides an easy scramble to round off an entertaining route.

ROUTE 31: THE TROTTERNISH HIGH-LEVEL ROUTE

ROUTE START: Portree (NG 481436, L23/E408 & E410, or Harvey's Storr); end point Duntulm (NG 411741). Other start/end points are possible.

ROUTE LOG: 26ml/42km, 2410m/7900ft, one day or more, with shorter options.

	1	2	3	4	5
Grade	▓	▓			
Terrain	▓	▓			
Navigation			▓		
Seriousness		▓			

ROUTE OVERVIEW: one-way long hill walk (or backpack). This is the finest long walk/backpacking route in the Hebrides – a grand skyline promenade along the undulating spine of Skye's longest peninsula.

From Portree to the north coast of Skye the backbone of the Trotternish peninsula forms a high escarpment (the Trotternish Ridge), with gentle slopes rolling down to Loch Snizort on the west and a more savage line of cliffs fronting the Sound of Raasay on the east. The walk along the crest of the escarpment, known as the Trotternish High-Level Route, is one of the finest end-to-end expeditions in Scotland. The ridge reaches the 600m/2000ft contour at five points and crosses several other tops over 500m/1650ft high. Short turf makes for excellent going as the ridge undulates from top to top, with magnificent coastal views all around and the 'tangle o' the isles' to lighten your step.

The full route leaves the A855 roadside at the bridge over the River Chracaig c.1½ml/2km north of Portree. It begins unenterprisingly with a boggy moorland stomp over the minor tops of Pein a' Chleibh and A' Chorra-bheinn to Ben Dearg, where the ridge begins to delineate itself and the line of eastern cliffs that will be with you for the remainder of the trip first appears. The band of summit crags that bars the direct descent from Ben Dearg is outflanked by a long dog-leg to the

> To make the trip more manageable, use transport to cover the initial 1½ml/2½km road walk from Portree at the south end. Save another 4ml/6km of low-level bogtrot by beginning further up the road at a parking area opposite Loch Leathan beside a small waterfall (NG 495510). From here, cross the moor to find a grassy rake that climbs diagonally left to the Bealach Mor, south of The Storr.
>
> Similarly, if transport can be arranged, you can save a few miles at the north end by descending north or north-east to the coast road rather than north-west across the moor to Duntulm. The route can also be split into two shorter walks at the Bealach Ollasgairte on the Uig-Staffin road.

west. Two passes (Bealach Mor and Bealach Beag) follow as the ridge undulates northwards and climbs steeply to the summit of the Storr (Route 27).

On the far side of The Storr a steep descent and re-ascent across the Bealach a' Chuirn gains the summit of Hartaval, the second highest peak in Trotternish, and then comes a more gentle section culminating in Baca Ruadh and Sgurr a' Mhadaidh Ruaidh (Route 28). Continuing northwards, the ridge undulates over a succession of tops to Beinn Edra, the most northerly 600m/2000ft hill on Skye, before losing height at the Bealach Uige above lonely Loch Corcasgil at the foot of the cliffs.

A steep climb over the summit of Bioda Buidhe then deposits you at the Bealach Ollasgairte on the Uig-Staffin road. The descent to the bealach passes the craggy lump of Cleat, which is separated from the main ridge by landslips and towers over Loch Cleat.

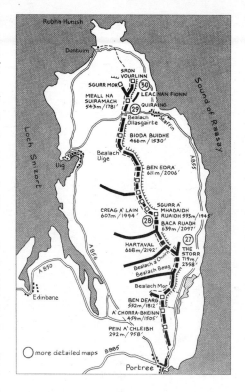

North of the Bealach Ollasgairte the ridge reaches Meall nam Suiramach above the Quiraing (Route 29) and forks. On the left branch lies Sgurr Mor, whose yielding moss makes tough going and whose convex slopes curtail views. The better route is the right branch, where a spacious walk leads out along the narrow summit ridge of Sron Vourlinn above Leac nan Fionn (Route 30). Continue past the summit to the north top, beyond which lie only flat moors and the sea, and descend across the moor to the A855 coast road. Duntulm, a few miles away on the north coast, makes a fitting end point to the route.

> 'Then onwards, ever northwards, down into the valleys and up again to the hill-tops . . . It was a walk along the top of the world, with glorious vistas of seas, islands and mountains.'
>
> Ben Humble (*Tramping in Skye*, 1933)

COAST WALKS: INTRODUCTION

Many Skye coast walks are remote and serious undertakings. The rewards include wild and spectacular coastal scenery on an unprecedented scale, but there are dangers of which the uninitiated may be unaware.

Much of the Skye coastline is distant from the nearest road. Cliffs often overhang, undercut by the sea. Their vertiginous edges are often crumbling and honeycombed by rabbits. Sudden gusts of wind can turn cliff-tops into dangerous places. There is rarely any shelter from the elements.

Cliff-top terrain is often undulating, requiring constant ascent and descent, sometimes on steep, exposed hillsides of grass that become slippery when wet. Such is the height of Skye cliff-tops that total ascent for a route can easily equal that for a hill walk. A different mental attitude from hillwalking is required, as the end point of the walk is hardly ever in view.

Cliff-top rivers may cut deep gorges as they fall to the sea, requiring appreciable inland detours to outflank. In spate rivers may be dangerous or impassable. In many places sheep paths at the cliff edge make for excellent going but may also induce a false sense of security, for sheep have small feet and no sense of vertigo (in fact no sense at all). Use their trails with care.

Shoreline coast walks have a different set of dangers from cliff-top coast walks. Shoreline rocks may be greasy and require care if a twisted ankle or worse is to be avoided. Shoreline crags may be awkward to negotiate. Stonefall, sometimes induced by seabirds, is always a danger at the foot of cliffs. Note also that some nesting birds can be aggressive and have been known to swoop down from a sea-cliff to attack someone walking along the shoreline below. And the greatest danger of all: becoming trapped at the cliff-foot by an incoming tide.

In short, as much preparation and care is required for coast walking as for mountain walking. The more difficult coast walks in Routes 32-42 following should be attempted only in dry weather in good footwear by well-equipped walkers. Heed the warnings in the text. Stay away from dangerous cliff edges. This advice also applies to some of the short walks in Routes 43-47.

Sections of walks that are underwater at high tide and can be undertaken at low tide only are unmistakably marked in the text: AT LOW TIDE ONLY. A tide timetable is an indispensible item of equipment. Tide tables for the west coast of Scotland are published by Clunie Group Ltd (CGL) in Oban. Their booklet can be obtained from Island Cycles on The Green in Portree (tel: 01478-613121) or from CGL (www.cg-ltd.co.uk, tel: 01631-565485). Alternatively consult www.tidetimes.org.uk or enquire at Tourist Information Offices (see Visitor Information on p.13).

ROUTE 32: SUISNISH AND BORERAIG

ROUTE START: Loch Cill Chriosd
(NG 615205, L32/E411 or E412)

ROUTE LOG: 10ml/16km,
420m/1400ft, 6+hrs

ROUTE OVERVIEW: circular moor
and coast walk. Ancient moorland
paths link to form an exploratory
circuit that visits limestone scenery, sea
cliffs, stacks and caves, old marble quarries, deserted villages, duns, Druidical sites
and many other features of interest.

	1	2	3	4	5
Grade	▓				
Terrain	▓				
Navigation			▓		
Seriousness		▓			

No part of Skye is more fun to explore than the stub of land that juts seawards
between Loch Slapin and Loch Eishort in the south of the island. Two ancient
moorland paths and a fine coastal path link the cleared villages of Suisnish and
Boreraig and enable a circular walk that is as fascinating as any on Skye.

The outward path is now much reclaimed by the land and is shown on
E411 and E412 only. Signposted Suisnish, it begins at a passing place on a
corner of Loch Cill Chriosd, on
the A881 Broadford-Elgol road
in Strath Suardal (park without
causing obstruction). It runs beside
a fence, crosses the shoulder of
a grassy knoll and doubles back
to the ruined village of Kilchrist,
where only the walls of the old
Manse remain standing. The village
site is unmistakably limestone – a
beautiful oasis of green turf and
rock outcrops in the midst of the
dull granite moor.

In front of the ruined Manse
the path bears right and becomes
very boggy. Aim south-west across
the moor, slightly downhill, to
reach more ruins at another green
limestone oasis. At the near edge
of these ruins pick up an indistinct
path that climbs left (south) onto

*From Suisnish and Boreraig hundreds
of people were evicted during the
Clearances, their dwellings razed to
the ground to prevent their return.
In October 1853, with snow on the
ground, elderly crofters died after being
evicted. The Suisnish clearances were
given special poignancy by the evocative
eye-witness account of Sir Archibald
Geikie, the geologist. Returning from
a ramble, Geikie heard the cries of the
evicted crofters: 'the long plaintive wail
like a funeral coronach . . .'*

*It is impossible to walk through the
ruins of Suisnish today without the same
sense of loss that so moved Geikie: 'Not
a soul is to be seen there now, but the
green patches of field and the crumbling
walls mark where an active and happy
community once lived.'*

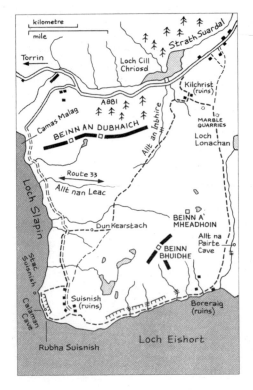

the moor, initially heading slightly away from the Allt an Inbhire, then doubling back to cross the stream. If you cannot find the path, follow the riverbank.

The path re-crosses the stream (back to the true right bank) and crosses a watershed to reach the head of the valley of the Allt nan Leac. The Allt nan Leac is crossed ten metres above the point where it sinks underground to form the Uamh Cinn Ghlinn, the longest limestone cave on Skye (see Route 33).

Continuing south-west, the path rises across the far side of the valley onto open moor once again, becoming increasingly difficult to follow. It then heads directly southwards, staying well above Glen Boreraig, but at this point it is more interesting to leave it and head down the glen to the prominent grassy knoll formerly crowned by Dun Kearstach.

From Dun Kearstach continue down to the Land Rover track that runs along the coastline from Camas Malag to Suisnish. Near the track is a ruined hut circle that further testifies to the area's ancient importance – the land bordering the coastline was at one time the Druidical centre of Skye. Turn left along the track to reach Suisnish. N.B. This track provides an easier approach, 2½ml/4km each way, for a shorter excursion to Suisnish (see Route 33).

Beyond a gate the track continues down into the deserted village. After investigating the forlorn ruins, scramblers may wish to consider more exciting fare by exploring the stretch of coastline below. Cut down the fields to dumpy Stac Suisnish, whose two 5m/16ft-high tops provide good sport for boulderers.

Continue along an occasionally greasy rock pavement at the foot of overhanging 30m/100ft sea cliffs around the point of Rubha Suisnish and past the impressive Calaman Cave among others. This is a thrilling shoreline trip that can be undertaken AT LOW TIDE ONLY, with no escape for the next ½ml/1km, until the point has been rounded.

There are various ways out of Suisnish, depending on where your explorations end, to pick up the continuing coastal path to Boreraig. Avoiding the shoreline diversion, the most common way now begins at a gate on the track (NG 591160). From here go left

On the hillside above Kilchrist marble was mined from the early eighteenth century until 1912 and transported by narrow-gauge railway to Broadford. The marble was used for the main altar in Iona Abbey, as well as at Armadale Castle and, if tradition is to be believed, in the building of the Vatican and the Palace of Versailles. The stone is still quarried in nearby Torrin.

around fencing to reach the excellent Boreraig path. Evolved by generation upon generation of travellers communing between the rich pastures of Suisnish and Boreraig, it holds initially to high ground before wending its way down to the shores of a beautifully curving bay beneath the cliffs of Beinn Bhuidhe. The dramatic Cuillin skyline is now left behind for the less severe horizons of Sleat, with the whitewashed cottages of Ord prominent across the upper reaches of Loch Eishort.

One or two waterfalls are passed before reaching verdant Boreraig, where streams meander across green meadows to a lovely bay. As at Suisnish, so at Boreraig; one cannot help but be moved by the sheer number of ruined buildings here. Using E411 or E412 as a guide, seek out the dun and the solitary standing stone (NG 619163). There was also once a Druid temple here.

Take care on this route not to be overtaken by darkness, for Strath Suardal is haunted by the malevolent goblin Ludag who, according to tradition, hops about on his one leg dealing 'heavy blows on the cheeks of benighted travellers'!

The path back to Kilchrist is overall in a much better state and easier to follow than the outward path. To find its start, begin at the standing stone and head up to the right of some ruins. The path climbs steadily above the gorge of the Allt na Pairte, passing a large tree-filled hollow that is the entrance to Allt

na Pairte Cave (a 190m/630ft-long cave that is a no-go area for non-cavers). Above here the path passes through a new native woodland project, re-crosses the watershed and reaches limestone country once more on the descent towards Strath Suardal.

The hillside at this point is dotted with spoil heaps from old marble quarries. At a waymarked fork (NG 621196) branch left to more mine workings, then cross a short stretch of moor to rejoin the outward route in Kilchrist.

ROUTE 33: LIMESTONE CAVES OF STRATH

ROUTE START: Camas Malag (NG 583193, L32/E411 or E412)

ROUTE LOG: 4ml/6km, little ascent, 3+hrs

ROUTE OVERVIEW: return coast and glen walk. An unusual and entertaining excursion visits the little-known limestone centre of Skye.

	1	2	3	4	5
Grade					
Terrain					
Navigation					
Seriousness					

The limestone areas of Strath are a delight to explore on the surface. The porous rock is carved into all sorts of fantastic shapes, the going is always dry, often on lush green grass, hollows (known as shakeholes) dot the moor and streams disappear underground (at sinks) and reappear (at resurgences). Much fun can be had searching for cave entrances, even if you don't enter the caves themselves.

WARNING: The caves of Strath are rough, strenuous, constricted and convoluted, and many carry icy streams where air space may be restricted. They should not be entered by anyone without caving experience. However, in the vicinity of the glen of the Allt nan Leac, there are four 'through' caves whose underground meanderings can be followed safely on the surface from one entrance to the other.

The route to the Allt nan Leac begins at the bay of Camas Malag, reached by a minor road that leaves the A881 just east of Torrin. Beyond the bay the road continues as a rough Land Rover track to Suisnish. Around the first corner is the Allt na Garbhlain, which sinks into a large hole on the right to form the upper entrance of Camas Malag Cave, the first of the 'through' caves. Lower down the hillside the stream reappears at other entrances, before exiting from the system at a fissure in a shoreline cliff, which can be reached by a short scramble.

Continuing along the track to Suisnish, the next stream reached is the Allt nan Leac itself. Aim for the small waterfall that can be seen less than 100m

> *CAVE LENGTHS:*
>
> *1. Camas Malag Cave c.250m/830ft*
> *2. Uamh Sgeinne c.105m/305ft*
> *3. Beinn an Dubhaich Cave*
>   *c.175m/570ft*
> *4. Uamh Cinn Ghlinn c.365m/1200ft*

upstream. To its left a small stream emerges from the hillside, disappears underground and reappears again. The upper resurgence (a low arch of rock) is the lower entrance to Uamh Sgeinne (Cave of the Knives). The upper entrance burrow lies less than 100m further upstream but

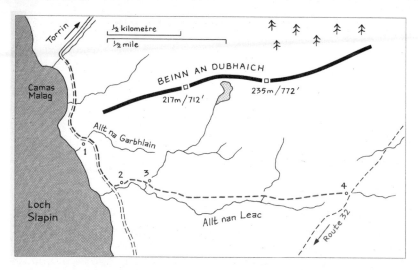

is hard to find. It is hidden among limestone outcrops, about 10m up the hillside from a point where trees stand on each side of the Allt nan Leac, just below a small waterfall and pool.

Above Uamh Sgeinne the glen levels off. Fifty metres beyond the point where a fence crosses to the near bank (left-hand side), there is a resurgence a few metres to the left. This is the rising for Beinn an Dubhaich Cave, whose main entrance, a 3m/10ft deep tree-covered hole, can be found about 30m diagonally uphill further right.

The Allt nan Leac caves lie on the south side of Beinn an Dubhaich. On the north side Uamh an Ard Achadh (High Pasture Cave, NG 594197), with a length of c.320m/1050ft, is the second longest cave on Skye. However, its insignificant entrance hole is hardly worth seeking out for the non-caver, and the surrounding area is the subject of archaeological excavation (see www.high-pasture-cave.org).

There are also some minor limestone caves in the banks of the Allt Lochain Cruinn near Broadford.

Further right still is the upper entrance, where the stream sinks underground.

Beyond the level section of glen containing Beinn an Dubhaich Cave, a slight rise leads to another long flat section, and then the glen narrows and climbs to yet another short flat section where an old wall is crossed. One hundred metres beyond the wall, a tree marks the spot where the young Allt nan Leac emerges from a hole at the foot of a line of crags. This is the lower entrance of Uamh Cinn Ghlinn, the longest and finest cave on Skye. The two upper entrances can be found by following the dry valley up onto the moor.

ROUTE 34: RUBH' AN DUNAIN

ROUTE START: Glen Brittle campsite (NG 414205, L32/E411)

ROUTE LOG: 7½ml/12km, little ascent, 4½hrs

ROUTE OVERVIEW: return or circular coast walk. A scenic stroll along the shores of Loch Brittle, in the shadow of the Cuillin, ends at a

	1	2	3	4	5
Grade					
Terrain					
Navigation					
Seriousness					

headland and viewpoint where there are many features of historical interest.

Rubh' an Dunain (Headland of the Dun) is the headland on the south side of Loch Brittle. From Glen Brittle campsite its low-lying moors do not appear as inviting as the majestic Cuillin which tower above them, yet the path to the point provides a pleasant and popular coastal walk with fine views of Rum, Canna and the southern Cuillin corries, and with many sites of historical interest to explore.

From Glen Brittle campsite, climb briefly up the path behind the toilet block to reach a track that runs along the coast on the south side of Loch Brittle. It crosses the Allt Coire Lagan, which in spate can be crossed dryshod by a bridge downstream, and ends at the second stream beyond. A path continues to a fork at the stream just before Creag Mhor, whose 15m/50ft basalt crags provide sport for rock climbers when the Cuillin are in cloud.

Keep right here to reach the northern end of the wide depression known as the Slochd Dubh (Black Pit), a fault line that cuts right across the headland. Easy ground then continues around the north and west slopes of Carn Mor (Big Cairn) to reach the north side of Loch na h-Airde. From here at least one more hour should be allowed to explore the headland itself.

In front of the wall beside the loch is a well-preserved chambered cairn, with a 3m long, 1m high passageway leading into the central chamber, now roofless. When the chamber was excavated in 1931 and 1932 the remains of six adults and pieces of pottery were unearthed, dating its use to the Beaker and Neolithic periods. From here walk out to the point of the headland, where a cairn caps small sea-cliffs and there

> *Adventurous walkers can extend the walk along the shores of the Soay Sound to An Leac (The Flagstone), the old ferry point for crossings between Skye and Soay. Note, however, that the moorland crossing from there back to Glen Brittle is much rougher than the stroll out to Rubh' an Dunain.*

are fine views of Rum (only 8ml/13km away across the Cuillin Sound) and northwards along the Minginish coast to Stac a' Mheadais north of Loch Eynort (Route 35).

From the point continue around the coastline to the southern shore of Loch na h-Airde. At the mouth of the loch will be seen a channel that was built long ago to link the loch with the sea and enable it to be used as an anchorage. The waters of the loch are only just above sea-level, and tradition has it that MacLeod galleys used to shelter here. The dun for which the headland is named crowns a knoll on the far side of the channel, its landward wall still 4m/13ft high, its seaward side guarded by cliffs.

East of Loch na h-Airde a shallow cave can be seen on the hillside. More of an overhang than a cave, it nevertheless revealed Beaker pottery and an Iron Age forge during the 1932 excavation. By following the stream left of the cave up towards a smaller lochan, the ruins of Rhundunan House (the old MacAskill home) can be seen. To return to Glen Brittle campsite, re-cross the headland via the Slochd Dubh and rejoin the coastal path. To vary the return route from the Allt Coire Lagan if the ground is dry, drop down below the bridge to a lower path that passes some interesting rocky inlets on its way back to the campsite.

Until the Clearances of the nineteenth century, Rubh' an Dunain was held by the MacAskills. In 1811 Kenneth MacAskill and a large party of tenants were forced to emigrate to North and South Carolina. In 1883 there were still twenty or more families living in the area, but today nothing remains of their occupation but ruins.

ROUTE 35: BRITTLE TO EYNORT

ROUTE START: foot of Glen Brittle (NG 409210, L32/E411).

ROUTE LOG: 7½ml/12km miles, 490m/1600ft, 6hrs.

ROUTE OVERVIEW: circular cliff-top coast and moor walk. A rough and serious cliff-top coast walk undulates along a crumbling cliff top past a remarkable sea stack. The route involves no scrambling but is graded 4 to reflect its challenging nature.

	1	2	3	4	5
Grade	■	■	■	■	
Terrain	■	■	■	■	■
Navigation	■	■	■		
Seriousness	■	■	■	■	

North of Loch Brittle are to be found the first great sea cliffs of the west coast of Skye and one of the island's most fantastic sea stacks – Stac an Tuill (Stack of the Hole). The cliff-top walk, however, is a serious one, as the convex, crumbling cliff edge is one of the most dangerous on the coast and the return across the Minginish moors is rough.

The route begins near the foot of Glen Brittle, at the sharp bend where the road turns left to run alongside the River Brittle (parking spaces). Go through a gate, cross the bridge over the river and turn immediately left on a path down to the river. Follow the riverbank, then the shore of Loch Brittle, below fields and fences until you can pick up a path that runs along a grass shelf above the shore. Keep to this shelf until it crosses a stream that cascades from the moor above and begins to peter out on increasingly steep slopes, then make a steep rising traverse onto the moor, aiming for the top of an open gully seen ahead.

Once onto the cliff top continue out towards the headland at the mouth of Loch Brittle, passing two fine lochans. The coastline now turns north-west and the cliff top becomes undulating and complex. To save time and energy it is probably best to keep well back from the edge, aiming for the rocky high point of Dunan Thearna Sgurr that can be seen some distance ahead.

Beyond Dunan Thearna Sgurr the cliffs become more awesome and the direct route onward is immediately barred by the deep gorge of the Allt Mor and its waterfall. To negotiate the gorge,

> 'Like a lady dressed in a monstrous sized hoop and petticoat, such as are worn at the court of St James's, having a very large hole quite through the middle of the hoop.'
>
> Redoubtable traveller Sarah Murray's view of Stac an Tuill when she sailed past it on her way from Rum to Loch Eynort in 1802.

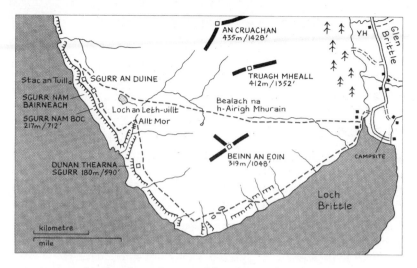

contour into the glen above the waterfall and cross the stream there (normally possible dryshod). From the far side the waterfall is worth a closer look. It has an impressive free fall of some 15m/50ft and is flanked by great fissures in the rock.

Beyond the gorge the cliff-top terrain is excellent – turfed with short grass and honeycombed by rabbit burrows. The very edge of the cliff, however, is extremely dangerous. Its convex nature makes views over the edge impossible, and in places crumbling earth perilously overhangs the abyss.

The cliff top reaches its highest point at Sgurr nam Boc, but do not attempt to view the plunging 217m/712ft cliff face until you get to Sgurr nan Bairneach, the next headland beyond. From here also the intricate, perfectly sculpted Stac an Tuill can be seen for the first time beneath the next headland. The complete sculpture resembles a gothic cathedral, complete with spire and vaulted window (the 'hole'). For a closer view continue to the headland above it (but do not attempt to view it from here) and descend to the next headland beyond.

Beyond here the cliffs diminish in size towards Loch Eynort and are something of an anti-climax, so now is a good time to consider returning to Glen Brittle. The shortest return route heads almost due east across the moor following the course of streams and is the obvious route on the map. Go past the marshy shores of Loch an Leth-uillt and follow the Allt Mor up to the long, flat pass of the Bealach na h-Airigh Mhurain, right (south) of the unimposing moorland top of Truagh Mheall. The bealach is barely a couple of miles from the coast and only 40m/130ft higher than Sgurr nam Boc, but the tramp to it across the rough moor requires one final determined push before it is underfoot and the Cuillin burst into view once more to beckon you homewards.

ROUTE 36: EYNORT TO TALISKER

ROUTE START: foot of Glen Eynort (NG 379264, L32/E411)

ROUTE LOG: 13½ml/21km, 440m/1450ft, 10hrs

ROUTE OVERVIEW: circular cliff-top coast and moor walk. A long and thrilling route negotiates complex cliff-top terrain that is exposed, serious,

	1	2	3	4	5
Grade	■	■	■	■	■
Terrain	■	■			
Navigation	■	■	■	■	■
Seriousness	■	■	■	■	

lonely and full of stirring situations above awesome cliffs. The route involves no scrambling but is graded 5 to reflect its challenging nature.

Peaceful Glen Eynort is the ironic starting point for the most spectacular of the Minginish coast walks, northwards along the cliff top to Talisker Bay. The route is a major undertaking, passing through some of the loneliest country on Skye and involving the crossing of steep grass slopes on the edge of awesome cliffs. It should be done only in good footwear, in good weather and when the ground is dry, and will not be appreciated by anyone who suffers from vertigo. For those prepared to meet its challenges, however, it provides a sensational cliff-top walk that will linger long in the memory.

The route begins at the end of the surfaced road at the foot of Glen Eynort. Go through a gate and continue along an unsurfaced road past a cottage to a farmyard. On the far side of the farmyard cross a field to pick up the track again beside a ruined church and follow it to the ruined buildings on the small peninsula of Faolainn (Sea-gull). Beyond here follow a good sheep path along a grass shelf above small waterside crags and then take to the beach beyond.

At the point beyond Faolainn (NG 374247) you are faced with a choice. The hillside above the shore, ominously named Biod na Fionaich (Shaggy Cliff), steepens and you must decide whether to take the high route across its top or the low route along its foot (and climb to higher ground around the point). The high route is easier, although it still involves avoiding small crags on the ascent of very steep grass slopes.

The low route is even more exciting but requires care and

Preshal Beg (345m/1132ft) is one of the most outstanding of the many hidden surprises on this route. Despite its lowly height, it crowns the moor like an impregnable rock fortress, a dun fit for a giant. Its south-west face, remote and rarely seen, is ringed by fluted basalt pipes in comparison with which the similar formations at the Giant's Causeway in Antrim seem but an inferior imitation.

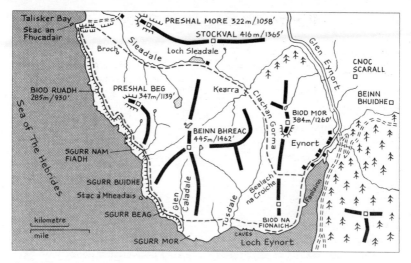

should be undertaken only if the shoreline rocks are dry and you are not of a nervous disposition. The going continues to be good on boulders and rock pavement, but easy progress is given counterpoint by the curiously thrilling sensation of clinging to the edge of the land, leaving behind the sheltered safety of the deeply indented loch for the wide horizons of the open sea. When Sarah Murray sailed into Loch Eynort from Rum during her tour of the islands in 1802 she described the mood of the place exactly: 'as silent and forlorn as an uninhabited island'.

As far as the point beyond Biod na Fionaich (NG 368244) it is necessary to leave the shoreline only once to bypass a small crag, but then cliffs begin to bar the way and it is finally necessary to take to higher ground by climbing the steep grass slope above. The first few metres are very steep indeed and, unless you are sure of your adhesion, retrace your steps along the shoreline until less steep slopes present themselves.

Keeping well away from the crumbling cliff edge, you are forced upwards on short turf to a height of 90m/300ft at the headland above the sea caves marked on the map. From here descend into the hanging valley of Tusdale, a grassy bowl backed by a fine waterfall and drained by a series of smaller waterfalls, then keep high above steep grass slopes at the mouth of Loch Eynort to regain the cliff top at Glen Caladale.

Between the Caladale River and the next headland of Sgurr Beag (Little Peak), a fine wide bay backed by a line of 90m/300ft vertical cliffs gives a taste of the excitements still to come, for the route now develops into a wonderful cliff-top stravaig to Talisker Bay. Short grass and good sheep tracks make excellent going, and numerous headlands provide excellent safe viewpoints, so avoid the temptation to go too near the crumbling cliff edge.

As you progress, the coastal architecture becomes increasingly impressive. Looking back towards Glen Caladale from Sgurr Beag a huge cave (marked only on E411) can be seen holing the cliff face. Beyond Sgurr Beag the great grass-topped stump of Stac a' Mheadais is passed en route to the airy viewpoint of Sgurr Buidhe (Yellow Peak). From here the next 2ml/3km of coastline, a line of unbreached cliffs soaring up to 280m/920ft at Biod Ruadh (Red Cliff), can be studied in detail. An iron fencepost provides security for the nervous.

It takes longer to reach Biod Ruadh than anticipated, as the route undulates across the slopes of Beinn Bhreac (Speckled Mountain), over the huge cliff face of Sgurr nam Fiadh (Deer Peak) and around craggy Preshal Beg. The cliff-edge summit of Biod Ruadh, the highest point on the walk, is simply an airy tuft of grass teetering on the edge of the abyss.

Beyond here the cliffs diminish in height towards Talisker Point, and if you do not wish to continue it is possible to take a short cut inland into Sleadale for the return journey to Eynort. The continuation to Talisker, however, holds much interest.

Descend along the cliff edge, detouring around one or two rock bands, to reach the headland above Stac an Fhucadair at Talisker Point (see Route 37). From this eagle's viewpoint the stack looks very impressive and the wide strand of the bay extremely attractive. The cliffs prohibit a direct descent, however, and it is necessary to turn right and head east to outflank them.

Access to the bay is possible further along, down the steep grass slopes of Leathad Beithe but, unless transport awaits at Talisker, make a rising traverse into Sleadale beneath the prow of Preshal More. From Sleadale the return route to Eynort takes a long but surprisingly level route through the hills, with the Cuillin occasionally soaring into view ahead.

Follow the Sleadale Burn up to remote Loch Sleadale, hidden deep on the moor, then descend across the broad basin of Cearra and continue through the curious grassy corridor of the oddly named Clachan Gorma (Blue Stones). When the river begins to descend into Tusdale, contour left onto the Bealach na Croiche (Pass of the Cross) and descend to the ruined church at Eynort to complete an unforgettable round.

Towering over Talisker is the impressive prow of Preshal More (320m/1050ft), whose columnar basalt supports mirror those of Preshal Beg. While staying at Talisker House in 1773 James Boswell climbed the hill after dinner. His admirable scrambling route, to the right of the left-hand skyline, is today known as Boswell's Buttress.

ROUTE 37: TALISKER TO FISKAVAIG

ROUTE START: Talisker Bay (OS 32, NG 326306, L32/E410)

ROUTE LOG: 7½ml/12km, 290m/950ft, 5hrs

ROUTE OVERVIEW: circular cliff-top coast walk. A rough coast walk crosses craggy moorland above superb sea-carved cliffs and waterfalls. The

	1	2	3	4	5
Grade					
Terrain					
Navigation					
Seriousness					

route involves no scrambling but is graded 3 to reflect its challenging nature.

North of Talisker the cliffs of the Minginish coastline continue to Fiskavaig before they give way to the less severe scenery of Loch Bracadale. The walk from Talisker to Fiskavaig is shorter and less vertigo-inducing than its two neighbouring coast walks to the south (Routes 35 and 36), but the coastal scenery is equally spectacular. Moreover, a cross-country cart track makes the return journey easy.

From the end of the public road at Talisker, take the track on the right past a cottage and farmyard, then follow a signposted path around another house to regain the track and climb to its first hairpin bend. Leave the track here to climb diagonally across the hillside on good sheep paths to reach the plateau above. Follow the edge of the plateau until above the beach, where the cliffs begin. There is a stunning view from here around the next cliff-girt bay to the 120m/400ft headland of Rubha Cruinn (Round Headland), with a fine waterfall dropping from the plateau into the centre of the bay.

At Rubha Cruinn the coastline turns northwards, away from Talisker Bay. There is no continuous shoreline route past McFarlane's Rock, seen below, so stay high over Sgurr Mor (Big Peak). Beyond Rubha Dubh a' Ghrianain (The Black Headland of the Sunny Place) a huge cauldron

Of all the bays on the Minginish coast, Talisker is the most exquisite and worthy of investigation. It lies at the foot of Gleann Oraid in a flat-bottomed U-shaped trench dominated by the prow of Preshal More. Its beautiful sandy beach is hemmed in by cliffs and given counterpoint by Stac an Fhucadair (The Fuller's Stack) at Talisker Point on the south side of the bay. The stack has a fine rock pavement beneath it.

To reach the bay from the road-end take the left-most track, signposted 'To the beach', through the grounds of Talisker House. To make a round trip, return along a path on the south bank of the Sleadale Burn. Note that the stack can be reached AT LOW TIDE ONLY.

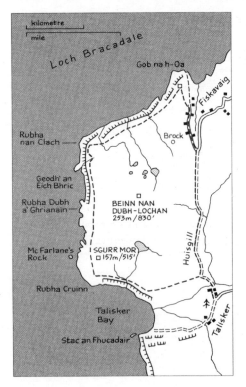

carved by the sea can be seen on the shore. At the headland just beyond Geodh' an Eich Bhric (Cove of the Speckled Horse) a short diversion away from the cliff edge is required to outflank lines of small crags and a curiously deep-cut gorge carved out of the plateau by a small stream.

At Rubha nan Clach (Stony Headland) the coastline turns eastwards, leaving the open sea for the inner recesses of Loch Bracadale. The cliff top now becomes more complex and route-finding more interesting. Small crags dot the moor and there is another substantial gorge to negotiate. The easiest going is to be found far back from the cliff edge, which is cut deeply by a number of streams.

As Gob na h-Oa (Beak of the Cave) is approached a broch can be seen in a superb position crowning an eminence on the right. It is possible to take a short cut back to Talisker via the broch, but it is worth continuing to the headland above the Gob for the fine view back along the coast to Rubha nan Clach, which includes numerous waterfalls dropping from the plateau.

The route back to Talisker lies directly southwards. Various grassy paths lead to a short farm track that reaches a gate on the Fiskavaig road, just before its end at the last house (NG 321339). Walk up the road to a hairpin bend, then keep straight on along an excellent cart track that descends Huisgill to your starting point, surprisingly less than 2ml/3km distant.

> *The remoteness of this stretch of coastline was highlighted by the discovery of the Uamh an Eich Bhric (Cave of the Speckled Horse) as recently as 2006. An awkward-to-reach rock shelter above the shoreline 400m south of Geodh' an Eich Bhric, it has yielded a number of archaeological finds, including part of a human skull and bone fragments of animals such as pig and wolf.*

ROUTE 38: MacLeod's Maidens

ROUTE START: Orbost House (NG 257431, L23/E407)

ROUTE LOG: 10ml/16km, 370m/1200ft, 5+hrs (excluding time spent at the Maidens)

ROUTE OVERVIEW: return coast walk. An easy, classic coast walk leads to the highest sea stack on Skye (and optionally onwards to even more spectacular scenery – see Route 39).

	1	2	3	4	5
Grade	▓				
Terrain	▓				
Navigation	▓	▓			
Seriousness	▓	▓			

At the southern tip of the Duirinish peninsula, just around the corner from Idrigill Point, stand the three most famous sea stacks on Skye – MacLeod's Maidens, the tallest of which (the tallest stack on Skye) reaches a height of 63m/207ft. The delightful walk to the dramatic viewpoint on the adjacent cliff-top is one of the island's classic coast walks. For most of the way there is an excellently contoured path which makes the going extremely pleasant, and in addition a short detour (missed by most people) enables a stunning view to be had of the unique double arches south of Brandarsaig Bay. Although the path is easy, good footwear is essential in the vicinity of the Maidens, where the airy cliff edge requires great care.

The route begins at Orbost House, at the end of a minor road south of Dunvegan. There are parking spaces beside the entrance drive to the house. Take the continuing Land Rover track, signposted to Rubha Idrigill and all points beyond, down to the shores of Loch Bharcasaig and a bridge over the Abhainn Bharcasaig. Loch Bharcasaig is a lovely bay of Loch Bracadale, bounded on the left by the headland of Meall Greepa (see Route 44e).

Since the first edition of this guidebook the landscape beyond the bridge has been much altered by maturing forestry plantations, and the old path has been obliterated by a new forest track. This development has improved the going but curtailed the views over Loch Bracadale (although clearings are opening up again). At the time of writing the track runs to the Forse Burn.

> *If you fancy your chances of climbing the Mother stack you must first abseil from the cliff top of Rubha na Maighdeanan to the shore below (preferably leaving the rope in place). The only other approach is from the sea, and this is often made treacherous by the heavy swell and current around Idrigill Point. Graded Severe, the climb to the summit was first completed in 1959 by I. S. Clough and J. McLean, who named their route The Old Lady.*

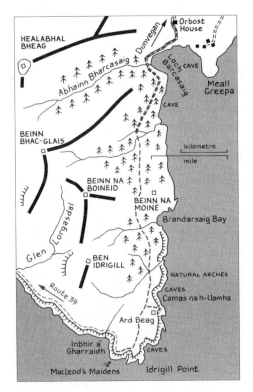

At a fork on the far side of the Forse Burn, branch right on the continuing old path. It climbs onto the low bealach between Beinn na Boineid (Bonnet Mountain) and Beinn na Moine (Bog Mountain) and traverses high above Brandarsaig Bay. The complex contortions of the coastline around Brandarsaig Bay can be explored by those with an excess of time and energy, perhaps on the return trip. It is the only place en route where access to the shore is possible.

The path continues over the next rise to the Idrigill Burn, where it leaves the trees behind, passes the abandoned village of Idrigill and goes through the Glac Ghealaridh (Defile of the White Shieling, i.e. the level defile between Steineval and Ard Beag; named only on E407). From the near end of the defile a short detour leads to one of the most stunning coastal views on Skye.

Leave the path and climb to an obvious clearing at the cliff edge half-way up the slopes of Ard Beag (Little Height). The view from here back across Camas na h-Uamha (Bay of the Cave) includes caves and stacks galore, but what makes it exceptional even by Skye standards are the remarkable double arches on the headland beyond, here seen in profile one behind the other.

After returning to the path, continue through the Glac Ghealaridh to reach more ruins, beyond which, at the time of writing, the path loses itself among sheep tracks. The path marked on the map as continuing all the way around the coast is a figment of the mapmaker's imagination. Leave the ruins to

According to the legend that gave rise to their name, the three stacks are the wife and daughters of the Fourth Chief of the MacLeods, who were shipwrecked off Idrigill Point.

your left and, using the map as a guide, head straight across the moor to the headland above the Maidens (Rubha na Maighdeanan, The Maidens' Headland; named only on E407).

The terrain is complex, with many knolls that make it difficult to hold to a direct line. You are most likely to reach the cliff top just before the Maidens, in which case follow the cliff edge until they come into view. If you reach the cliff edge at a very large bay with cliffs rising westwards, this is Inbhir a' Gharraidh (Cove of the Walled Enclosure) beyond the Maidens.

The crumbling cliff edge at Rubha na Maighdeanan demands extreme caution. The setting is dramatic. The cairn on the cliff top is perched some 70m/230ft above the crashing waves below. The tallest Maiden (the Mother) stands close by. Beyond her stand her two daughters, one a dumpy pinnacle, the other seen from most angles as a thin rock blade.

The best view of the Maidens is obtained from further round Inbhir a' Gharraidh, from where the three stacks appear in profile, the leaning summit block of the Mother resembling a head nodding to the two daughters. From this angle, and from the sea, the Mother has a truly human appearance that has been likened to a statue of a seated Queen Victoria. Across Loch Bracadale the Cuillin rear above the Minginish coastline to complete a picture of nature at its grandest.

After a sojourn at the Rubha the pleasant walk back to Loch Bharcasaig awaits. If it is late in the day, this is best taken at a leisurely pace in order to enjoy the views over Loch Bracadale and its islands, warmed by slanting evening light.

ROUTE 39: THE SOUTH DUIRINISH COAST WALK

ROUTE START: Orbost House (NG 257431, L23/E407); route end: Ramasaig (NG 165441)

ROUTE LOG: 14ml/22km, 720m/2350ft, 9+hrs (includes Route 38 to MacLeod's Maidens)

ROUTE OVERVIEW: one-way

	1	2	3	4	5
Grade					
Terrain					
Navigation					
Seriousness					

cliff-top coast walk, add-on to Route 38. This is simply the finest cliff-top coast walk in the British Isles – awesome and breathtaking. The route involves no scrambling but is graded 5 to reflect its challenging nature.

The rarely visited South Duirinish coastline between Idrigill Point and Lorgill Bay is another of the hidden wonders of Skye. The coastal scenery is spectacular, the terrain is excellent and every headland reveals some new exciting surprise. The route guards its secrets well, however, for it begins 5ml/8km from the nearest road-end at Orbost House and ends 2ml/3km from the nearest road-end at Ramasaig. The point-to-point walk therefore demands a certain amount of pre-planning, although it is possible to curtail it at more than one point and strike back across the moors to Orbost.

Note that the cliff-top path marked on maps does not exist, but there are plenty of sheep paths and the going is excellent anyway. Good footwear is nevertheless essential and all the usual coast-walking precautions apply.

From MacLeod's Maidens (see Route 38 for access from Orbost House) continue around the cliff top above Inbhir a' Gharraidh and across the slopes of Ben Idrigill, reaching a height of 200m/650ft. Descend slightly across a stream to reach the next headland, where there is a pinnacle low down on the cliff face. From here the route ahead can be seen stretching to Lorgill Bay and beyond, the cliff-top like a bowling green – wonderful walking country.

The treacherous Black Skerry has claimed many a passing boat and in former times attracted unscrupulous types in search of plunder. The wrecker and smuggler Campbell of Ensor even lit false beacons here to lure ships to their doom. Nowadays it sees more traffic as a scuba-diving site.

Descend further into Glen Lorgasadal to reach perhaps the finest stretch of coastline on the whole route, studded with stacks and pinnacles. The first pinnacle passed clings to the cliff face like a huge Cleopatra's Needle that seems ready to peel away into the sea. Next

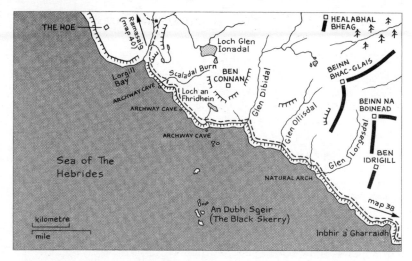

comes an arête that is topped by two pinnacles, and on the cliff top above is a perfect green that would make an idyllic (though precarious) campsite.

From the small promontory just beyond the arête the view back is stunning. The arête is seen to be holed at sea-level, forming the natural arch marked on maps (NG 222380). Beside the arch are two stacks, one a wedge with a knife-edge summit ridge. Between the stacks the Lorgasdal River plunges into the sea. The scene is the epitome of all that is best in Skye coastal architecture.

At the next headland, named Biod a' Mhurain (Bent Grass Cliff) on E407, MacLeod's Maidens come into view once more. Next comes Glen Ollisdal at the foot of Healabhal Bheag, then another headland, named Creag na Cuail (Firewood Crag) on E407, then Glen Dibidal (Deep Glen). Across the Geodha Mor (Big Cove) at the foot of Glen Dibidal can be seen a lovely cove whose sandy beach and crystal clear waters are inaccessible on foot.

As its name implies, Glen Dibidal forms a deep gorge through which the Dibidal River plunges into the sea, and it is necessary to lose height by taking a diagonal line down across the hillside to cross the river above the gorge.

Beyond Glen Dibidal, if possible the coast becomes even more awesome, with the map noting a number of caves and natural arches. The caves are massive, reaching almost the height of the cliff, and great care is required on the crumbling cliff edge above them. The arches are similarly on the grand scale, being in reality enormous archway caves that tunnel through headlands. None of the arches or caves can be reached from the cliff top and are best viewed from the headlands between them. Adding to the fearsomeness of the scene is the treacherous An Dubh Sgeir (The Black Skerry) offshore.

A study of the map will show two ways to turn this point-to-point route into a round trip from Orbost House. The shorter option, which unfortunately entails omitting the most awesome scenery, leaves the coastline at Biod a' Mhurain (the headland between Glen Lorgasdal and Glen Ollisdal). Contour into Glen Ollisdal and, staying right of boggy ground higher up around the Ollisdal Lochs, cross the Bealach Bharcasaig. Descend rough ground on the far side to reach the north side of the forest and a path that follows the fence down to Loch Bharcasaig (round trip: 13ml/20km, 600m/2000ft, 8+hrs).

The longer option completes the full cliff-top walk to Biod Boidheach (the headland above Lorgill Bay) before turning inland. Head east, following the Scaladal Burn up onto the moors. Stay right of Loch Glen Ionadal to cross the low bealach between Beinn na Loch and Ben Connan, then contour around upper Glen Dibidal to reach the Bealach Bharcasaig as above (round trip: 17ml/27km, 700m/2300ft, 11+hrs).

From Glen Dibidal regain the cliff top and reach the stream that drains Loch an Fhridhein, from where the first archway cave can be seen cutting through the headland beyond. A fence leads on along the cliff edge above another deeply recessed cave (unviewable), then the second archway cave comes into view – an enormous tunnel some 30m/100ft long through which the sea pounds mercilessly. On the next rise the cliffs reach 90m/300ft and MacLeod's Maidens can be seen for the last time.

Continuing along the cliff edge, descend to the Scaladal Burn to view the largest cave of all, cutting deep into the cliff face ahead. Beneath your feet, but not viewable until you reach the far side of the Scaladal Burn, is the third archway cave – another huge tunnel some 15m/50ft long.

The crossing of the gorge formed by the Scaladal Burn requires care. Follow the edge of the gorge a short distance inland until you find a sheep path that descends into the gorge above a waterfall and climbs back along a rock ledge on the far side. Follow the far side of the gorge down to the cliff edge to view the third archway cave, then climb the steepest slope of the day to reach the vertiginous grassy summit of Biod Boidheach (Beautiful Cliff, NG 176408, again named only E407). An iron fence-post provides security for the nervous.

Beyond Biod Boidheach lies tranquil Lorgill Bay, whose beach and verdant pastures are balm to the eyes after the ferocity of the South Duirinish coastline, and beyond the bay rise the cliffs of The Hoe (Route 40). Descend to the bay and stroll across the pleasant riverside pastures to Lorgill shepherd's bothy.

To continue to Ramasaig, pick up a path heading north-west past the ruins of Lorgill village (see p.118) onto the moor. The path becomes an excellent cart track to Ramasaig road-end.

ROUTE 40: MOONEN BAY HEIGHTS

ROUTE START: Ramasaig (OS 23, NG 165441, L23/E407)

ROUTE LOG: 8½ml/14km, 590m/1950ft, 5hrs

ROUTE OVERVIEW: circular cliff-top coast walk. A short moorland crossing leads to a scenic, mostly grassy stroll over the three highest

	1	2	3	4	5
Grade		▓			
Terrain	▓	▓			
Navigation	▓				
Seriousness		▓			

points on a line of great sea cliffs that front one of Skye's largest bays.

The west coast of Duirinish contains the highest sea cliffs on Skye, stretching for mile after mile as a more or less vertical wall unbroken by caves and stacks, and this gives the coastline a purity of line that is quite different from that of the South Duirinish coastline described in Routes 38 and 39. North of Lorgill Bay the cliffs ring the large, crescent-shaped Moonen Bay. The road from Glendale to Ramasaig runs close to the cliff top and gives ready access to a magnificent cliff-edge walk.

There are three high points on the cliff top: The Hoe, Ramasaig Cliff and Waterstein Head. Each lies only a short distance across the moor from the roadside and can easily be climbed independently of the others, but a walk that clings to the cliff top and crosses all three makes a much finer outing, with excellent going and superb seaward views.

The Hoe stands immediately north of Lorgill Bay and is approached via the cart track from Ramasaig to Lorgill Bay described in Route 39. Park without causing obstruction at the road-end at Ramasaig, at the last house or at the bottom of the hill just beyond the last house. Follow the track as far as its high point, then bear right over boggy ground to climb to The Hoe's mossy summit plateau, which is a wonderful lookout point for views both up the coastline to Ramasaig Cliff and Waterstein Head and down the coastline to MacLeod's Maidens and the distant Cuillin. The summit itself is set well back from the cliff edge.

From here, turn northwards for a magnificent descent along the cliff top on beautiful short green turf to

> *The huge coastal cliffs of north-west Skye are the best place on the island to view seabirds. The vertical cliffs surrounding Moonen Bay provide a safe home for colonies of fulmar, black guillemots and terns. During the breeding season at Hoe Rape especially, beware of aggressive fulmars nesting on its seaward face. They have sharp claws and spit a foul liquid.*

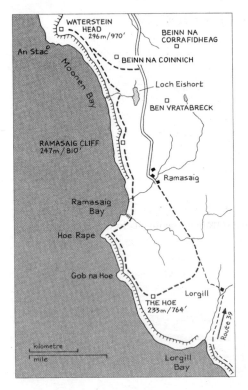

Ramasaig Bay (a Norse name, as are many on this coastline, meaning Raven's Bay). The headland of Hoe Rape halfway along makes a fine vantage point from which to view 30m/100ft Ramasaig waterfall and 105m/350ft Loch Eishort waterfall ahead. Both plunge over the cliff edge to the shoreline. At Ramasaig Bay you can descend to the shore to obtain close-up views of the waterfall. This is the only shore access en route.

North of the bay, keep to the cliff edge and climb steeply up the lush grass beside a fence to the top of Ramasaig Cliff. Between here and Waterstein Head the cliff edge becomes more indented and complex, especially at the point where the stream draining Loch Eishort plunges over the cliff edge, but navigation is easy if you keep to the right of the cliff-edge fence.

The cliffs at Waterstein Head are the highest on Skye apart from Biod an Athair (Route 41). The cliff face drops dramatically to a lone sea stack (called simply An Stac) and the crashing waves far below, but the fence stops you from getting too close to oblivion. There are great views from here across the northern reaches of Moonen Bay to Neist Point (Route 45a), especially when it is silhouetted by the westering sun.

Lorgill was once a thriving community, but the ten families who lived there in 1830 were summarily evicted to make way for sheep during the Highland Clearances. Threatened with imprisonment unless they left, they were forced to emigrate to Nova Scotia.

The least eventful way back across the boggy moor from Waterstein Head to the Ramasaig road is to contour around the right-hand (southern) side of Beinn na Coinnich to reach the roadside north of Loch Eishort. A short walk then leads back to Ramasaig.

ROUTE 41: SKY CLIFF

ROUTE START: Galtrigill (NG 181546, L23/E407)

ROUTE LOG: 4½ml/7km, 270m/900ft, 3½hrs

ROUTE OVERVIEW: circular moor and cliff-top coast walk. An easy ascent to the highest sea cliff on Skye is optionally followed by a rougher coast walk to a remarkable natural arch.

	1	2	3	4	5
Grade	▓				
Terrain		▓	▓	▓	
Navigation	▓	▓			
Seriousness	▓				

The extreme northern spur of the Duirinish peninsula between Loch Pooltiel and Loch Dunvegan forms a large subsidiary peninsula in its own right, whose entire western coastline is one continuous line of cliffs. This coastline makes a fine long walk but, as there is a road up the east side of the peninsula, the highest cliffs on Skye at Biod an Athair near Dunvegan Head can be reached more conveniently from the road-end at Galtrigill. Park with care so as not to obstruct the turning circle.

Viewed from here, the gently rising moor and seemingly inconsequential summit of Biod an Athair make the ascent appear deceptively simple, but the airy cliff edge demands great respect and the usual coast-walking precautions apply, especially if the recommended but much rougher continuation to the natural arch of Am Famhair (The Giant) is included. Initial access to the moor

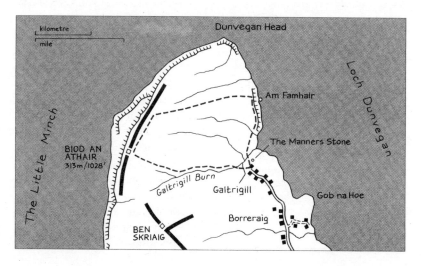

is complicated by fencing and the extensive ruins of old Galtrigill village, which stretch both east and west of the road. The track on the left at the road-end heads west to reach open ground.

To find the best route across the heathery moor, aim for the Galtrigill Burn and follow its banks up the hillside, veering right higher up to reach the cliff edge and the summit. The best way to view the

> In the ruined village of old Galtrigill below the road-end stands the Manners Stone, a large flat 1m square stone on which, according to tradition, you sit to find your manners. To locate it, cross a fence (stile) to find a short path leading to another fence (and stile), then walk through the fields among the ruined buildings for a hundred metres or so until you reach the isolated rock.

stupendous cliff face that suddenly bursts into view, and to appreciate its Gaelic name (meaning Sky Cliff), is to lie down (carefully!) on the grass and peer over the edge at the miniature Atlantic breakers far below. Such is the scale of the face that its dimensions are hard to take in. To gain some perspective, wander northwards along the cliff top beyond the summit and look back. Views across the Little Minch to the Outer Hebrides are superb.

A good sheep path leads onwards along the cliff top towards Dunvegan Head but, as you progress, the cliff edge becomes less well delineated, the going becomes increasingly heathery and tough and the struggle to reach the undistinguished point of Dunvegan Head is hardly worthwhile. It is better at this point to aim straight across the moor to Am Famhair on the east coast – an interesting navigational exercise, as all points on the cliff top look the same on approach.

> At the south end of Galtrigill Bay, reached by a rocky path from below the Manners Stone, is a prominent 'pipers' cave' where students from the MacCrimmon Piping School in nearby Borreraig could practise in peace. The MacCrimmons were hereditary pipers to the MacLeods. A prominent monument stands on the hillside north-west of the village and historical artefacts can be viewed at Borreraig Park Museum (NG 192524).
>
> Further south, expert and seaworthy scramblers who are adept at using limpets for footholds may find a careful sea-level exploration of the headland of Gob na Hoe more than exciting. The shoreline can be reached at the bay north of the headland.

Am Famhair is yet another of Skye's seemingly inexhaustible supply of remarkable natural arches. It stands high and dry on the beach, completely unconnected to the cliff face and abandoned long ago by the sea, stranded like some prehistoric sculpture. To return to Galtrigill from here, head south along the coast but stay slightly away from the cliff edge in order to outflank the gorge formed by the Galtrigill Burn.

Pinnacles of the Sanctuary; the Old Man of Storr is in the centre (Route 27)

Sgurr a' Mhadaidh Ruaidh (right) and Baca Ruadh (centre left) from near Loch Cuithir (Route 28)

The fantastic pinnacles of the Quiraing from the Table (Route 29)

The pinnacled south-west ridge of Leac nan Fionn (Route 30)

Beinn Edra (left) and Bioda Buidhe (right) (Route 31)

Rubh' an Dunain and Rum from across Loch Brittle (Route 34)

An eerie day at Moonen Bay, with wispy cloud on Ramasaig Cliff (Route 40)

MacLeod's Maidens from across Inbhir a' Gharraidh (Route 38)

Looking past Unish ruins and the lighthouse at Waternish Point to the mountains of Harris (Route 42)

The imposing entrance canyon of Spar Cave at low tide (Route 43c)

Dunscaith Castle, with Bla Bheinn behind (Route 43g)

Sunset over Neist Point from Waterstein Head (Route 45a)

Dun Caan from Loch na Mna cliffs (Route 48)

Dun Caan and the east coast of Raasay from the track to Hallaig (Route 49)

Above Loch Arnish at the north end of Raasay, looking south along the spine of the island to Dun Caan (Route 50)

ROUTE 42: WATERNISH POINT

ROUTE START: Trumpan (NG 225612, L23/E407)

ROUTE LOG: 10ml/16km, 220m/720ft, 7hrs

ROUTE OVERVIEW: circular clifftop coast and moor walk. An easy walk to the end of the loneliest and most spacious peninsula on Skye is optionally

	1	2	3	4	5
Grade		▓			
Terrain		▓		▓	
Navigation		▓			
Seriousness		▓			

followed by an exploration of the much rougher Raven's Coastline. This option involves no scrambling but is graded 3 to reflect its challenging nature.

The Waternish peninsula is a remote, unfrequented and untamed land of wide horizons still echoing to the clash of claymores. The unmanned lighthouse at Waternish Point and ruined brochs and memorials to long-forgotten clan battles add to the feeling of a land abandoned. The walk to the point is made easy by an excellent track, but the continuation along the east coast (the 'Raven's Coastline') is a much more serious proposition, involving rough going and an airy cliff-top walk. The route begins just north-east of Trumpan at a right-angled bend in the road (NG 229616). Parking on the corner is limited so it is normal to begin the walk 600m down the road at Trumpan Church car park.

From the bend a Land Rover track goes left to run up the west side of the peninsula for 3ml/5km to the ruined house at Unish. The sea-cliffs along the way reach a height of 80m/250ft, but they cannot be viewed until beyond Unish as the track lies well back from the cliff edge.

To compensate for the lack of views of the cliffs there are glorious views westward across the sea to the hills of the Outer Hebrides, strung out like beads on the horizon. In addition there are some interesting short detours to be made along the way to view a number of sites of historical significance. The first

In 1578, according to tradition, Trumpan Church was the site of an infamous massacre – a revenge attack for the suffocation of 395 MacDonalds in a cave on Eigg when the MacLeods lit a fire at the entrance. When the church was packed with MacLeods the MacDonalds landed in Ardmore Bay, barricaded the doors and set fire to it. Only one woman escaped to raise the alarm, which led to the MacDonalds themselves being massacred in turn. Their bodies were laid beside a stone dyke that was then tumbled over to bury them. The incident has ever since been known as the Battle of the Spoiled Dyke.

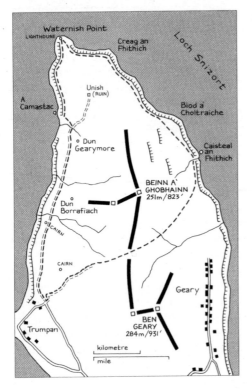

of these (NG 233623) is a prominent cairn on the moor on the right. This is a memorial to John MacLeod of Waternish, who was killed here c.1530 during the Second Battle of Waternish (contested by the MacLeods and the MacDonalds, naturally). Further along on the left a second cairn (NG 230632) commemorates the death of his son Roderick MacLeod of Unish, who fell in the same battle.

It is not difficult to imagine these windswept moors ringing with the sound of battle and haunted by the ghosts of the slain, but as at Trumpan and elsewhere on Skye one feels appalled, angered and saddened by the senseless loss of life in clan society. The cairns, with inscriptions in both Gaelic and English, were restored by the Clan MacLeod Society USA as recently as 1985, yet already the elements have begun to erode them, as time has eroded memories of that long ago battle.

Above the track beyond the second cairn stands Dun Borrafiach (NG 236637), one of the most beautifully constructed Iron Age brochs on Skye. The short tramp across the boggy moor to view it is worthwhile as it is remarkable both for the size of the stones used (up to 1m square) and for the quality of their placement, which is almost worthy of an Incan construction. Further along and closer to the track stands Dun Gearymore (NG 237649), a more dilapidated broch but one in whose north-west corner a low, narrow gallery can still be traced for 6m/20ft.

Beyond Dun Gearymore the track bears right away from the coast to the ruins of Unish House. The still standing walls and chimney stacks make a prominent landmark, but the ruins are dangerous and should be avoided. It is more interesting to leave the track when it turns right and go left to reach the coastline at the pinnacled stump of An Camastac (The Stack of the Bay). The going along the cliff top from here to the lighthouse at Waternish Point is excellent, and there are fine coastal views.

It was at Waternish Point that Bonnie Prince Charlie and Flora MacDonald first touched Skye after their journey across the Little Minch from South Uist in 1746. They tried to land at Ardmore Point (Route 45c) but were fired on by soldiers stationed there. The oarsmen managed to row out of musket range and the party took refuge in a cave at Waternish Point before crossing Loch Snizort to Trotternish.

In Trumpan churchyard the standing stone with the small hole in it is the Trial Stone. According to tradition, the innocence or guilt of an accused person was determined by his or her ability to insert a finger into the hole. Sounds easy . . . except that the accused was blindfolded first.

By far the easiest return route from the point is by the outward route, but keen coast walkers may choose to continue around the east coast of the Waternish peninsula to explore the Raven's coastline and return across the moor. This extension involves more serious terrain than the outward journey, but the coastal scenery is correspondingly more exciting.

Heading east, a shallow bay leads to the point called Creag an Fhithich (The Raven's Crag), where the coastline turns southwards into Loch Snizort and views of the outer isles are replaced by views of the Ascrib Islands and Trotternish. Beyond Creag an Fhithich a good sheep path through the heather clings to the cliff edge on the seaward side of an old fence. Composure is required. If in doubt stay further inland.

Approaching the headland of Biod a' Choltraiche (Razorbill Cliff) the going deteriorates and it is best to stay away from the cliff edge altogether, keeping to the moor until Caisteal an Fhithich (The Raven's Castle) comes into view. This is a grass-topped stack that is almost as high as the cliff itself, and which is connected to it by a short beach causeway. Great care is required when trying to view or photograph the stack. The most dramatic and safest view is obtained from just beyond it, where it can be viewed over a waterfall. The crag and castle are not named arbitrarily, as ravens do patrol this stretch of coastline.

To complete the circuit back to Trumpan it is necessary to cross the backbone of the Waternish peninsula from east to west. Head diagonally uphill, aiming for the low point on the skyline between Beinn a' Ghobhainn (Blacksmith Mountain) and Ben Geary (Enclosure Mountain). The going is rough, but as height is gained the views open out to compensate. Descend to pick up the grassy cart track marked on the map at NG 240624, which gives a pleasant end-of-day stroll back to the road.

ROUTE 43: SHORT WALKS, SOUTH SKYE

The routes described here cover five short walks on Sleat and three on the adjacent peninsula of Strathaird in the south of Skye. On Sleat the A851 Broadford-Armadale road runs down the east coast, while a twisting loop road gives access to the picturesque west coast. Strathaird is accessed by the B8083 Broadford-Elgol road. Routes 43a-43c on Strathaird are described from north to south as the road reaches them. Routes 43d-43h on Sleat are described in a clockwise direction, north-to-south down the east coast and south-to-north up the west coast.

Route 43a: Dun Ringill (NG 553173) L32/E412, 1+hrs

Dun Ringill stands atop some curious sandstone cliffs on the east coast of Strathaird near Kilmarie. The path to it begins at Kilmarie House, reached by a short minor road that leaves the B8083 Broadford-Elgol road on the south side of the bridge over the Abhainn Cille Mhairie. The gardens of Kilmarie House are notable for their fine trees, which can be seen from the roadside at the river mouth. Go through a gate in the fence on the opposite side of the road just before the house and cross the river by an ornate bridge. Turn immediately right along the far riverbank on a path that runs through woodlands to the river mouth and along the coastline to the dun.

Dun Ringill was the stronghold of the MacKinnons before they moved to Caisteal Moil at Kylerhea. It is typical of many duns on Skye in that it crowns a rocky headland surrounded by sea cliffs on three sides, but it is untypical in its landward entrance, an 8m/25ft passageway that is partly covered. Little else but the passageway remains, the top of the dun now being deep in nettles. On the moor above the dun are numerous remains of later habitations.

The shoreline beyond the dun is worth exploring for a few hundred metres, where brittle sandstone cliffs teeter precariously. There is a cave, and an arch whose supporting walls have been holed as if by giant punches. Beware falling rocks.

Route 43b: Prince Charles's Cave (NG 516135) L32/E411, 2hrs

Suidhe Biorach (Pointed Seat) at the south-west tip of Strathaird sports some exciting cliff scenery similar to that in the Spar Cave area (see next route) and is easily reached by a good cliff-top path from Elgol. It was here that Bonnie Prince Charlie ended his wanderings in the islands and quit Skye for the mainland on the night of 4 July, 1746, and the cave in which he spent his last hours there can be visited.

The path starts in the middle of the upper tier of the car park at Elgol jetty. If the car park is full there is additional parking at the upper car park or beside

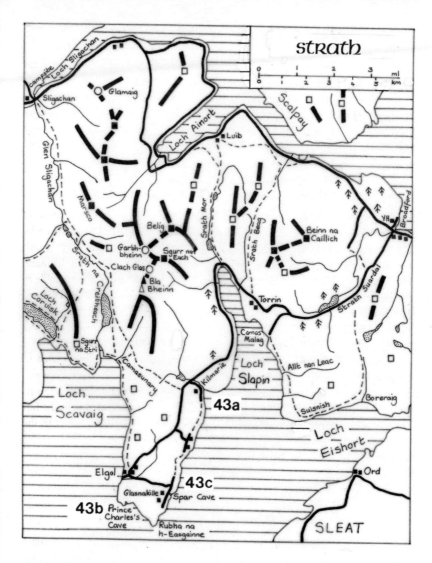

Elgol Hall a short distance along the road to Glasnakille. The path makes a short, gentle ascent to the cliff top and follows it all the way out to the point, with superb views of Rum and the Cuillin. The cliff top in the vicinity of the point is complex and sports a number of deep creeks, fissures and other interesting rock features. Suidhe Biorach was so named because it used to be the custom for childless women to sit there in the hope of becoming fertile.

Prince Charles's Cave lies beyond the point beside a shoreline rock platform on the west side of the bay of Port an Luig Mhoir (Harbour of the Big Hollow). To reach it continue beyond the platform in order to outflank the cliffs, then descend to the shore and return along the cliff foot. This is advisable **AT LOW TIDE ONLY**. The cave is a short but large 'through' cave floored by a pool, and it is not obvious until you have walked past it.

Route 43c: Spar Cave (NG 537129) L32/E411, 2hrs

Spar Cave is one of the natural wonders of Scotland. Beyond its huge entrance canyon on the shores below Glasnakille it forms a spectacular flowstone-encrusted passageway burrowing deep into the hillside. Its scale and formations are unprecedented and the trip to its innermost recesses high in the roof of the passageway is breathtaking. No caving skills are required, but the logistics of a visit should not be underestimated.

Reaching the entrance canyon requires scrambling along shoreline cliffs and over seaweed-encrusted rocks, and is possible **AT LOW TIDE ONLY**. Inside the cave itself the floor is in turns muddy, steeply ascending and pitted with transparent pools. A torch is required. For the sake of those who come after you, please, please do not remove or interfere with the calcite formations.

The route to the cave begins 100m south of the road junction in Glasnakille. Go though a gate, cross a field right of a stone byre and descend a funnel-like depression on a small path. The path descends directly to the edge of the shoreline cliffs, goes left for a short distance then winds down to a rocky inlet. Once on the shoreline, go left beneath the cliff face past a narrow flooded creek. The entrance to Spar Cave lies around the next headland. Reach it by edging around rocky ledges at the cliff foot and clambering across seaweed-covered rocks at the tidal limit. WARNING. This section of the route is passable for only a couple of hours each side of low tide.

The entrance canyon is around 60m/200ft long and up to 30m/100ft high, resembling 'some deep cathedral aisle' as John MacCulloch described it. The entrance itself lies at the landward end of the canyon and is guarded by a 3m/10ft high broken wall. This wall, complete with locked door, was built by an early nineteenth-century proprietor to prevent visitors from robbing the cave of its long pendant stalactites ('spars'). Unfortunately the wall did not serve its purpose; Sir Walter Scott, for instance, was able to climb it with the aid of a rope in 1814. The door was eventually demolished by a shot from an offshore gunboat. Today the cave is bereft of the stalactite formations for which it was once renowned.

Beyond the wall two passages lead off. That on the right soon degenerates into a crawl. The main passage is on the left. It is muddy for some distance but then develops into a fantastic flowstone staircase some 50m/160ft long, rising like a frozen marble cataract into the darkness of the roof high above. Everywhere – floor, walls, roof – is encrusted in creamy calcium carbonate ('spar'), which forms fine formations as it flows down the walls. There are no great stalactites left, and the roof is blackened from the smoke of ancient candles and torches, but it remains an awesome sight. The place has the aura and dimensions of a Gothic cathedral.

The corrugations in the flowstone provide a good grip, such that the scramble up the passageway is not as hard as it looks. At the summit, high in the roof, care is required on a short level section lined with transparent, almost invisible pools. Then the flowstone passage descends again to a very deep pool some 5m/16ft across, which marks the limit of exploration. The cave ends abruptly not far beyond the pool.

You will be loath to leave this magical spot, 'deep in Strathaird's enchanted cell', as Sir Walter Scott described it in Lord of the Isles, where 'dazzling spars gleam like a firmament of stars'. But make sure that you make the return trip while the tide is still low.

In Gaelic, Spar Cave is known as Slochd Altrimen (Nursing Cave) after a tale of the ninth century. The son of the chief of Colonsay was shipwrecked on the Strathaird coast and found by Princess Dounhuila of nearby Dun Glass, whose father was the sworn enemy of the chief of Colonsay. Young Colonsay was imprisoned in Dun Glass, but Dounhuila fell in love with him and bore him a child, which, to ensure its survival, she had a trusty servant keep in Spar Cave. Dounhuila visited the cave to nurse the child, hence the cave's name. The story had a happy ending, for the chiefs patched up their feud and the lovers married.

The bays to the immediate south of Spar Cave are also worth exploring, and they too can be reached by steep winding paths if you can find them. The sandstone cliffs here are awesome, full of overhangs, caves and honeycomb formations. Take care in their exploration.

Route 43d: Knock Castle (NG 671091) L32/E412, 1hr

The A851 down the eastern side of Sleat touches the coast at Isleornsay and again at Knock Bay, where a craggy headland is crowned by the gaunt ruins of Knock Castle, also known in Gaelic as Caisteal Chamuis (Cash-tyal Chammish, Bay Castle). Held at one time by the MacLeods, the stronghold was later captured by the MacDonalds and inhabited by them until they moved to Dunscaith (see below). One MacDonald tale tells of a fifteenth-

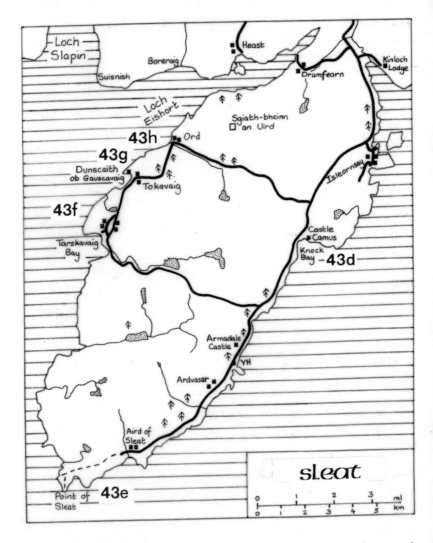

Loch Slapin

Suisnish

Boreraig

Heast

Drumfearn

Kinloch Lodge

Loch Eishort

Sgiath-bheinn an Uird

43h   Ord

43g

Dunscaith ob Gauscavaig

Tokavaig

Isleornsay

43f

Tarskavaig Bay

Castle Camus

Knock Bay   **43d**

Armadale Castle

YH

Ardvasar

Aird of Sleat

sleat

Point of Sleat   **43e**

0   1   2   3   ml
0   1   2   3   4   5   km

century siege by the MacLeods, during which one Mary of the Castle inspired her MacDonald clansmen to hold out and defeat the enemy. Another tradition says that the castle is haunted by a glaistig (a female sprite). Among the eerie ivy-clad ruins of the castle today, where remnants of wall perch at the cliff edge, such tales are not beyond belief.

To reach the castle, park at the end of the very short minor road that leaves the main road just south of Toravaig House hotel. From here a track descends past houses to a cottage on Knock Bay. From here another track branches left over a bridge and up the hillside on the far side of the river. Follow it around a fence and cross fields to reach the dun (new fencing permitting).

Route 43e: Point of Sleat (NG 588007) L32/E412, 5ml/8km, 3+hrs

Beyond Knock Bay the A851 continues down the east coast of Sleat to the ferry terminal at Armadale pier, then a minor road continues above the rocky coastline to Aird of Sleat. Many of the bays and headlands along this stretch of coast are well worth exploring, notably the cliffs of Tormore and the stack on the west side of Port na Long. The road ends at Aird Old Church Gallery just beyond Aird of Sleat, and from here a path runs to Point of Sleat at the lonely southern tip of Skye.

From the road-end take the track that continues straight on across the rising moor. Follow it for c.1½ml/2½km across a landscape of craggy knolls to a footbridge over a stream (NG 567004). Just beyond here branch left on a rocky path signposted Point of Sleat and follow this up the hillside and beside a fence.

At a waymarked junction c.50m beyond the end of the fence branch right on a path that becomes boggier and more indistinct as it crosses heathery moorland.

It descends concrete steps to a rocky bay on the west side of the peninsula (NG 561994) and goes left along the beach. Finally it crosses a narrow isthmus and climbs to Point of Sleat lighthouse, perched on a rocky headland at this most southerly point on Skye. Note the contorted folding of the rock and the honeycombed overhangs below the lighthouse on the right (west). Much time could be spent exploring the coastline around the Point before returning to Aird of Sleat.

Route 43f: Tarskavaig Bay to Tokavaig Bay (NG 583097) L32/E412, 3ml/5km, 2+hrs

The wild west coast of Sleat is mostly remote and untracked country, relatively flat but indented by numerous rocky bays that are a delight to explore. The wave-lapped shoreline ramble from Tarskavaig Bay to Ob Gauscavaig especially repays investigation, with the Cuillin in constant view across Loch Eishort.

From the car park at the road end on the north shore of Tarskavaig Bay, continue along a track to an old church hidden further round the bay. Beyond here keep walking to reach Tarskavaig Point – a fascinating rock playground of labyrinthine creeks, canyons, beaches, rock shelves and other formations.

Beyond Tarskavaig Point take to the beach and boulder-hop up the coast.

The going is relatively easy (though tiring) on rounded sea-worn boulders. The route follows the foot of shoreline cliffs past a variety of interesting coastal scenery, here seen on a more intimate scale than in the north of Skye.

The only coastal feature marked on the map is Uamh Tarskavaig (Tarskavaig Cave). It is only one of many caves but it is the largest and is unmistakable when it comes into view. The covered portion of the cave is some 20m/65ft deep by 5m/16ft high, not large by Skye standards but nevertheless impressive enough and made something out of the ordinary by its entrance canyon, in whose southern wall (facing on approach) is a natural arch.

Not far beyond the cave Dunscaith Castle on the north shore of Ob Gauscavaig comes into view, and soon afterwards the cliffs begin to peter out and the shoreline rocks become sharper. At this point it is easier to take to the grass above the beach in order to reach the roadside at Ob Gauscavaig. Without transport at both ends the walk can be curtailed once the best scenery is passed at Uamh Tarskavaig for a short return trip across country to your starting point.

Route 43g: Dunscaith Castle (NG 601118) L32/E412, 1+hrs

The ruined castle of Dunscaith crowns a rocky headland on the north side of Ob Gauscavaig, in a commanding position at the entrance to Loch Eishort. To reach it, park at the roadside on the north side of the bay and take the track signposted 'Footpath to Castle'. When the track ends at a house, go left around the fence and continue along the shore.

Few castles have such a dramatic situation. The rock on which it stands rises 13m/40ft from the sea and is surrounded by water on three sides. On the landward side it is separated from the mainland of Sleat by a ravine bridged by two arched walls, whose intervening bridge has long since collapsed, making access to the castle awkward. This may be a blessing in disguise for the modern visitor, for Ossianic tradition tells that the old bridge 'narrowed until it became as narrow as the hair of one's head, and the second time it shortened until it became as short as an inch, and the third time it grew slippery as an eel of the river, and the fourth time it rose up on high against you until it was as tall as the mast of a ship'.

The bridge must have shrunk considerably in recent times for the gap across the ravine is now only 2m/6ft long. Nevertheless, the crossing should not be attempted by those of a nervous disposition as it requires edging along a narrow ledge beside either arched wall. Once across, a winding staircase leads past a still standing 5m/16ft high section of wall to the now grassy summit of the rock. An alternative route to the top goes via an exposed scramble from the beach to the left of the bridge.

Dunscaith is one of the oldest fortified headlands in the Hebrides, its origins lost in the mists of time and steeped in legend. Once a stronghold of the MacLeods, the castle itself was later inhabited by the MacDonalds until they too abandoned it in the early seventeenth century for Duntulm in the more prosperous north end of Skye. One dark episode from this period was the murder of Donald Galloch, third chief of the MacDonalds, by his half-brother Black Archibald on the shore nearby in 1508.

It is with Cuchullin, the legendary Irish warrior-hero, however, that Dunscaith will forever be associated. Before the MacDonalds took up residence it was the legendary home of Sgathach, an Amazon queen famed for her skill in battle training. It was here that Cuchullin came to complete his education, and with the help of Sgathach and her attendants, 'thrice fifty handsome marriageable girls', completed it was. Many were the deeds of Cuchullin at Dunscaith. The grass-topped rock on the shore beneath Dunscaith is Clach Luath (Luath's Stone), where Cuchullin tied his hound Luath on return from the hunt.

Dunscaith is listed as an Ancient Monument, but is not maintained and disintegrates a little more each year in its battle against Skye storms. In places the wall still reaches a height of 5m/16ft, but like the bridge it cannot last forever. Long may it remain standing as a haunting reminder of times long past.

Route 43h: Ord (NG 617132) L32/E412, 1+hrs

North of Ob Gauscavaig the road winds through Tokavaig village and climbs through its famous ashwood, once a sacred Druid grove. The shore is reached again at the sands of Ord Bay, where the view across Loch Eishort to the coast of Suisnish and Boreraig, with Bla Bheinn and the Cuillin beyond, has been described as the most magnificent in Scotland. It was here that Alexander Smith stayed when he wrote his classic book *A Summer in Skye* in 1865. Of Loch Eishort he wrote: 'On a fine morning there is not in the whole world a prettier sheet of water.'

One of the offshore islands north of Ord has a fine 'coral' strand, similar to those at Claigan (Route 45b), which can be reached dryshod **AT LOW TIDE ONLY**. To reach it, begin just up the hill from the bay on the road to Ord House. Walk past Ord House to pick up a well-built stone path along the coast. The path reaches some holiday chalets and continues left of the last chalet to a bay. At the far end of the bay at low tide a spit of sand leads out to the coral strand.

The road between Ord and the east coast runs between the lowly Sgiath-bheinns (Skee-a Vain, Wing Mountain), whose extensive quartzite pavement summits glisten from afar in the sunlight. North of the road, the 295m/968ft Sgiath-bheinn an Uird (of Ord) gives the easiest ascent and has the best views.

ROUTE 44: SHORT WALKS, LOCH BRACADALE

With its sweeping vistas and varied scenery, Loch Bracadale is considered by many to be the most beautiful of all Skye lochs. In its inner recesses between Idrigill Point to the north and Rubha nan Clach to the south are a number of photogenic islands and promontories which interlock in such a way that from every angle they form a perfect composition, their landscapes so intricate that each turn in the coastline reveals some new surprise. At any time of day the sun illuminates something of interest, and there is often sunlight on these low-lying shores when there is cloud elsewhere in Skye.

The student of Skye history will find much of interest around Loch Bracadale, for its sheltered shores have long been coveted by both inhabitants and invaders. It was here, in the days when the loch was known as Vestrafjord (the Western Fjord), that Haco's beaten fleet took shelter in 1263 on its way back north from the Battle of Largs. When Pennant came in 1772 he judged it to be the best site on Skye for a town, although that honour later went to Portree, surprisingly only 8ml/13km away as the eagle flies on the opposite coast of the island.

From the walker's point of view the outstanding features of Loch Bracadale are its promontories and peninsulas, on all of which there is something special to see. The five routes described here are listed from south to north.

Route 44a: Ardtreck Point (GR 338354) L32/E410, 1½+hrs

Lonely Ardtreck Point juts out into southern Loch Bracadale at the northern tip of Minginish above Portnalong. The walk out along the short, stubby peninsula to the point is rough but passes a dun and a lighthouse and gives good views of Oronsay and the Fiskavaig coastline. From the B8009 Portnalong-Fiskavaig road follow the minor road signposted 'Ardtreck' until it bears left across the peninsula and becomes unsurfaced.

Leave the car here, walk a short distance further then turn right alongside a fence and head across the moor towards Dun Ardtreck, which can be seen ahead on the west coast of the peninsula. Keep close to the fence in order that a transverse fence can be crossed by a stile of stones at the fence junction, then aim for the cliff top on which the dun stands.

The walls of the dun are only 2½m/8ft high, but they are equally thick, and remains of the gallery between inner and outer walls can still be seen. Beyond the dun, descend to a small bay and continue along the bouldery shore beneath cliffs to reach the lighthouse at the point. A return route via the east coast of the peninsula is made awkward by steep vegetated slopes and seaweed-encrusted rocks and, as the backbone of the peninsula is also very rough, it is best to return

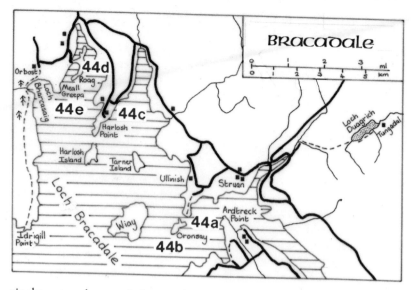

via the outward route. A sheep path along the cliff top from the lighthouse to the dun gives some slight variation.

Route 44b: Oronsay and Vicinity (NG 322374) L23 or L32/E410, 1½+hrs

The tidal island of Oronsay consists entirely of the finest stretch of greensward on Skye, sweeping up from the shore at the mainland end of the island to vertical 72m/236ft cliffs overlooking Loch Bracadale. The ground soon dries out after rain, making the walk to the high point of the island a pleasant excursion even when the going elsewhere may be heavy. On a sunny day the walk around the cliff top gives wonderful views over Loch Bracadale, and there are some delightful spots simply to pause and enjoy the peace and solitude.

Like its namesake in Sleat, Oronsay (Ebb-tide island) can be reached by a beach causeway **AT LOW TIDE ONLY**. To reach it take either of the minor roads to Ullinish that leave the A853 Sligachan-Dunvegan road just north of Struan. A few hundred metres east of Ullinish Lodge hotel, take the road on the south and park just before the last house. Go through a gate on the right, signposted 'Footpath to Oronsay' and follow a track (becoming a path) to Ullinish Point and the causeway.

Once onto the island follow the left-hand (south-east) cliff top above fine small creeks and crags until forced up to the highest tuft of grass at the end of the island, where the cliffs form an imposing wall. Beneath the high point is a wave-lashed skerry where two stacks hold out against the elements. To the south there are fine close-up views of the Talisker-Fiskavaig coastline. To the west MacLeod's Maidens peer over the island of Wiay, while to the north-west there is a perfect view of the natural arch at the south end of Tarner Island. To complete a circuit of Oronsay return via the north-west coast.

While in the vicinity of Struan, Dun Beag (NG 339387) is worth a visit. It stands right beside the A853 immediately north of the Ullinish turn-off and it is easily reached by a path from a car park. As recently as 200 years ago its walls still stood 6m/20ft high. Local re-use of the stones over the centuries has reduced that height to only 4m/13ft, but between inner and outer walls can still be seen a cell and sections of gallery, complete with access steps. The site was excavated earlier this century and the stonework restored to give some indication of its former glory. Standing inside the central enclosure today certainly gives some idea of the security it must have afforded when the building was intact.

There is one further place nearby that all Cuillin lovers with a sense of history and nostalgia may wish to visit, and that is old Struan cemetery (NG 355388; not the one marked on the map, but the one at the back of the church 100m west of the A853). Here are the graves of John MacKenzie, marked simply 'Cuillin Guide', and Norman Collie, buried close beside his great friend at his own request.

At the head of Glen Bracadale, hidden beneath the featureless moors that form the heartland of Skye between east and west coasts, is the 8m long Tungadal souterrain (NG 407401). The bleak approach route begins at Totardor road end east of Struan, follows a cart track up Glen Bracadale to Loch Duagrich, then crosses the extremely marshy mouth of the loch to gain a path along the south-east shore. The entrance lies among boulders in the middle of a grassy knoll, around 150m from the head of the loch.

WARNING. The marshy ground around Loch Duagrich can become perilously marshy, so only adventurous souterrain-tickers and masochists need apply. Others will be more than content to sample the more accessible and longer souterrains at Claigan (Route 45b) and Kilvaxter (Route 47b).

Route 44c: The Piper's Cave (NG 284409) L23/E407 or E410, 2hrs

The Piper's Cave at Harlosh Point is the longest sea cave on Skye and its exploration requires a torch. Reaching it on foot is an exciting excursion in itself, to be attempted AT LOW TIDE ONLY. Yet the very existence of the cave is becoming lost in the mists of time. It is not marked on L23 and is marked but not named on E407, but it was famous as long ago as 1773, when Johnson and Boswell visited it, and the tale of the eponymous piper is one of the most famous in Skye folklore.

To reach Harlosh Point, take either of the minor roads to Harlosh that leave the A853 Sligachan-Dunvegan road just north of Caroy. The surfaced road ends at Ardmore and there are parking spaces on the left just beyond. From here a grassy track goes to a gate in a fence, then a path continues. Beyond the gate, on the rise immediately to the right, are the almost imperceptible ruins of an old chapel.

The direct route to the Piper's Cave goes south along the cliff top, but it is worth making a detour via the north-west coast in order to view Dun Neill. The walls of Dun Neill are barely discernable, but then Neill hardly needed any – his dun crowned a promontory which is surrounded by sea cliffs on three sides, while on the landward side any attacker would need both hands to scramble up. In the bay beyond Dun Neill are further signs of habitation, and beyond here is the most westerly point of the peninsula, from where there are fine views of the Idrigill Point coastline and the beautiful sandy beach on the north coast of Harlosh Island.

Continuing around the coastline, Harlosh Point is soon reached, and here the excitement begins, for the sea cliffs along the south-east coast soon reach a height of 20m/65ft. Beyond a deep-cut inlet a 10m/30ft finger of basalt points the way to the Piper's Cave. From the cliff top directly opposite the pinnacle a well-worn easy scramble leads down to the shoreline, and **AT LOW TIDE ONLY** it is possible to scramble left along the cliff foot to the cave entrance.

Beyond the huge arch that forms the entrance a 3m/10ft square tube burrows into the hillside. With a torch it is possible to follow it to its abrupt end (watch your head!) some 50m/160ft from the entrance. Without a torch you will readily appreciate the feelings of the piper, who was heard to mutter as he entered: 'I doot, I doot, I doot I'll e'er come oot!'

The Piper's Cave must have been longer in the days of the piper. Having been given the gift of music by a fairy queen, he was finally called to task and, having passed on the gift to his sons (thus founding the hereditary school of piping at Borreraig), he entered the cave with his dog, pipes blasting. Followers above ground followed the sound of the pipes as far as Fairy Bridge north of Dunvegan, where the music stopped. The piper's dog reappeared, hair completely singed off, at Uamh Oir (Route 47b). Beyond the cave it is possible to scramble a short distance further along the shoreline, but the only way back to the cliff top is by the route of approach.

Route 44d: Roag Island (NG 272433) L23/E407 or E410, 2hrs

Roag Island is not really an island, as it is connected to the mainland of Skye by a causeway that carries a road. Nevertheless, it feels like an island, and that is good enough. It is mostly flat except at its southern end, where a large table-like rock bastion is separated from the rest of the island by another, shorter stone causeway that makes it almost another island in itself. This table is bounded by crags up to 10m/35ft high and makes a delightful playground for all who enjoy clambering around on shoreline rocks.

To reach Roag Island take the road to Roag village that leaves the A853 Sligachan-Dunvegan road at Roskhill south of Dunvegan. From Roag take the road to Ardroag and park on the landward side of the causeway, as parking is not allowed on the island itself. Follow the road across the causeway to the last house, from where only a short stretch of moor separates you from the stone causeway leading to the table top. The most interesting formations are at the south-west point, where the deeply fissured tangle of rock is like giant eroded crazy paving.

Route 44e: Meall Greepa (NG 257431) L23/E407, 1½+hrs

At the headland of Meall Greepa (Precipice Hill) is one of those exciting surprises of which Skye seems to have an unending store, in this case the largest archway cave on the island. The walk to the cave should be attempted **AT LOW TIDE ONLY** and to be appreciated to the full it should be saved for the evening of a fine day, when the sun irradiates the cliffs.

Access to Meall Greepa is from Orbost House, as for MacLeod's Maidens (Route 38). Take the Land Rover track down to Loch Bharcasaig then go left along the shoreline on a delightful rock platform beneath sea cliffs. At one point the cliffs fall directly into the sea but at low tide the section can be crossed dryshod on stepping stones to reach the mouth of the cave.

Only now is the cave revealed in its true glory as a huge archway cave tunnelling right through Meall Greepa, forming a beautifully arched cavern some 40m/130ft long by 10m/30ft high, in whose dark recesses echo the swirling waters of Loch Bracadale. Brave souls who do not fear the prospect of a wetting can cross the channel at the cave's entrance and scramble some distance up the centre of the channel on large blocks that have fallen from the roof. Beyond the cave is a natural arch visible from certain angles during the approach walk but not reachable on foot.

The summit of Meall Greepa makes a fine viewpoint for Loch Bracadale that can be reached by following the cliff top rather than the cliff foot. N.B. Do not attempt to reach the cliff top via the steep earthy rake to the left of the cave as this is loose and dangerous, and do not go nearer the cliff edge than the fence used to keep sheep away. It is also worth crossing the neck of the headland to view the coastline of Loch na Faolinn, the next loch to the east, where cliff buttresses, indented by caves, fall vertically into the sea.

ROUTE 45: SHORT WALKS, NORTH-EAST SKYE

The five routes described here cover short walks on and near the peninsulas of Duirinish and Waternish in north-east Skye. They are described in a clockwise direction from west to east.

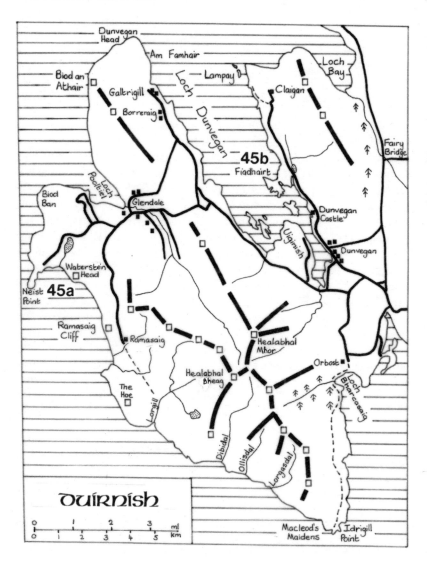

Route 45a: Neist Point (NG 133478) L23/E407, 1+hrs

Across Moonen Bay from Waterstein Head (Route 40) the curious appendage of Neist Point (originally An Eist, The Horse) juts out into the sea like a giant knobbly arm, ending in rocky fingertips between which the surf pounds. There is much to see in the area, and a well-surfaced access path, complete with concrete steps and handrail, makes it a popular excursion.

The path begins at the car park at Neist Point road-end west of Glendale on the B884. It descends through a break in the cliffs and contours around the craggy lump of An t-Aigeach (The Stallion, NG 129475, named only on E407) to reach Neist Point lighthouse, a beautiful 1929 building perched on the cliff top above the sea. Since the first edition of this guidebook the lighthouse has been automated and the former keepers' cottages are now holiday homes.

Between the lighthouse and the point a vast, cleanly-faulted, three-dimensional rock pavement provides delightful scrambling. There are magnificent views southwards across Moonen Bay to Waterstein Head, Ramasaig Cliff and The Hoe and westwards across the Little Minch to the Outer Hebrides (stunning at sunset).

The east coast of the Neist Point peninsula is relatively flat, but on the west coast cliffs reach a height of 90m/300ft at An t-Aigeach, and beyond here a two-tiered cliff reaches 120m/400ft. This latter cliff top can be reached from the road-end by a path that affords good views of the point as it heads west along the cliff edge. The walk can be extended to a ruined coastguard lookout station, beyond which can be seen the top of Biod Ban (White Cliff), a stupendous mural precipice 196m/645ft high. For an unimpeded view of the whole cliff face, continue across the plateau past the lookout to the edge of Oisgill Bay. Return to the car park from the lookout by a path that goes straight across the moor.

Route 45b: Dunvegan and Vicinity (NG 447491) L23/E407

North of Dunvegan Castle there are a number of features of interest on the minor road that runs for 4ml/6km up the east shore of Loch Dunvegan to Claigan.

The small Fiadhairt peninsula immediately beyond the castle is completely surrounded by water except for a narrow isthmus that connects it to the rest of Skye. Because of its isolation and the rough-looking moorland approach it is rarely visited, and as a consequence it boasts one of the best preserved brochs on Skye and a shoreline beloved of Loch Dunvegan seals.

Although the peninsula itself is quite rough, the approach walk from the south-west corner of Loch Suardal (NG 239509) is surprisingly pleasant. From the roadside follow a short dirt track up the hillside, then bear right to some ruins seen ahead. At the ruins pick up an old track that contours right of the high point of the moor to reach the isthmus.

On the moor just beyond the isthmus stands the broch, whose inner and outer walls, although only 2m/6ft high, are complete, with steps leading down between them to a partially-covered gallery. The dun is unusual on two counts: it has two entrances (one a channelled passageway from the moor) and its excavation in 1914 uncovered a Roman artefact – a terracotta model of a bale of hides or fleeces. The shores of the peninsula can be explored at will, from the vegetated sea cliffs at the northern end to the low-lying rocks at the complex southern tip. If there are seals on the rocks, approach quietly, for they are easily disturbed (1+hrs).

At the end of the minor road, Claigan Coral Beaches are a popular tourist destination, even if the sand is not true coral but sun-bleached bits of a red alga called Lithothamnion calcareum. To find the car park at the start of the walk (NG 233537), turn left at the T-junction just beyond the houses in Claigan. A track (signposted 'Claigan Beaches') leads down to the shore and along

With its café and shops, the busy tourist destination of Dunvegan Castle is no place for outdoor lovers to commune with nature, but it is nevertheless worth a visit. Built on a rocky outcrop on the shores of Loch Dunvegan, which originally surrounded it completely, it is the only one of Skye's old fortresses that is still intact and still occupied. The ancestral home of the Chiefs of Clan MacLeod for over seven centuries, it is said to be the oldest continuously inhabited castle in Scotland. You can explore the castle buildings, stroll around the eighteenth-century gardens, take a boat trip to see the seal colony or simply take time out from your island wanderings to visit the café and shops.

There is much history here. The most treasured MacLeod possession is the legendary, if somewhat tattered, Fairy Flag, which confers victory on the clan when unfurled in battle. Also to be found here, among other important relics, are the Dunvegan Cup, dating from the Middle Ages, and a lock of Bonnie Prince Charlie's hair.

The castle is open to the public from the beginning of April to the middle of October, 10–5.30, and for groups by appointment during the rest of the year. For further information see www.dunvegancastle.com or tel 01470-521206.

to the first beach, beyond which a path continues to the more extensive second beach opposite the tidal island of Lampay (1½hrs).

Most people stop here, but you can explore further. Walk on to the point beyond (Groban na Sgeire) and look for the mini natural arch, climb the minor highpoint of Cnoc Mor a' Ghrobain above it (only 28m/92ft high and named only on E407) and, **AT LOW TIDE ONLY**, walk out to Lampay.

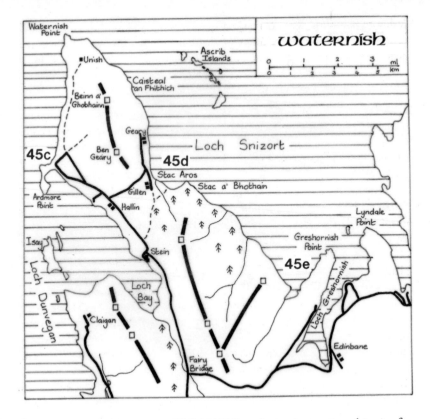

Nearby Claigan souterrain (NG 238539) makes an interesting objective for a short walk off the regular tourist itinerary, but take a torch if you intend to investigate the dark, muddy interior. From the coral beaches car park, walk back across the T-junction and, when the road bends sharp left, follow the track that goes straight on. The souterrain will be found c.500m along, not far from where the track bears right. Its exact position is about 20m beyond the bend and 15m to the left, at the back of a small depression. The entrance is a low, lintelled burrow that leads to a narrow rising tunnel almost 10m/35ft long (1hr).

Route 45c: Ardmore Point (NG 225612) L23/E407, 2+hrs

Immediately west of Trumpan Church in Waternish (see Route 42) the small peninsula of Ardmore sports some sizeable sea cliffs at the headlands of Ard Beag and Rogheadh. To reach them, walk down the road from the church car park to the first corner, then follow a track down to and along the shore of

Ardmore Bay. Turn right beside a fence to cross the neck of the peninsula and reach the north shore, then follow the cliff top around to Ardmore Point at the peninsula's south end. The double arches at Rogheadh are especially pleasing.

Route 45d: Loch Losait (NG 268597) L23/E407, 2+hrs

Loch Losait, an inner bay of Loch Snizort on the east coast of the Waternish peninsula, sports some little-visited sea stacks and caves. Park at the road-end in Gillen so as not to obstruct the turning area. Continue along a grassy track, bear left at a fork to join another track at a gate and follow this down to a forestry track, which descends to the bay.

The shoreline can be followed in either direction, west to Stac Aros (House Stack) or east to Stac a' Bhothain (Bothy Stack). Of the two stacks, Stac Aros, a fine lump of rock some 10m/35ft high, is the nearest and the most interesting. To reach it, boulder-hop along the beach. The far side of the stack yields an exposed scramble up through thick vegetation to a guano-encrusted summit platform. Ten minutes further along the beach is a fine 30m/100ft deep sea cave, which can be reached AT LOW TIDE ONLY by a short scramble. Unfortunately, there is no way beyond to the rock platforms of Aros Bay.

To reach Stac a' Bhothain go round the point east of Loch Losait. The going is initially good, on level grass above the beach, but eventually degenerates into a boulder-hop along the shore. The 15m/50ft stack appears grassy and uninteresting at first, but the vertical cliff face on its far side is very impressive. The stack is connected to the shore by a high neck that yields a straightforward if vegetated and exposed scramble. Beyond the stack the beach stretches away to the headland of Biod nan Laogh (Calf Cliff), which bars further shoreline progress.

Route 45e: Greshornish Point (NG 341541) L23/E408, 4ml/6km, 3hrs

The small, stubby Greshornish peninsula between Waternish and Trotternish is remote and rarely visited. The trip out to Greshornish Point nevertheless makes a fine tramp along a wild coastal cliff top, with an interesting dun and a number of stacks and caves to be viewed *en route*.

The walk begins at Greshornish House hotel, reached by a minor road that leaves the A850 Portree-Dunvegan road at Upperglen. 100m beyond the hotel's entrance drive there is a sharp right-hand bend with parking spaces. Start here on the track that goes through the gate on the left. When it bears right to a clump of trees and forks, take the left branch. This becomes a path across the neck of the peninsula to its west coast, which is reached at Loch Diubaig, an inner bay of Loch Snizort that separates Greshornish from Waternish. Across the loch the map marks a natural arch but it is indistinguishable by eye, and the long walk around the head of the loch to attempt to view it from the dangerous slopes above is unrewarding.

From the bay follow good sheep paths along the west-coast cliff top towards Greshornish Point. In the next bay are a number of caves and a 15m/50ft finger of basalt, and in the bay beyond that stands a broader, grass-topped stack. The cliffs gradually increase in height and force the coast walker up to the high point of the peninsula at 98m/322ft, from where there are fine views in all directions. Beyond here the cliffs diminish in height towards Greshornish Point, where small crags fringe an area of lush green moss.

Turning southwards, the return to Greshornish House follows the east coast of the peninsula along the shores of Loch Greshornish, a finger-like inner loch of Loch Snizort. The loch is a long way from the open sea, yet there have been stories of icebergs and walruses here, and it is recorded that in one summer long ago it was so full of sharks that no-one dared bathe in it. Another curious incident occurred in the First World War when the loch was bombed by a plane that suspected a U-boat of lurking in its depths. This must have been a truly surreal sight.

The first feature of interest reached on the return trip is ruined Dun na h'Airde (Dun of the Point), which occupies a fine position on a rock promontory surrounded on three sides by 15m/50ft sea cliffs. Surprisingly this is marked on L23 but not the larger-scale E408. AT LOW TIDE ONLY it is possible to clamber along the shoreline beneath the dun, where water-worn holes in the rock give some indication of the power of the sea.

The remainder of the east coast is mainly flat, and good going above the beach soon leads back to Greshornish House. On reaching the grounds at Greshornish a wall runs down to the shore. Follow it up right to a gate on a track that leads back to your starting point.

ROUTE 46: SHORT WALKS, TROTTERNISH EAST

Trotternish is the largest and most northerly of the peninsulas of Skye. The mountainous ridge that runs along its spine and reaches its highest point at the Storr (719m/2358ft) is described in Routes 27-31. The A855 coast road completely encircles the peninsula (46m/75 km round trip from Portree) to give easy access to both the mountains and the coast.

On the coast are to be found mile after mile of stacks, caves, natural arches, waterfalls and other coastal features which cannot be seen from the road but which provide endless opportunities for rewarding short walks. The eight routes described here along the east coast of the peninsula are listed in an anti-clockwise direction, travelling north. All lie north of Portree except the first, which, although it lies outside Trotternish, is included here because of its proximity.

Route 46a: The Braes (NG 526349) L32/E409 or E410, 1½+hrs

The Braes north of Loch Sligachan are more renowned for their historical associations than their walking potential, for it was here on 17 April 1882 that the Battle of the Braes was fought between local crofters and an imported police force. The Braes crofters had reached the end of their tether when summonsed for grazing on land that had been taken away from them and, when the local constabulary arrived with 48 extra policemen from Glasgow to arrest the ringleaders, a running fight broke out, truncheons versus sticks and stones. The police were beaten back to Portree. Widespread newspaper coverage highlighted the grievances of Scotland's crofters and led indirectly to the Napier Commission of 1883 (see History).

Nothing could be further removed from those hectic scenes of yesteryear than the tranquil Braes of today, isolated from the summer bustle of modern Skye by the B883 road from Portree and a path from Sligachan. Few walkers come this way, for neither the map nor the view from the roadside give any indication of the coastal playground to be found on the seaward side of the small wing-shaped peninsula of An Aird that juts out into the Narrows of Raasay opposite the Braes. Here you will find in one short, exciting, cliff-fringed stretch of coastline one of the most tantalising collections of secret caves, pinnacles and strange coastal formations on Skye.

To find the start of the path to An Aird, take the minor road signposted Gedintailor from the B883 and park on the roadside verge opposite the peninsula, just beyond a passing place with a red post box in it. From the post box a renovated path crosses the moor and descends to the beach. Follow the beach across the neck of the peninsula and walk round to the ruined dun at its

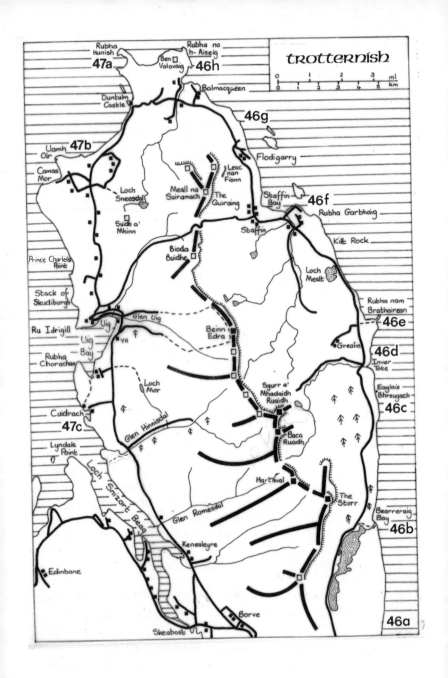

TROTTERNISH

Rubha Hunish **47a**
Ben Volovaig
Rubha na h-Aiseig **46h**
Duntulm Castle
Balmacqueen
46g
Uamh Oir **47b**
Camas Mor
Flodigarry
Loch Sneasdal
Meall na Suiramach
Leac nan Fionn
The Quiraing
Staffin Bay **46f**
Rubha Garbhaig
Suidh a' Mhinn
Staffin
Prince Charles's Point
Bioda Buidhe
Kilt Rock
Stack of Skudiburgh
Loch Mealt
Ru Idrigill
Uig
Glen Uig
Rubha nam Brathairean **46e**
Uig Bay
YH
Beinn Edra
Grealin **46d**
Rubha Chorachan
Loch Mor
Inver Tote
Sgurr a' Mhadaidh Ruaidh
Eaglais Bhreugach **46c**
Cuidrach **47c**
Glen Hinnisdal
Baca Ruadh
Lyndale Point
Hartaval
The Storr
Glen Romesdal
Bearreraig Bay **46b**
Loch Snizort Beag
Kensaleyre
Edinbane
Borve
Skeabost
46a

northern point. There is often sunshine here when the Red Hills and the Cuillin are in cloud, and the view of them across Loch Sligachan can be dramatic. The main area of interest lies south along the cliff top, beyond the cove formed by the dog-leg in the coastline.

The first feature reached is a cave that can be explored **AT LOW TIDE ONLY**. The entrance is a 30m/100ft long canyon whose 10m/30ft high walls are a trap when the tide comes in. Access is from the shore, which at low tide can be reached via a small bay just beyond the cave. Also of interest in this bay is a stack left high and dry on the beach.

In the next bay is a similar but even larger cave whose entrance canyon can be reached by a scramble down a gully on the far side. The back of the cave splits into three or four arched caverns, in the deepest of which it is possible to stand upright some 20m/65ft from the cave entrance.

Beyond the far bounding wall of the cave's entrance canyon is a deep hole into which the sea flows through a natural arch. Just beyond here is the most remarkable formation of all – a 3m/10ft long, eroded concertina of rock that stretches across a canyon like a fragile bridge. Please help its preservation (and yours!) by not attempting to cross it.

Next comes a 3m/10ft tall gendarme that adorns the end of a short ridge. Brave souls can reach its table-top by a step across from the ridge and a mantelshelf manoeuvre. Beyond the gendarme the cliffs become smaller and provide bouldering problems galore.

Route 46b: Bearreraig Bay (NG 513524) L32/E408 or E409, 1+hrs

Bearreraig Bay, at the foot of the Storr, is the first place north of Portree where access to the shore is easy, and it is worth visiting for its waterfall, its fossils, its views of Holm Island and its unique approach route – a steep descent beside a pulley-operated railway to an electricity generating station 140m/450ft below.

Begin at the Storr Lochs Dam access road, which leaves the A855 *c.*6mls north of Portree at the north end of Loch Leathan beside a bus shelter. Park by the dam without causing an obstruction. Until recently the route down to the bay descended no fewer than 674 concrete steps beside the railway, but these are now considered dangerous. Instead, go through a gate right of the main building to find a path that descends to the shore. The path is steep and can be slippery when wet, but there's a handrail when it gets too close to the cliff edge.

Once on the curving beach, go left to view the waterfall below the dam, still impressive although diminished by the hydro-electric scheme, then go round the corner on the right to view the craggy lump of Holm Island. There are many fossils to be found in the shoreline rocks, including abundant ammonites, curled up like Catherine wheels. There have been other finds here as well. In 1891 a Norse treasure hoard was discovered, including silver bracelets and rings, and coins from as far away as Samarkand. By fording the Bearreraig River, the equally fossiliferous north shore of the bay can be explored.

In 2011 some of the fossils were hacked out of the rock and looted. Elsewhere on Skye fossilised dinosaur footprints have also been removed. Please behave responsibly and follow the Scottish Fossil Code (www.snh.gov.uk/docs/B572665.pdf).

Route 46c: Eaglais Bhreugach (NG 516605) L32/E408, 3hrs

The Eaglais Bhreugach (False Church) is an enormous shoreline boulder split by a churchlike archway. It is guarded by coastal cliffs on both sides, but **AT LOW TIDE ONLY** can be reached by a walk along the shoreline. At high tide the initial section is impassable and there is no alternative way back.

The route begins at the car park above the bay of Inver Tote, c.13mls north of Portree. Walk back across the bridge over the Lealt River and, after c.50m, take a gated track on the left for another c.50m to a junction. Go left here for c.25m to a large rectangular rock, then turn right on the near side of a fence to follow the edge of the trees that line the gorge of the Lealt River. Eventually you'll find a path that descends past the impressive lower Lealt waterfall to the shore.

To view the Eaglais Bhreugach from above, leave the path to follow the cliff top right to Dun Grianan, whose few remaining stones perch airily at the cliff edge. To visit the rock, follow the path down to the shore and go right beneath Dun Grianan, with mainly good going on rock pavement and large boulders.

The Eaglais stands in a shallow bay c.1ml/1½km along the beach. It is 12m/40ft high and has a circumference of about 36m/120ft. Holing its centre is the huge arch that gives it its name, although according to tradition there is more to the name than mere appearance, for there are tales of pagan rites here, involving the roasting of cats.

Beside the main arch is another smaller passageway, still large enough to walk through, and on the beach nearby is an isolated pinnacle some 5m/16ft high whose name adds to the legends, for this is the Cubaid (Pulpit) of Satan. The scramble up the landward or seaward end of the Eaglais may tempt some, but the vegetated higher slopes are steep and dangerous.

It is worth continuing a short distance further along the beach to a 20m/65ft long sea cave whose near wall is holed by another large arch and whose entrance is guarded by deep ankle-grabbing seaweed. In some weathers a curtain of water falls across the entrance to give the place the air of a secret grotto, but beware the loose and waterlogged cliffs above, which are prone to rockfall. This cave marks the limit of shoreline progress. The natural arch further along, which is prominent during the walk to the Eaglais, cannot be reached. Return to Inver Tote while the tide is low.

Route 46d: Lealt Waterfall (NG 516605) L32/E408 or E409, ½hr

The Lealt River drops steeply between the roadside and the shore at Inver Tote to form some impressive waterfalls. The two-tiered upper fall is best viewed from the north bank of the river. Park in the car park as for Route 46c and simply follow the gravel path. Beyond waterfall viewpoints the path continues to a viewpoint overlooking the bay and the prominent chimney of old diatomite workings, where diatomite from Loch Cuithir was dried and shipped (see Route 28). A steep, rough, little path continues down the grassy hillside to the shore, but go down AT YOUR OWN RISK, as it is quite exposed and is dangerous in wet or windy conditions. From the shore it is possible to walk north along the beach, past an impressive needle-like pinnacle and Sgeir Dhubh skerry, to Rubha na Brathairean (see next route for details).

Route 46e: Rubha nam Brathairean (NG 516625) L32/E408, 2½hrs

Rubha nam Brathairean (Brothers' Point) is one of the most delightful spots on the Trotternish coastline, yet reaching it involves some unexpectedly exciting scrambling on a narrow arête and exposed paths. To reach the Rubha, park in the lay-by just north of the Glenview Hotel and Grealin turn-off. Take the track opposite the hotel through one or more gates and turn right on a signposted path that curves down to the bay below, where there are some ruined buildings and numerous creeks and small crags on which to scramble around.

A somewhat exposed path goes right above the crags and around the bay towards the point, which is guarded by a curious dun-like knoll that cannot be circumvented. Moreover, the ridge that leads out to the knoll narrows to a sharp arête and sports two gendarmes. The scramble over the gendarmes is moderate but exposed. Sheep paths contour below the crest for the less gymnastic. Care is required also on the scramble over the knoll to the green table-like pastures at the point beyond.

The knoll is said to be the site of an Iron Age fort named Dun Hasan. In later times the promontory may have been settled by early Christians, hence its name. Alternatively, according to tradition, the name derives from its occupation by Donald Mac Dubh Ruaraidh and his brothers. The brothers survived by remaining neutral in the many disputes between the MacLeods and the MacDonalds until they could see the likely outcome, when they would join the winning side in order to obtain any booty that was going. On the shore below the knoll is the Preas Dhomhnuill Dhuibh, a deep opening where the booty was stored (*preas* means cupboard).

From the landward side of the two gendarmes an exposed path cuts diagonally down the cliff face to the shore, from where it is possible to walk out along flat shoreline rocks to Sgeir Dhubh (Black Skerry) at the next point. Sgeir Dhubh has a tragic history that testifies to the dangers of the Trotternish coastline. In 1812 sixteen people were killed here when a boat from Portree struck the rocks in darkness; winds drove the boat to Gairloch, and only one body was ever recovered. The cliff face south of Sgeir Dubh boasts a slender pinnacle some 50m/160ft high, behind which the Old Man of Storr forms a perfect backdrop. As noted above, it is possible to walk along the beach past the needle all the way to Inver Tote.

Route 46f: Staffin Slipway (NG 494681) L32/E408, 1+hrs

By the roadside north of Rubha nam Brathairean is Kilt Rock, a 60m/200ft waterfall that is worth a look if you can find somewhere to park among the tour coaches. North of here the sea cliffs diminish in size towards the wide sandy shores of Staffin Bay, which looks magnificent when the north wind fuels the crashing waves. On the south side of the bay a minor road from Stenscholl cuts around the foot of the cliffs to Staffin Slipway, where there are a number of features of interest.

At the headlands of An Corran and Rubha Garbhaig there are some small shoreline crags, while on the landward side of the road an easily accessible cliff face provides good sport for rock climbers. At low tide at An Corran it is sometimes possible to see fossilised dinosaur footprints in the mudstone right of the large boulders. The dinosaur may have been the 10m-long Megalosaurus that lived here 165 million years ago. To see more dinosaur fossils, visit Staffin Museum at Ellishadder near Kilt Rock (borve.net/staffin-museum.co.uk, tel 01470-562321).

Above the slipway a grass track, paved with rocks, meanders up through a break in the cliffs. This is the Cabhsair (Causeway), constructed in 1846 to provide work during the potato famine. It climbs onto the moor, where there is a collapsed chambered cairn, and continues as a path to Staffin.

The most fascinating place to explore is a giant crazy pavement south of the slipway, reached by walking across the flat marshy ground above the shore. The pavement is littered with huge boulders that have rolled down from the cliffs above, and in places the going is labyrinthine. A scramble around the boulders along the pavement edge above 5m/16ft sea cliffs involves some interesting moves. Some of the cracks in the pavement are considerable, and it takes nerve to reach all the small promontories that jut out into the sea.

Route 46g: The North-east Stacks (NG 450737) L32/E408, 1+hrs

A few miles north of Staffin Slipway, between Creag na h-Eiginn and Port Gobhlaig, the coastline bristles with amazing sea stacks. The cliff top is easily reached by a short track that leaves the A855 at a high point beside an old building. The going along the cliff top in either direction is good and the views are exciting. **WARNING**. The cliff edge is dangerous and requires extreme care. Avoid when windy.

Southwards, the cliff top should be followed at least as far as the bay before Galta Mor (Big Pig), where there is some fine basalt piping. Beyond here the going remains easy as far as Steall a' Ghreip (Waterfall of the Precipice), but neither the waterfall nor the cave marked on the map can be seen from the cliff top.

Northwards, the first features of interest reached are the outstanding twin stacks of Stacan Gobhlach (Forked Stacks), which are linked to the shore by a double line of great flat rocks like giant stepping stones. Around the next headland stands the great needle of Stac Buidhe (Yellow Stack), with a precariously balanced boulder at its summit. Continuing along the cliff top, a small inlet hides a fine 20m/65ft stack whose summit is only about 6m/20ft from the cliff top and seems almost close enough to jump onto (the author disclaims all responsibility for failed attempts!). Beyond here the cliffs peter out into the rocky bay of Port Gobhlaig.

Route 46h: Stac Lachlainn (NG 436751) L32/E408, 1½+hrs

After the North-east Stacks the flat moor of Rubha na h-Aiseig at the extreme north-east tip of Skye comes as something of a disappointment. This remote, desolate and featureless spot will be appreciated only by seekers of solitude and lovers of wild wave-lapped shores. Others may be content with a visit to sturdy Stac Lachlainn (Lachlan's Stack) just north of Port Gobhlaig.

Take the minor road that leaves the A855 just beyond the Connista turn-off, signposted Aird. At the head of the bay at Port Gobhlaig is a car park with a picnic table. From here follow grass slopes above the shoreline to reach the stack. Just before it there's a deep enclosed pool formed by a natural bridge through which the sea enters. On the stack's seaward side is a natural arch that can only be seen from further along the coast.

ROUTE 47: SHORT WALKS, TROTTERNISH WEST

The short walks described here are found on the west cast of the Trotternish peninsula. They follow on from the east coast routes described in Route 46 and are described in an anti-clockwise (north-to-south) direction.

Route 47a: Rubha Hunish (NG 423743) L23/E408, 3+hrs

Rubha Hunish (Bear Point), the most northerly point on Skye, is a long, grassy, crag-fringed headland, lonely and breezy, fringed by beautiful stacks and almost completely cut off from the rest of the island by the 100m/330ft cliffs of the appropriately named Meall Tuath (117m/383ft, North Hill). The walk to it appears in some tourist guidebooks, but it is hardly a straightforward route and the most interesting parts are certainly not attainable by the average tourist.

There are two ways to reach the Point and they are best combined into a round trip. Go prepared for boggy going and you won't be frustrated by the moorland terrain. The outward route begins at a car park 100m up the road to Shulista at the northernmost point of the A855 coast road. The signposted 1½ml/2½km path begins just beyond. It has been partly renovated but at the time of writing remains mostly a boggy morass. Persevere.

Approaching Meall Tuath, branch right at a fork to the old coastguard lookout station at the summit, now a small bothy that makes a welcome shelter on a stormy day. As you might expect, there's a fine view from here across Rubha Hunish to the Shiant Islands and Lewis, with the curiously shaped islet of Lord MacDonald's Table further left.

The cliffs of Meall Tuath fringe the coastline eastwards towards Rubha na h-Aiseig and westwards towards Rubha Voreven. There is no shoreline access from the east, and from Rubha Voreven chaotic rockfalls make shoreline access from the west awkward, especially at high tide. The only easy access to Rubha Hunish is from the dip between the summit of Meall Tuath and its south-west top. From the far (south-west) side of this dip a rocky path disappears behind a large, conspicuous boulder and zigzags down to the shore. The descent is not technically difficult but it is scrambly, exposed and not for the nervous.

If you do make it down, the most interesting features of the headland lie hidden on its north-east side, where there are some fine sea cliffs, stacks and deep creeks to explore. Near the neck of the peninsula is a fine blade-shaped stack, and further out towards the point stands magnificent Bodha Hunish (Bear Reef), a 30m/100ft stack that is one of the most perfectly proportioned on Skye.

Back at the dip between Meall Tuath's summit and south-west top, the return trip to the roadside begins on a marshy path that curves over the south-west top and down to Tulm Bay on the far side. It continues along the grass above the beach, heading for Duntulm Castle and Duntulm Castle Hotel at the south end of the bay. When you reach a wall on approach to the hotel, go left to reach a track that takes you back to the coast road c.800m from your starting point.

The ghostly ruins of Duntulm Castle, situated on a craggy headland overlooking the Little Minch, are all that remain of a once grand building that was the chief residence of the MacDonalds from the sixteenth to the early eighteenth centuries. The castle was dismantled (and on one occasion blown up with gunpowder) in order that its stones could be reused, and the remaining fragments of wall give scant indication of its former size and magnificence. This forlorn place has witnessed many scenes of glory and tragedy, revelry and bloodshed. It echoes with the ghosts of the past and is worth the short walk from the nearby car park.

On the rocky shore of Port Duntulm below, reached by a path from the castle, is a long groove said to have been made by the keels of MacDonald galleys. Beside the ruins is a memorial to the MacArthurs (hereditary pipers to the MacDonalds), with an inscription whose poignancy is enhanced by the surrounding ruins: Thig crioch air an t-Saoghal, Ach mairidh gaol is ceol (The World will end, But love and music endureth).

Route 47b: Uamh Oir and Vicinity (NG 378717) L23/E408, 3+hrs

West of Duntulm the low-lying shores of the broad bay of Lub Score are more suitable for roadside picnics than coast walks. At the end of the bay stands the headland of Ru Bornesketaig, which according to tradition was the scene of yet another dispute between the MacLeods and MacDonalds. Both clans claimed ownership of the land, and to avoid bloodshed it was agreed that the dispute be settled by a race between their best war galleys, whosoever's hand touched land first being deemed the winner. When the race got underway the MacLeods gained the advantage, but a MacDonald cut off his hand with his dagger and threw it ashore, thus becoming the first to touch land.

There are several caves in the vicinity of Ru Bornesketaig, some of which were used by smugglers in former times. One in particular, the magnificent Uamh Oir, is the closest Skye comes to having a cave to rival the wonders of Fingal's Cave on Staffa. The cave's name (meaning Cave of Gold) derives from its legendary use for the secretion of valuables in times of trouble.

The shortest approach to the cave is from the end of the more westerly of the two roads in Bornesketaig (NG 376715), but the local community would prefer visitors to approach from the end of the more easterly road (NG 378717). From the car park at the road-end follow the north coast cliffs westwards around the headland of Ru Bornesketaig, or take a short cut left of the highpoint, to reach the west-facing coast. If you stick to the cliff top you'll pass a magnificent needle stack and natural arch.

Your objective is a break in the cliffs left (south) of the highpoint and a cliff-top dun (completely dismantled). This spot is recognisable by an old fence post sticking out of a boulder. Descend steep, grassy slopes from here to the shore (take care when wet). Uamh Oir lies just around the corner on the right, its hexagonal basalt columns forming a perfect rectangular entrance to the deep-water channel beyond. Beside the entrance is a crazy basalt pavement reminiscent of the Giant's Causeway in Northern Ireland. It is not possible to enter the cave nor cross to the far side of the entrance. In the opposite direction from the cave, back along the shore towards Camas Mor, it is possible to walk some distance along a fine rock pavement at the cliff foot well above the waterline, but there is no through route.

While in the vicinity of Bornesketaig, the 17m long souterrain at Kilvaxter (NG 389696) is worth a visit if you can duck-walk with a torch along the low passage. Also just up the road is the grave and monument of Flora MacDonald (NG 399719) and the Museum of Highland Life (NG 395718; www.skyemuseum.co.uk), with its reconstruction of a township of blackhouses (traditional thatched cottages).

Route 47c: Hugh's Castle and Vicinity (NG 380591) L23/E408, 1+hrs

South of Uamh Oir the low-lying shores of Loch Snizort are flat and uninteresting, given over to farmland. The main feature of historical interest here is Prince Charles's Point (NG 374667), where the Bonnie Prince and Flora MacDonald landed in 1746.

South of here the coastline is indented by Uig Bay, whose two headlands – Ru Idrigill to the north and Ru Choracahan to the south – both make good viewpoints. Ru Idrigill is reached by a path from the hairpin bend north of Uig (NG 383640). The walk can be extended north for close-up views of Stack Skudiburgh, an inaccessible 15m/50ft rock finger on the shore below. Ru Choracahan is reached from the crossroads in Earlish (NG 385612) via secluded Camas Beag (Little Bay) and its waterfall.

East of Uig Bay, Glen Uig penetrates deep onto the moors and is worth a detour to view its curious landscape of 'fairy hills', like giant anthills, in the midst of which the fortress-like rock of Castle Ewen towers over a picturesque roadside lochan. The glen is marketed to tourists as the 'Fairy Glen', but the cone-shaped hillocks, rather than being supernatural real estate, are the result of landslide and glaciation.

From the road end, adventurous walkers can climb Beinn Edra, Skye's most northerly 600m/2000ft hill (see also Route 31). A cart track continues for some way, then it is necessary to cross the Abhainn Dhubh and follow a stone-and-turf dyke up to the skyline south of the summit (6ml/10 km, 500m/1650ft return).

South of Uig Bay stands a most unusual historical edifice that is well worth the short walk to it. Hugh's Castle (Caisteal Uisdein on maps) was built by Hugh MacDonald in the early seventeenth century. It was a curious construction in that it contained no door, entry being by some kind of retractable wooden structure (i.e. a glorified ladder). Even today reaching the inside of the ruins is problematical.

The walk to the castle begins in Cuidrach to the north. The minor road through Cuidrach runs from the coast road south of Uig to the sheltered bay of Poll na h-Ealaidh. When the road forks at the bay, take the left-branching track (signposted South Cuidreach) to another fork and to parking spaces just along the left branch. If access changes, you may have to park before this point. The track continues and becomes a path to a highpoint on the moor. The castle crowns some sea cliffs just beyond.

The castle ruins form a sturdy rectangular enclosure some 16m/52ft long by 10m/32ft wide, with walls up to 5m/16ft high and 3m/10ft thick. The easiest way in is through a narrow chest-high window aperture on the landward side, through which it is possible to squeeze sideways. Inside are only nettles and fallen stones.

Hugh built the castle as part of his plot to attain the leadership of the clan, then held by his uncle, Donald Gorm. He planned to invite Donald Gorm to his castle and then murder him. Unfortunately for Hugh, the invitation was inadvertently sent to an accomplice and the details of the plan to Donald Gorm. His end, in Duntulm dungeons, was a terrible one, given salt beef to encourage his thirst and then walled up to die in agony. The details are gruesome.

South of Hugh's Castle, the most southerly section of the west coast of Trotternish follows the low-lying shoreline of Loch Snizort Beag. The main interest here is again historical. Of note is the best-preserved standing stone on Skye – Clach Ard, which stands beside the road at Peinmore (NG 421491). It is much weathered but it is still possible to make out the mysterious Pictish symbols: a 'V' rod at the top and double circles crossed by a 'Z' rod beneath. At Borve (NG 452480) there are five standing stones beside the road in the shape of a cross, and in a field near Eyre (NG 414525), accessible by a gate in a fence, are two more prominent stones.

RAASAY INTRODUCTION

General Description

The picturesque island of Raasay lies only a couple of miles off the east coast of Skye across the Sound of Raasay. With an area of 60 sq. ml (155 sq. km) and a size of 14ml/22km long by 3ml/5km wide it packs a wealth of geographical and historical features into a relatively small space.

Geologically, apart from a lack of gabbro, the same rocks are found here as on Skye. The south is mainly sandstone and shale, the north gneiss and granite. The south is green and gentle, the north rocky and barren. Unlike on Skye, the high ground is in the middle of the island, sloping down on all sides.

The island's early history closely follows Skye's too, with evidence of equally early occupation. The visitor can explore Dun Borodale above Inverarish and souterrains at Suisnish and near Raasay House. The Vikings left their mark on the island in the form of numerous place-names, including the name of the island itself (meaning Isle of Roe Deer).

In clan times the MacLeods ruled the roost, building Brochel Castle in the north-east before moving to Raasay House in the south. More than a hundred clansmen fought at the disastrous battle at Culloden in 1746, following which Bonnie Prince Charlie hid for a while on the island and government troops searching for him committed many atrocities, including the burning of Raasay House. By 1773, however, the island was peaceful enough again for Johnson and Boswell to visit and have a good time in a rebuilt Raasay House.

The population reached a peak of c.900 in the early nineteenth century but declined following the hardships that resulted in the Highland Clearances. The bankrupt chief sold the island in 1843 and emigrated to Australia. The villages of Hallaig (Route 48) and Screapadal (Route 49) were abandoned at this time.

Ownership of the island changed many times until it was finally bought by the government in 1979 and Raasay House was turned into an outdoor centre. As on Skye, there are an increasing number of holiday homes and tourism is one of the most important areas of employment.

The highest point on Raasay is Dun Caan. Although only 443m/1453ft high its distinctive castellated summit dominates the island (Route 48). Elsewhere, the craggy east coast gives a walk as wild as they come (Route 49), while a trip to the rocky northern reaches has an almost Aegean ambience (Route 50).

Visitor Information

The ferry to Raasay is operated by Caledonian MacBrayne and runs from Sconser, 2ml/3km east of Sligachan on the A87 at the southern mouth of Loch Sligachan

(NG 525323). It carries up to twelve cars and runs all year round. There are several ferries daily from Monday to Saturday and two on Sunday, making day trips possible (crossing time 25 minutes). Until 2010 the ferry arrived at Suisnish near the southern tip of the island but it now arrives at a new terminal in Churchtown Bay a couple of miles further north. Further information from Caledonian MacBrayne: www.calmac.co.uk (tel: 0800-066-5000).

Route 48 (Dun Caan) can be undertaken as a day trip between ferries without transport, but a car or bicycle is required for Route 49 (Raasay East Coast) and Route 50 (Raasay North End). Maps L24 and E409 cover all routes.

With a population of c.200 there are few visitor facilities. The only sizable village on the island is Inverarish, which has one shop/post office: Raasay Stores. A leaflet on island walks and forest trails is obtainable there. Further information: www.raasay.com/rstores.html (tel: 01478-660203).

There are no public services on Sundays or public transport except the ferry, only allowed to run on a Sunday since 2004. There are no petrol stations.

Hotels: Borodale House (formerly Isle of Raasay Hotel, www.isleofraasayhotel. co.uk, tel: 01478-660222). At the time of writing Raasay Outdoor Centre is being rebuilt following a fire in 2009. Up-top-date information: www.raasay-house.co.uk (tel: 01478-660266).

There are also holiday cottages, B&Bs and an SHYA Youth Hostel (www. syha.org.uk or tel direct: 01478-660240). There is no campsite.

Access considerations are as for Skye (see p.15). Deer stalking is unlikely to interfere with walking activities but take note of any roadside notices. Further information: Raasay Crofters Association (www.raasay.com/rcrofter.html).

For up-to-date visitor information consult www.raasay.com.

RONA

Rona is a small island, 10ml/16km long by a mile wide, that stretches to the north of Raasay across the half-mile narrows of the Kyle of Rona. It was evacuated in the 1920s, but a permanent settlement (Rona Lodge) was re-established in 1993 and visitors are now welcome again. Expect no traffic, no shops and as much peace as you can handle.

Climb the highest point, Meall Acairsaid (126m/414ft), explore bays and sea-cliffs and visit landmarks such as Church Cave, the grave of the Viking princess and the ruins of a fourteenth century chapel.

Accommodation: cottages, B&B, bothy, camping. Boats cross from Portree and Raasay in the summer season. For details on facilities and access contact Rona Lodge (www.isleofrona.com, tel: 07831-293963) or enquire on Skye at Portree Tourist Information Office and on Raasay at Borodale House Hotel.

ROUTE START: Raasay ferry terminal (NG 545362, L24 or L32/ E409)

ROUTE LOG: return by outward route: 9ml/14km, 460m/1600ft, 6hrs; round trip via Hallaig and Eyre Point: 12½ml/20km, 560m/1850ft, 8hrs

ROUTE OVERVIEW: return or circular hill walk. A spacious walk leads to scenic summit of Raasay's highest hill, whose lowly height belies its rugged stature.

	1	2	3	4	5
Grade	■				
Terrain	■	■			
Navigation	■				
Seriousness	■				

Dun Caan is an exceptional little hill that has the character and prominence of a much higher mountain. Its castellated summit rises above an array of picturesque lochans that nestle at various levels on the hillside as though constructed by a landscape artist. The walk to the summit can be completed on foot in a day between ferries from Skye.

From the ferry terminal follow the road through Inverarish in the direction of North Fearns to a car park beside an old iron ore mine (NG 555343), which operated from 1912 to 1919 with the help of First World War prisoners-of-war. Take the forest track signposted Burma Road for *c*.600m, until shortly after it crosses the Inverarish Burn, then bear right on a path signposted Dun Caan.

The path climbs steeply beside the stream to the upper forest fence, then continues up onto the moor. It has some boggy and indistinct sections but remains easy enough to follow. Eventually it reaches a line of cliffs overlooking Loch na Mna at the foot of Dun Caan's upper slopes, where it forks. Branches go left along the top of the cliffs and right beneath them by the shoreline, to meet up again at the far end of the loch. The high path gives better views and better going on rock pavement.

At the end of the cliffs the high path joins another path that comes up from the road to the north-west. Here you'll find a curious little

Renowned native poet Sorley MacLean (1911–96) wrote a haunting elegy on the cleared village of Hallaig, in which he pictured the deserted village populated again by the ghosts of the past, 'their laughter a mist in my ears, and their beauty a film on my heart'. On the return coastal route described you'll pass a poignant memorial cairn on which the poem is displayed in both Gaelic and English.

View a film of Hallaig, with a soundtrack of MacLean reading his poem in the original Gaelic, at www. sorleymaclean.org/video/hallaig.wmv.

lochan that has no outlet and is preserved only by a minor swell in the surrounding land. In a dip below it lies the larger Loch na Meilich. The path passes the head of Loch na Meilich before zigzagging 130m/400ft up a final steep grass slope to reach Dun Caan's craggy summit with its enormous all-round view.

A return via the old township of Hallaig on the deserted east coast is recommended if time allows and you don't mind some off-path terrain. Retrace steps to Loch na Mna then follow a moorland terrace between the loch and a band of cliffs to its left (east). When the cliffs give out, descend easily to the lush pastures and forlorn ruins of Hallaig.

The path out of Hallaig is difficult to distinguish at first among sheep paths. After descending slightly to cross the Hallaig Burn, look for it around the 100m contour, about level with the cliff foot of Beinn na Leac ahead. It contours along a shelf through natural woodland and rounds the foot of Beinn na Leac below a huge rock pillar, passing a memorial cairn displaying Sorley MacLean's poem 'Hallaig'. The path eventually becomes a fine grassy track that leads to the road at North Fearns.

If time allows you can continue around the coast to the lighthouse at Eyre Point and the coast road back to Inverarish. At the second house in North Fearns a path leads down to the shore. Walk along the pebble beach or take a small path through the woods above it.

> We mounted up to the top of Duncaan, where we sat down, ate cold mutton and bread and cheese and drank brandy and punch. Then we had a Highland song... then we danced a reel.'
>
> James Boswell describing his famous jig on Dun Caan in 1773 during his tour of the Hebrides with Samuel Johnson.

ROUTE 49: RAASAY EAST COAST

ROUTE START: North Fearns (NG 593360, L24/E409); end point near Brochel Castle (NG 578461)

ROUTE LOG: 7ml/11km, undulating, 5hrs

ROUTE OVERVIEW: one-way coast walk. A 'walk on the wild side' of Raasay follows an adventurous old path along the island's remote eastern shoreline. The route involves no scrambling but is graded 3 to reflect its challenging nature.

	1	2	3	4	5
Grade					
Terrain					
Navigation					
Seriousness					

To avoid the logistical problems posed by a one-way walk, the route can be split and undertaken as two return walks from each end to a mid-point such as the cave-like recess (NG 586411). Alternatively the northern reaches of the route beyond Screapadal make an easy return walk from the roadside at Brochel.

There are few wilder places to coast-walk in the British Isles than the craggy, rarely visited east coast of Raasay. There was once a surprisingly good shoreline path here, built for deer stalking in the nineteenth century, but these days the old path is best described as 'sporting' (although it may be improved in the future). Landslides have carried sections of it away, while elsewhere it is sometimes so overgrown that rucksacks snag on trees and make it necessary to take to the shore. If the thought of such exploits brings a smile to your face, one of the most adventurous shoreline routes in the country awaits its next challenger.

In the direction south to north, the route begins at the road end at North Fearns. The fine path from here to Hallaig is described in Route 48. Beyond Hallaig the path descends to the shoreline, continues along the edge of the beach and climbs again around a shoreline cliff to reach the mouth of the stream that drains Loch a' Chadha-charnaich. Alternatively you can stay high by the shores of the loch

The rock that forms the cliffs and boulders at Creag na Bruaich is a slimy sandstone, which was quarried at one time. Until exposed to air it was so soft that it could be cut with an axe. In stormy weather the sea pounds the coastline here mercilessly. On one occasion it was recorded that water was forced upwards out of a fissure with such force that a passing boat reported the discovery of a new volcano on Raasay.

and follow the stream down to the shoreline.

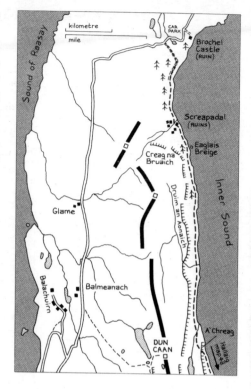

Continuing northwards, the line of cliffs that fringes the central east coast of Raasay gradually closes in. The going on the steep hillside beneath them becomes rougher, even forcing you down onto the rocky shoreline in one place. At the next point (NG 586411) there is a chaotic jumble of giant boulders and a stream crosses the path at the back of a deep cave-like recess. This marks the onset of the toughest part of the route.

Trees and thick vegetation crowd the steep hillside beneath Druim an Aonaich, forcing the path to weave a contorted route. Its precise line is dependent on the current state of landslides and fallen trees. When the going gets too tough it again takes to the shore. At the point beyond this section is another jumble of huge boulders and beyond here the path improves at last to provide wonderful coast walking.

On approach to Screapadal the fantastic rock pillars of Creag na Bruaich tower overhead. Huge boulders hiding deep fissures rest at all angles on the hillside. On the shoreline at the next point is the Eaglais Breige (False Church), an enormous boulder whose name derives from its vaulted shape.

The Eaglais Breige signals your arrival at the green fields of South and North Screapadal which, like Hallaig, are cleared townships whose forlorn ruins stand on a series of terraces that rise up the hillside. The path continues across the fields and becomes a forest track that runs parallel to the shoreline through a forestry plantation. The track turns sharp left at a hairpin bend and climbs to a car parking area on Raasay's 'main' road, around 600m from Brochel Castle car park.

ROUTE 50: RAASAY NORTH END

ROUTE START: Arnish (NG 594480, L24/E409)

ROUTE LOG: 10ml/16km + detours, undulating, 6hrs

ROUTE OVERVIEW: return moor and coast walk. A scenic walk on an historic path leads through complex, picturesque terrain to the remote northern tip of Raasay.

	1	2	3	4	5
Grade	■				
Terrain		■			
Navigation	■				
Seriousness	■				

> *Brochel Castle perches on a volcanic plug that gives it a commanding position on the main sea route between Kyle of Lochalsh and Lewis. Piracy was a popular pursuit. It was built by the MacLeods, probably in the fifteenth century, and was occupied until some time in the seventeenth, when the chief moved to Raasay House in the south of the island. The castle is now in a ruinous state but remains, in the words of John MacCulloch, 'a very whimsical and picturesque structure'.*

> *To help save his dwindling local community, Malcolm (Calum) MacLeod of Arnish built the 1¾ml stretch of road from Brochel to Arnish almost single-handedly in the 1960s and 1970s using little more than a pick-axe, a shovel and a wheelbarrow. It has become famous as Calum's Road. Previously, between 1949 and 1952, he also constructed the fine path that links Fladday to Torran.*

The rocky, indented coastline and emerald waters of north Raasay give the landscape the character of a Greek island, and the walk to the northern tip is a wonderful excursion, full of interest. From parking spaces at the end of Calum's Road, the route to the north tip of the island begins on a track that branches left to Torran. Follow the track down through birch woods and around the seashore of Loch Arnish to a fork behind old Torran schoolhouse (now a holiday home).

The left-hand branch here goes to Fladday and makes a possible return route. Take the right branch to climb out of the woods and around a cliff face to another junction. Calum told the author that the cliff was known as the Piper's Cliff because the outline of a piper can be discerned on the rock, but the author has yet to see it.

Again take the right branch at the junction. It climbs to a high point of 150m/500ft before undulating and winding along the knolly spine of the island to the old northern townships (marked as 'shielings' on the map).

Beyond Lochan nan Ghrunnd, in the vicinity of a shepherd's hut, the path becomes very boggy and indistinct for a while (although it may be improved in the future). Look northwards to see a raised section that marks its continuation. The path ends at a small cove on Raasay's north coast.

Beyond the cove lies the rocky little island of Eilean Tigh, which can be reached **AT LOW TIDE ONLY** by a slippery causeway a short distance to the left. The island consists entirely of one hill, which at 111m/365ft makes a good viewpoint over nearby Rona. To reach the very north

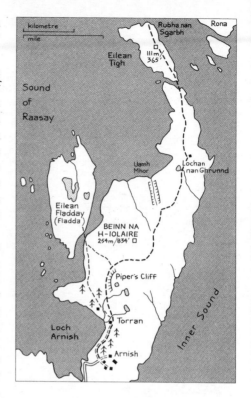

tip of Raasay, descend to Rubha nan Sgarbh on the far side. It's an unremarkable spot on the right of a small cove but it makes an adventurous and satisfying end to the route northwards.

On the return journey to Arnish, two interesting detours can be made. On the ascent beyond (south of) Lochan nan Ghrunnd, when the path turns sharp left up a boggy defile, a rough scramble down the defile on the right will take you down to shoreline cliffs and Uamh Mhor (Big Cave). This is a false cave formed by a huge boulder jammed into the top of a gully. Behind the boulder hangs another large needle-shaped rock, poised as though ready to prise the chockstone down onto your head.

The second (and easier) detour branches right at the junction at the Piper's Cliff to visit the tidal island of Fladday, again accessible **AT LOW TIDE ONLY**. From the near side of the slippery causeway to the island a fine path hewn out of a steep hillside goes southwards along the coast to rejoin the outward route at old Torran schoolhouse. When Fladday and the north of the island were inhabited, schoolchildren had to repeat the walk you have just done every day.

GLOSSARY/INDEX

Note: entries are indexed by route number, not page.

A' Chorra-bheinn, A Chorra Ven, The Mountain of the Corrie 31

A' Chreag, A Chraik, The Crag 49

Abhainn nan Leac, Avin nan *Lyechk*, River of Slabs 14, 22

Allt a' Chaoich, Owlt a *Cheu*-ich, the Mad Burn (named after its appearance in spate) 18a

Allt a' Mhuillin, Owlt a Voolin, Mill Stream 9

Allt Aigeann, Owlt *Aik*en, Stream of the Abyss 22

Allt an Fhraoich, Owlt an *Hreu*-ich, Heather Stream 18a

Allt an Inbhire, Owlt an *Iny*irra, Stream of the Rivermouth 32

Allt Daraich, Owlt *Darr*ich, Stream of Oak Timber 20

Allt Dearg Mor (Beag), Owlt Jerrak Moar (Bake), Big (Little) Red Stream 1, 3, 18b

Allt Mor, Owlt Moar, Big Stream 35

Allt Mor an Fhionn Choire, Owlt Moar an Hyoon Chorra, Big Stream of the Fair Corrie 4

Allt na Dunaiche, Owlt na *Doon*ich-ya, Burn of Sorrow 13

Allt na Garbhlain, Owlt na *Garra*vlin 33

Allt na Measarroch, Owlt na Mess-arroch, Stream of Temperance 21

Allt na Pairte, *Parsh*-tya, Stream of the Part 32

Allt nan Leac, Owlt nan Lyachk, Stream of the Flat Stones 32, 33

Am Basteir, Am *Bash*-tyir, traditionally translated as The Executioner, but the name may be fanciful based on the resemblance of the Basteir Tooth to an axe-head; the Gaelic word Bas means Death 3

Am Famhair, Am *Fah*vir, The Giant 41

Am Fraoch-choire, Am Freuch Chorra, The Heather Corrie 15, 21

Am Mam, The Moor 14

An Aird, An Arj, The Point 46a

An Caisteal, An *Cash*-tyal, The Castle 5

An Camastac, from Gaelic Camas Stac, The Stack of the Bay 42

An Corran, The Sickle (from its shape) 46f

An Cruachan, An *Croo*-achan, The Little Mound 35

An Diallaid, An *Jee*-alitch, The Saddle 7

An Dorus, An *Dorr*us, The Door 7

An Dubh Sgeir, An Doo Skerr, The Black Skerry 39

An Garbh-choire, An Garrav Corra, The Rough Corrie 19c

An Glas-choire, An Glass Chorra, The Grey Corrie 2

An Leac, An Lyechk, The Slab 34

An Sgurran, An *Skoor*an, The Rocks 25

An Stac, An Stachk, The Stack 9 (Inaccessible Pinnacle), 40 (Moonen Bay)

An t-Aigeach, An Tag-yach, The Stallion 45a

Ard Beag, Ard Bake, Little Height 38

Ardmore Point 45c

Ardtreck Point 44a

Baca Ruadh, *Bach*ka *Roo*-a, Red Bank 28, 31

Bad Step, The 16, 17

Basteir Tooth, The 3, 4

Bealach a' Bhasteir, *Byala*ch a *Vash*-tyir, Pass of the Executioner 3

Bealach a' Chuirn, *Byala*ch a Hoorn, Pass of the Rocky Heap 31

Bealach a' Garbh-choire, *Byala*ch a *Garra*v Corra, Pass of the Rough Corrie 11, 19c

Bealach a' Mhaim, *Byala*ch a *Va*-im, Pass of the Moor 4, 18b

Bealach Beag, *Byala*ch Bake, Little Pass 31

Bealach Coir' a' Ghrunnda, *Byala*ch Corra Ghrunnda, Pass of the Floored Corrie 10, 11

Bealach Coir' a' Tairneilear, *Byala*ch Coira *Tarny*ela, Pass of the Corrie of the Thunderer 5

Bealach Coir' an Lochan, *Byala*ch Corran Lochan, Pass of the Corrie of the Lochan 11, 19b

Bealach Coire Lagan, *Byala*ch Corra *Lah*kan, Pass of the Corrie of the Hollow 9

Bealach Coire na Banachdich, *Byala*ch Corra na Banach-ich, Pass of the Smallpox Corrie 8, 19a

Bealach Coire Sgreamhach, *Byala*ch Corra *Scree*-avach, Pass of the Loathsome Corrie 23

Bealach Mor, *Byala*ch Moar, Big Pass 31

Bealach Mosgaraidh, *Byala*ch *Moska*rry, Pass of the Dry-rot Shieling 20

Bealach na Beiste, *Byala*ch na *Baish*-tcha, Pass of the Beast 22

Bealach na Croiche, *Byala*ch na *Croich*-ya, Pass of the Cross 36

Bealach na Glaic Moire, *Byala*ch na Glachk

Moara, Pass of the Big Defile 5, 6, 18b

Bealach na h-Airigh Mhurain, *Byala*ch na Harry
Voorin, Pass of the Bent-grass Shieling 35

Bealach na Sgairde, *Byala*ch na *Skarr*-stcha,
Pass of the Scree 20

Bealach nam Mulachag, Pass of the Hilly Place
24

Bealach nan Lice, *Byala*ch nan *Leeka*, Pass of
the Slabs 4

Bealach Ollasgairte, *Byala*ch Olla*skarr*-stcha,
poss. from Gaelic for Wool and Scree 31

Bealach Udal, *Byala*ch Udal, poss. Gloomy
Pass 24

Bealach Uige, *Byala*ch *Oo*-iga, Pass of Uig 31

Bearreraig Bay 46b

Beinn a' Mheadhoin, Ben a *Vay*-an, Middle
Mountain 32

Beinn a' Ghobhainn, Ben a *Gho*-in, Mountain
of the Blacksmith 42

Beinn an Dubhaich (Cave), Ben an *Doo*-ich,
Mountain of Darkness 33

Beinn an Eoin, Ben an *Yai*-awn, Mountain of
the Bird 35

Beinn Bheag, Ben Vake, Little Mountain 24

Beinn Bhreac, Ben *Vrai*-achk, Speckled
Mountain 36

Beinn Bhuidhe, Ben *Voo*-ya, Yellow Mountain
25 (MacLeod's Tables), 32 (Suisnish)

Beinn Dearg Mhor (Bheag), Ben *Jerra*k Voar
(Vake), Big (Little) Red Mountain 20
(Glamaig), 23 (Beinn na Caillich)

Beinn Dearg Mheadhonach, Ben *Jerra*k *Vay*-
anach, Middle Red Mountain 20

Beinn Dubh a' Bhealaich, Ben Doo a *Vyali*ch,
Black Mountain of the Pass 24

Beinn Edra, Bain *Ett*era, The Between
Mountain 31, 47b

Beinn na Boineid, Ben na *Bonna*j, Bonnet
Mountain 38

Beinn na Caillich, Ben na *Kyle*-yich, Mountain
of the Old Woman 23 (Broadford), 24
(Kylerhea)

Beinn na Coinnich, Ben na *Coan*-yich,
Mountain of the Moss 40

Beinn na h-Uamha, Bain na *Hoo*-aha,
Mountain of the Cave 25

Beinn na Leac, Ben na Lyechk, Mountain of
the Slab 48

Beinn na Moine, Ben na *Moan*-ya, Mountain
of the Bog 38

Beinn na Seamraig, Ben na *Shem*raik,
Shamrock Mountain 24

Belig, Birch Tree Bark 22

Ben Aslak, Mountain of the Ridge or Hollow 24

Ben Cleat, Ben Clait, Mountain of the Cliff 17

Ben Dearg, Ben *Jerra*k, Red Mountain 31

Ben Geary, Ben Gyarry, Mountain of the
Enclosure 42

Ben Leacach, Ben *Lyech*kach, Slabby Mountain
17

Ben Tianavaig, Ben *Tchee*anavaig, Mountain of
the Sheltering Bay 26

Bidein an Fhithich, Beejan an *Ee*-ich, Raven
Pinnacle 17

Bidein Druim nan Ramh, Beejan Dreem nan
Rahv, Pinnacle of the Ridge of Oars 5, 18b

Biod a' Choltraiche, Beet a *Chol*trich-ya,
Razorbill Cliff 42

Biod an Athair, Beet an *Ah*-hir, Sky Cliff 41

Biod Ban, Beet Bahn, White Cliff 45a

Biod Boidheach, Beet *Baw*-yach, Beautiful
Cliff 39

Biod na Fionaich, Beet na Fee-*oni*ch, Shaggy
Cliff 36

Biod nan Laogh, Beet nan Leu-y, Calf Cliff 45d

Biod Ruadh, Beet *Roo*-a, Red Cliff 36

Bioda Buidhe, Beeta *Boo*-ya, Yellow Point 31

Bla Bheinn, also written Blaven, *Blah*-ven,
Blue Mountain 13, 14

Black Skerry, see Sgeir Dubh

Bloody Stone, The 2, 15

Bodha Hunish, *Boe*-a Hoonish, Bear Reef 47a

Boreraig, *Borre*raik, Castle Bay 32

Braes, The 26, 46a

Brochel, Rock Fort 49

Bruach na Frithe, *Broo*-ach na *Free*-ha, Hill or
Edge of the Deer Forest or Wilderness 4, 5

Caisteal a' Garbh-choire, *Cash*-tyal a *Garr*av
Chorra, Castle of the Rough Corrie 11,
12, 19c

Caisteal an Fhithich, *Cash*-tyal an *Ee*-ich, The
Raven's Castle 42

Caisteal Chamuis, see Knock Castle

Caisteal Uisdein, see Hugh's Castle

Calaman Cave 32

Camas Ban, Cammas Bahn, White Bay 26

Camas Malag 32, 33

Camas Mor, Cammas Moar, Big Bay 47b

Camas na h-Uamha, Cammas na *Hoo*-aha, Bay
of the Cave 38

Camasunary, in Gaelic Camas Fhionnairigh,
Cammas *Ee*-oonary, Bay of the Fair Shieling
14, 17

Candlestick Cave 38

Carn Liath, Carn *Lee*-a, Grey Cairn 27

Carn Mor, Big Cairn 34

Castle Camus, see Knock Castle

Choire a' Caise, Chorra a *Kash*a, Corrie of Steepness 13

Cioch, The, *Kee*-och, Breast 10

Clach Ard, Stone of the Height 47c

Clach Glas, Grey Stone 13, 22

Clach Luath, Clach *Loo*-a, Luath's Stone 43g

Clach na Craoibhe Chaoruinn, Clach na *Creu*-ya *Cheur*an, Stone of the Rowan Tree 15

Clachan Gorma, Clachan *Gorr*ama, Blue Stones 36

Claigan coral sands 45b

Claigan souterrain 45b

Cleat, Clait, Cliff 31

Cnoc Mor a' Grobain, Crochk Moar a Grobin, Big Hill of the Point 45b

Coir' a' Chaoruinn, Corra *Cheur*an, Corrie of the Rowan 19b

Coir' a' Ghrunnda, Corra Ghrunnda, Floored Corrie 11, 12, 19b, 19c

Coir' a' Mhadaidh, Corra Vatty, Corrie of the Fox 5, 18b

Coir' a' Tairneilear, Corra *Tarny*ela, Corrie of the Thunderer 5

Coir' an Eich, Corran Yich, Horse Corrie 7

Coir' an Lochan, Corran Lochan, Corrie of the Lochan 19b

Coir' an t-Seasgaich, Corran *Tchays*-kich, Corrie of the Reeds 28

Coir' an Uaigneis, Corran Oo-*aig*-nis, Corrie of Solitude 18b

Coir-uisg, Cor*ooshk*, Water Corrie 16, 17, 18, 19

Coire a' Bhasteir, Corra *Vash*-tyir, Corrie of the Executioner 3, 4

Coire a' Chruidh, Corra a *Chroo*-y, Horseshoe Corrie 12

Coire Beag, Corra Bake, Little Corrie 12

Coire Faoin, Corrie *Feu*-in, Empty Corrie 27

Coire Gorm, Corra *Gorr*am, Blue Corrie 33

Coire Lagan, Corra *Lah*kan, Corrie of the Hollow 9, 10

Coire na Banachdich, Corra na Banach-ich, Smallpox Corrie 8, 19a

Coire na Creiche, Corra na *Craich*-ya, Corrie of the Spoils 6

Coire nan Laogh, Corra nan Looh, Calf Corrie 12, 18 (Sgurr nan Eag), 21 (Marsco)

Coire Odhar, Corr *Oa*-ar, Dun-coloured Corrie 23

Coire Riabhach, Corra *Ree*-avach or *Ree*-ach, Brindled Corrie 1 (Sgurr nan Gillean), 16 (Coruisk)

Coire Scamadal, Corrie of the Short Valley 27

Coire Uaigneich, Corra Oo-*aig*nich, Remote Corrie 13

Coireachan Ruadha, *Corr*achan *Roo*-aha, Red Corries 19a

Creag an Fhithich, Craik an *Ee*-ich, The Raven's Crag 42

Creag Mhor, Craik Voar, Big Crag 34

Creag na Bruaich, Craik na *Broo*-ich, Crag of the Slope or Hill 49

Creag na h-Eiginn, Craik na *Haik*in, Crag of Distress or Violence 46g

Cubaid, Coobaj, Pulpit (of Satan) 46c

Cuillin, The, Coolin, poss. High Rocks (from the Norse *Kjeulen*), Holly (from the Gaelic *Cuilion*, referring to the serrated skyline) or Worthless (from the Celtic, referring to their agricultural potential). The name is unlikely to be derived from Prince Cuchullin of Antrim.

Druim an Aonaich, Dreem an *Eun*ich, Ridge of the Steep Place 49

Druim Hain, Dreem *Hah*-in, Ridge of Hinds 15, 16

Druim na Ruaige, Dreem na *Roo*-ig-ya, Ridge of the Hunt 20

Druim nan Ramh, Dreem nan Rahv, Ridge of Oars 16, 18b

Dun Beag, Dun Bake, Little Dun 44b

Dun Borrafiach 42

Dun Caan (for a Danish king) 48

Dun Fiadhairt, Dun *Fee*-achursht, Dun of the Grassland 45b

Dun Gearymore 42

Dun Kearstach, *Kyar*stach, Dun of Justice 32

Dun na h'Airde, Dun na *Harj*a, Dun of the Point 45e

Dun Ringill, Dun of the Point of the Ravine 43a

Dunan Thearna Sgurr, *Doon*an *Hyarn*a Skoor, poss. Sloping Heap Peak 35

Dunscaith Castle, Dun*scaa*, poss. Dun of the Battle 43g

Duntulm Castle 47a

Dunvegan Castle 45b

Eag Dubh, Aik Doo, Black Cleft 7

Eaglais Bhreugach (Trotternish), Ecklish *Vree*-agach, False Church 46c

Eaglais Breige (Raasay), Ecklish *Breeg*a, False Church 49

Eas Mor, Ess Moar, Big Waterfall 8

Eilean Reamhar, Ailen *Rav*ar, Fat Island 18a

Eilean Tigh, Ailen Ty, Island of the House 50

Elgol 14, 17, 43b

Faolainn, Feulin, Exposed Place by the Shore 36

Fiadhairt, see Dun Fiadhairt

Fingal's Pinnacles 30

Fionn Coire, Fyoon Corra, Fair Corrie 4

Fladday, Flat Island 50

Flora MacDonald monument 47b

Galta Mor, Big Pig 46g

Galtrigill 41

Garbh-bheinn, *Garrav* Ven, Rough Mountain 22

Gars-bheinn, Garsh-ven, Echoing Mountain 12

Geodh' an Eich Bhric, Gyo an Yich Vreechk, Cove of the Speckled Horse 37

Geodha Mor, *Gyo-*a Moar, Big Cove 39

Glac Mhor, Glachk Voar, Big Defile 18b

Glamaig, *Glah-*mak, Deep Gorge 20

Glen Brittle, Broad Dale 4, 5, 6, 7, 8, 9, 10, 11, 12, 18, 19, 34, 35

Glen Caladale, Cold Dale 36

Glen Dibidal, Deep Dale 39

Glen Lorgasdal 39

Glen Ollisdal 39

Glen Sligachan 2, 15, 16, 20, 21

Gob na h-Oa, Gope na *Hoe-*a, Beak of the Cave 37

Gob na Hoe, Gope na Hoe, Beak of the Hill or Spur 41

Great Stone Shoot, The 10

Greshornish Point, Point of the Promontory of the Pig 45e

Groban na Sgeire, Groban na Skeera, Point of the Skerry 45b

Hallaig, Holy Bay 48, 49

Harlosh Point, Point of the Rock of the Fire 44c

Harta Corrie, Corrie of the Hart 2, 15

Hartaval, Hart Mountain 31

Healabhal Mhor (Bheag), *Hella*val Voar (Vake), poss. Big (Little) Holy Mountain (after its altar-like appearance) but more likely Big (Little) Flagstone Mountain 25

Hoe, The, The Hill or Spur 40

Hugh's Castle, in Gaelic Caisteal Uisdein, *Cash-*tyal Oosjin 47c

Inaccessible Pinnacle, The 9

Inbhir a' Gharraidh, Inyir a Gharry, Cove of the Walled Enclosure 38

Inver Tote 46c, 46d

Kilchrist 32

Kilmarie 13, 43a

Kilt Rock 46f

Kilvaxter souterrain 47b

Knight's Peak (for St Andrews theology professor William Knight) 1

Knock Castle, in Gaelic Caisteal Chamuis

(Cash-tyal *Chamm*ish, Bay Castle) 43d

Kyle Akin, *Ak*in, Strait of Acunn (a legendary Fienne) 24

Kyle Rhea, Ray, Strait of Readh, Acunn's brother 24

Lady Grange's Cave 38

Lampay 45b

Leac nan Fionn, Lyechk nan *Fee-*on, Fingal's Tombstone 30

Lealt Waterfalls, Leth-allt, Lai-*owlt*, Half-stream 46c, 46d

Loch a' Choire Riabhaich, Loch a Chorra *Ree-*avich, Loch of the Brindled Corrie 16

Loch an Fhir-bhallaich, Loch an Eer *Vall*ich, Loch of the Spotted Man 9, 10

Loch an Leth-uillt, Loch an Lai Oolt, Loch of the Half Stream 35

Loch Bharcasaig, Loch *Var*kasaig, Castle Bay 38, 44e

Loch Bracadale, Loch of the Meeting of Townships 37, 38, 44

Loch Brittle 34, 35

Loch Coruisk 16, 17, 18, 19

Loch Cuithir, Loch *Coo-*hir, Loch of the Cattle Fold or Rocky Area 28

Loch Eishort, Loch of the Icy Bay or Fjord 32, 43g

Loch Eynort, Loch of the Isthmus 36

Loch Hasco, Loch of the High Place 30

Loch Langaig, Loch of the Long Bay 30

Loch Leathan, Loch *Lyeh-*han, Broad Loch 27

Loch Lonachan, Marshy Loch 32

Loch Losait, Loch *Loss*aitch, Loch of the Small Stream or Hollow 45d

Loch na Cuilce, Loch na *Cool-*kya, Loch of Reeds 17

Loch na h-Airde, Loch na *Har*ja, Loch of the Point 34

Loch na Meilich, Loch na Mellich, Loch of the Bleating of Sheep 48

Loch na Mna, Loch na Mraa, Loch of the Wife or Woman 48

Loch na Sguabaidh, Loch na *Skoo-*aby, Sweeping Loch 22

Loch Scavaig 15, 16, 17

Loch Slapin, Muddy or Sluggish Loch 13, 22, 32, 33

Lochan nan Ghrunnd, Floored Lochan or Lochan of the Ground 50

Lorgill Bay, Bay of the Glen of the Deer Cry 39

Lota Corrie, High Corrie 2

MacLeod's Tables 25

Mam a' Phobuill, Mahm a *Foe-*pill, People's

Moor 21

Manners Stone, The 41

Maoladh Mor, *Meula* Moar, Big Bare Hill 29

Marsco, Sea-gull Rock 21

Meall Greepa, Mell Greepa, Precipice Hill 44e

Meall na Cuilce, Mell na *Koolka*, Hill of the Reeds 16

Meall na Suiramach, Mell na *Soora*mach, Maiden Hill 29, 31

Meall Tuath, Mell *Too*-a, North Hill 47a

Moonen Bay, named after the Ossianic hero Munan 40, 45a

Nead na h-Iolaire, Nyed na *Hill*era, Eagle's Nest 1

Neist Point (originally An Eist, An Eesht, The Horse) 45a

North-east Stacks 46g

Ob Gauscavaig, Gauscavaig or Tokavaig Bay 43f

Oisgill Bay 45a

Old Man of Storr, The 27

Ord 43h

Oronsay 44b

Pein a' Chleibh, Pane a Chlee, Mountain of the Chest 31

Pinnacle Basin 30

Piper's Cave, The 44c

Point of Sleat 43e

Port an Luig Mhoir, Porst an *Loo*-ik Voar, Harbour of the Big Hollow 43b

Port Gobhlaig, Porst Goalaig, Forked Harbour 46g

Preshal More (Beg), Big (Little) Preshal 37

Prince Charles's Cave 43b

Quiraing, The, Kwi-rang, The Round Cattle Fold (ie the Table) 29, 31

Ramasaig Cliff, Cliff of the Raven's Bay 40

Roag Island 44d

Rona 50

Ru Bornesketaig, Point of the Low Headland 47b

Ru Chorachan, Steep Headland 47c

Ru Idrigill, Idrigill Headland 47c

Ruadh Stac, *Roo*-a Stachk, Red Stack 21

Rubh' an Dunain, Roo an Doonan, Headland of the Dun 34

Rubha Ban, *Roo*-a Bahn, White Headland 17

Rubha Buidhe, *Roo*-a *Boo*-ya, Yellow Headland 17

Rubha Cruinn, *Roo*-a *Croo*-in, Round Headland 37

Rubha Dubh a' Ghrianain, *Roo*-a *Doo* a *Gree*-anin, The Black Headland of the Sunny Place 37

Rubha Garbhaig, *Roo*-a Garravig, Rough Headland 46f

Rubha Hunish, *Roo*-a Hoonish, Bear Point 47a

Rubha na h-Airigh Baine, *Roo*-a na Harry *Ban*-ya, Point of the White Shieling 17

Rubha na h-Aiseag, *Roo*-a na *Hash*ik, Ferry Point 46h

Rubha na Maighdeanan, *Roo*-a na *Ma*-ijanan, The Maidens' Headland 38

Rubha nam Brathairean, *Roo*-a nam *Bra*-huren, Brothers' Point 46e

Rubha nan Clach, *Roo*-a nan Clach, Stony Headland 37

Rubha nan Sgarbh, *Roo*-a nan *Skarra*v, Cormorant Point 50

Rubha Suisnish, Suisnish Point 32

Rubha Voreven 47a

Sanctuary, The 27

Screapadal, Rough Dale 49

Sgeir Dubh, Skeer Doo, Black Skerry 39 (South Duirinish), 46e (Trotternish)

Sgumain Stone Shoot, The 10

Sgurr a' Bhasteir, *Skoor* a *Vash*-tyir, Peak of the Executioner 4

Sgurr a' Choire Bhig, Skoor a Chorra Veek, Peak of the Little Corrie 12

Sgurr a' Fionn Choire, Skoor a Fyoon Chorra, Peak of the Fair Corrie 4

Sgurr a' Ghreadaidh, Skoor a Gretta, Peak of the Clear Waters 7

Sgurr a' Mhadaidh Ruaidh, Skoor a *Vah*ty *Roo*-y, Fox Peak 28, 31

Sgurr a' Mhadaidh, Skoor a *Vah*ty, Peak of the Foxes 7

Sgurr Alasdair, Skoor Alastir, Alexander's Peak (for Alexander Nicolson, who first climbed it in 1873) 10

Sgurr an Duine, Skoor an *Doon*a, Peak of the Person 35

Sgurr an Fheadain, Skoor an *Aite*nn, Peak of the Waterpipe 6

Sgurr Beag, Skoor Bake, Little Peak 2 (Sgurr nan Gillean), 36 (Loch Eynort)

Sgurr Buidhe, Skoor *Boo*-ya, Yellow Peak 36

Sgurr Coir' an Lochain, Skoor Corran Lochin, Peak of the Corrie of the Lochan 19a

Sgurr Dearg, Skoor *Jerr*ak, Red Peak 8, 9

Sgurr Dubh Mor, Skoor Doo Moar, Big Black Peak 11

Sgurr Dubh na Da Bheinn, Skoor *Doo* na *Dah Vain*, Black Peak of the Two Mountains 11

Sgurr Eadar Da Choire, *Skoor* Aitar *Dah Chorra*, Peak Between Two Corries 7

Sgurr Hain, Skoor *Hah*-in, Peak of Hinds 15

Sgurr Mhairi, Skoor Varry, Mary's Peak (for a young local girl who perished on the mountain while looking for a stray cow) 20

Sgurr Mhic Choinnich, Skoor Veechk *Choan*-yich, Mackenzie's Peak (for John Mackenzie, the famous nineteenth-century Skye guide) 9

Sgurr Mor, Skoor Moar, Big Peak 31 (Trotternish), 37 (Talisker)

Sgurr na Banachdich, Skoor na *Banach*-ich, poss. Smallpox Peak (from the pockmarked rock) but more likely Milkmaid's Peak (cattle were grazed in the corries below) 7, 8

Sgurr na Bhairnich, Skoor na Varnich, Limpet Peak 5

Sgurr na Coinnich, Skoor na *Coan*-yich, Peak of the Moss 24

Sgurr na h-Uamha, Skoor na *Hoo*-aha, Peak of the Cave 2

Sgurr na Stri, Skoor na Stri, Peak of Strife 15

Sgorr nam Boc, Skoor nam Bochk, Peak of the He-goat or Roe-buck 35

Sgurr nam Fiadh, Skoor *Fee*-a, Deer Peak 36

Sgurr nan Bairnich, Skoor nan Barnich, Limpet Peak 35

Sgurr nan Each, Skoor nan Yech, Peak of the Horses 22

Sgurr nan Eag, Skoor nan Aik, Notched Peak 12

Sgurr nan Gillean, Skoor nan *Geel*-yan, Peak of the Gullies 1, 2

Sgurr nan Gobhar, Skoor nan *Goa*-ar, Goat Peak 8

Sgurr Sgumain, Skoor Skooman, Mound or Stack Peak 10

Sgurr Thearlaich, Skoor *Hyar*lach, Charles' Peak (for Charles Pilkington, who was the first to climb the Inaccessible Pinnacle, with his brother Lawrence, in 1880) 10, 11

Sgurr Thormaid, Skoor *Hurr*amitch, Norman's Peak (for Norman Collie, the great Cuillin pioneer and discoverer of the Cioch) 7

Sgurr Thuilm, Skoor *Hool*am, Peak of the Knoll or Holm 7

Skye, poss. Wing (from the Celtic *skeitos* or Gaelic *sgiath*), Indented (from the Celtic *sci*), Scots (from the old Gaelic *sgith*), Sword People (from the Celtic *skia* and *neach*), from the Norse *skith* (a tablet or log used during the Norse occupation) or Cloud Island (from the Norse *sky* and *ey*)

Slat Bheinn, Slaht Ven, Rod Mountain 14

Sligachan, Place of Shells 1, 2, 3, 4, 15, 16, 18, 20, 21

Slochd Dubh, Slochk Doo, Black Pit 34

Spar Cave 43c

Srath Mor, Stra Moar, Big Valley 22

Srath na Creitheach, Stra na *Cree*-ach, Valley of the Brushwood 13, 15

Sron na Ciche, Strawn na *Keech*a, Nose of the Cioch 10

Sron Vourlinn, Strawn Voorlin, Mill Nose 29, 30, 31

Stac a' Bhothain, Stachk a *Vaw*-in, Stack of the Bothy 45d

Stac a' Mheadais, Stachk a *Vait*ish 36

Stac an Fhucadair, Stachk an Uchkadair, The Fuller's Stack 36, 37

Stac an Tuill, Stachk an Tuyl, Stack of the Hole 35

Stac Aros, Stachk Arrus, House Stack 45d

Stac Buidhe, Stachk *Boo*-ya, Yellow Stack 46g

Stac Lachlainn, Stachk Lachlan, Lachlan's Stack 46h

Stac Suisnish 32

Stacan Gobhlach, *Stach*kan Goalach, Forked Stacks 46g

Stack Skudiburgh 47c

Staffin Slipway 46f

Steall a' Ghreip, Shtyowl a Greep, Waterfall of the Precipice 46g

Storr, The, from the Norse Staur, meaning Pillar or Stake 27, 31

Strath Suardal, Greensward Dale 32

Struan 44b

Suidhe Biorach, *Soo*-ya *Bee*rach, Pointed Seat 43b

Suisnish, *Soosh*nish, Seething Headland 32

Talisker Bay/Point, House at the Rock 36, 37

Tarskavaig, Cod Bay 43f

Tokavaig 43f

Truagh Mheall, *Troo*-a Vell, Wretched Hill 35

Trumpan 42, 45c

Uamh an Ard Achadh, *Oo*-a an Ard Acha, High Pasture Cave 33

Uamh an Eich Bhric, *Oo*-a an Yich Vreechk, Cave of the Speckled Horse 37

Uamh Cinn Ghlinn, *Oo*-a Keen Ghleen, Valley Head Cave 33

Uamh Mhor, *Oo*-a Voar, Big Cave 50

Uamh Oir, *Oo*-a *Oa*-ir, Cave of Gold 47b

Uamh Sgeinne, *Oo*-a *Skain*-ya, Cave of the Knives 33

Waternish Point, Vatternish, Water Promontory 42

Waterstein Head 40

Grading System: Grid

	1	2	3	4	5
Grade	■				
Terrain	■				
Navigation		■			
Seriousness	■				

An at-a-glance grid for each route indicates the route's overall difficulty, where difficulty consists not only of **grade** (i.e. technical difficulty) but also type of **terrain** (irrespective of grade), difficulty of **navigation** with a compass in adverse weather and **seriousness** (i.e. difficulty of escape in case of curtailment of route for one reason or another, based on criteria of length and restricted line of escape). These factors vary over the duration of the route and should not be taken as absolute, but they provide a useful general guide and enable comparisons to be made between routes. Each category is graded 1 (easiest) to 5 (hardest).

Grade
1 Mostly not too steep
2 Appreciable steep sections
3 Some handwork required
4 Easy scramble
5 Hard scramble

Navigation
1 Straightforward
2 Reasonably straightforward
3 Appreciable accuracy required
4 Hard
5 Extremely hard

Terrain
1 Excellent
2 Good
3 Reasonable
4 Rough
5 Tough

Seriousness
1 Straightforward escape
2 Reasonably straightforward escape
3 Appreciable seriousness
4 Serious
5 Very serious

Scrambling, involving use of hands for assistance, is categorised as easy or hard. A hard scramble has fewer handholds and footholds than an easy scramble, while still remaining below the level of what would normally be regarded as a rock climb. Such judgments are necessarily subjective, and although great pains have been taken to ensure that gradings are standard across routes, an easy scramble may seem hard to one person and a hard scramble easy to another, depending on individual factors such as physical build, reach and response to exposure.